LETTERS

TO A

TRINITARIAN;

OR,

THE DOCTRINE OF THE

TRIPERSONALITY OF JEHOVAH

INCONSISTENT WITH THE

TRUTH OF THE INCARNATION.

BY GEORGE BUSH.

BOSTON:
PUBLISHED BY OTIS CLAPP, 23 SCHOOL STREET.
NEW-YORK: LEWIS C. BUSH, 16 HOWARD STREET.
LONDON: J. S. HODSON AND W. NEWBERY.

1850.

PREFACE.

THE ensuing series of Letters, with the exception of the one on Atonement, first made its appearance in successive Numbers of the "New Church Repository," for 1848, conducted by the Author. They were addressed to a gentleman of high literary and theological repute, though not a clergyman, and whose strong adherence to that form of doctrine known in the American churches as orthodox and evangelical, rendered him, to my mental eye, an impersonation of the peculiar aspect of the Trinitarian dogma with which I would contrast the teachings of the New Church. The ideal presence with me, of the established system thus represented, has, in every stage of the discussion, probably given complexion to the tone of my arguments. But I trust, notwithstanding, that the Unitarian also may find, in the ensuing pages, a presentation of views that he will not turn from under a sinister impression founded on their advocacy of the doctrine of the supreme divinity of our Lord Jesus Christ. He will here find the doctrine set forth under entirely new aspects and relations, and arraying itself in equally strong antagonism with the Trinity which he rejects and the Unity which he defends.

If the Author has written at all in the spirit of the system which he has espoused and would fain commend to the attention of his fellow-Christians, he cannot well have made himself liable to the charge of an illiberal, uncourteous, or indecorous mode of conducting an inquiry upon a very important department of revealed truth.

He has only to ask of those who may condescend to notice the work, that they will not consider the argument of the Letters refuted simply by disparaging flings at the alleged visionary claims of Swedenborg. I could not well sink lower in the esteem of others than I should in my own, did I deem myself capable of giving credence or currency to a system of religious doctrines that relied mainly upon anything else than *its own intrinsic evidence of truth*, albeit I may not be willing to admit that this truth could have been discovered unless it had been previously revealed.

NEW-YORK, JAN. 1, 1850.

CONTENTS.

	PAGE.
LETTER I.—THE ANGEL JEHOVAH,	7
LETTER II.—THE ANGEL JEHOVAH,	14
LETTER III.—THE DIVINE HUMANITY,	22
LETTER IV.—THE DIVINE HUMANITY,	28
LETTER V.—JEHOVAH-JESUS,	42
LETTER VI.—JEHOVAH-JESUS,	53
LETTER VII.—THE INCARNATION,	61
LETTER VIII.—THE INCARNATION,	73
LETTER IX.—THE GLORIFICATION,	80
LETTER X.—THE GLORIFICATION,	99
LETTER XI.—THE ATONEMENT,	107
LETTER XII.—PRACTICAL RESULTS,	120
LETTER XIII.—PRACTICAL RESULTS,	130

LETTERS TO A TRINITARIAN.

LETTER I.

THE ANGEL JEHOVAH.

DEAR SIR,

In our frequent conversations upon the distinguishing features of Swedenborg's Theology, you have more than once intimated your objections to his doctrine of the Divine Trinity as being really subversive of the true tenet, while yet holding forth a show of sustaining and confirming it. The position so distinctly and emphatically maintained throughout his writings, that the Jesus of the New Testament is the Jehovah of the Old, and that in Him is concentrated the only Trinity we are taught to recognise in either, strikes you as so inconsistent with what you have been led to believe in regard to the Tripersonal distinction, in which Christ holds the second rank, that you are prompted to an instant rejection of the entire scheme, and scruple not to affirm that if reduced to the alternative of giving up either the personal Trinity or the absolute Unity, you should feel compelled to resign the latter. This is doubtless more than most Trinitarians would be willing to say, notwithstanding their firm assurance that a threefold distinction of *persons* is unequivocally taught in the pages of Revelation. They have never yet, I believe, intimated that they considered the doctrine of the Tripersonality *more clearly* taught by the sacred writers than that of the Unipersonality. Your views on this head are probably peculiar to yourself. But in what I propose to offer on the general subject I shall take no advantage of this ultraism of position. I shall address you and aim to reason with you as occupying simply the ordinary Trinitarian ground—that is, as admitting that Jesus Christ is in some sense possessed of divine attributes, while at the same time he is, as divine, the second *person* of the adorable Trinity, in which character he assumed our nature, and accomplished the work of redemption on our behalf.

In the ensuing series of letters I propose to canvass the general theme of the Supreme Deity of our Lord and Saviour, Jesus Christ, with a special reference to the established views of Trinitarians on that subject, and by a course of argument founded primarily upon the Old Testament Scriptures. In the prosecution of my purpose, I have the satisfaction of knowing that we shall agree as to the authority appealed to. In a controversy with a Unitarian I fear I could not promise myself this advantage, as I perceive in the leading writers of that class a striking backwardness, to say the least, to abide by the testimony of the Old Testament in respect to the central doctrine of our Lord's divinity. They evidently regard this portion of the Scriptures as a mass of ancient historical documents, venerable indeed by age, but embodying merely the statements and sentiments of fallible men, who have chronicled facts and given utterance to poetry, prophecy, and parable under the promptings of a certain religious fervor, which at the same time falls immeasurably short of any thing that can be properly called *an infallible divine inspiration.* With the advocates of this opinion it would of course be impossible to enter upon such a discussion as I now propose, without a long preliminary debate upon the claims of the old Testament Scriptures to a character of equal authority, as a standard of doctrine, with that of the New. But all this, in the present instance, I am happily spared. I require no concession on this head but such as you are prepared at once to make. I shall, however, venture to hope that if the eye of any candid Unitarian shall fall upon these pages, he will be somewhat arrested and impressed by an array of evidence drawn from this source, on the main position, of which perhaps he was but little aware, and the force of which, I trust, may not be diminished to his mind by any air of novelty in the form of its presentation. I trust, too, that he will at least be ready to admit that on the ground which we assume, of the inspired character of the Law and the Prophets, our grand conclusion is one that is not easily resisted. For the proof of our postulate, we refer him to the various writers on the canon who have treated it in all its bearings.

To one who has been so familiar as I have long known you to be with the original languages of the Scriptures, it must often have occurred as a query, what could be really intended by the remarkable phrase, מלאך יהוה, *Malak Yehovah,* or, *Angel of the Lord,* so frequently met with in the Pentateuch and the subsequent books. Who was the true personage intended by that appellation? Was it the veritable Jehovah himself who was thus indicated, and if so, whence or why the denomination? If it were a created angel, what relation does he sustain to Jehovah, and on what ground does he speak in His name and claim for himself His attributes? This is a feature of the sacred record too prominent not to have attracted the notice of commentators in all ages, and yet scarcely any one, I think, can fail to have been struck with the vague and vacillating air of their expositions. It has formed a problem that has defied their solution. Yet nothing is of more importance than to ascertain the grounds of this denomination. If it has any bearing at all on the grand question at issue, it is of an import the most momentous, as its relations are ramified, to a vast extent, over the whole compass of revelation; and, if I mistake not, it will appear that no adequate view can be obtained from the New Testament of the true character of Christ, which involves an omission of the testimony gathered from the earlier Jewish oracles. No other satisfactory clew, I am persuaded, can be obtained to the leading titles applied to our Lord by the Evangelists and Apostles. But the evidence of this remains to be adduced.

It is my intention, in the sequel of the discussion, to adduce from Swedenborg the true, and, as I believe, the only true solution of the problem involved in this remarkable form of speech, but my present object is to exhibit distinctly the usage itself as a basis for the final induction. To this end it will be requisite to accumulate ample proof that the title "Angel of the Lord" is applied in some sense to the Lord himself, or, in other words, that the terms are used interchangeably. Should the citations appear rather copious, the object in view will account for it. A great step is taken towards the main conclusion when the fact is established that Jehovah is called an angel.

"And the *Angel of the Lord* found her (Hagar) by a fountain of water in the wilderness, by the fountain in the way to Shur. And he said, Hagar, Sarai's maid, whence camest thou? and whither wilt thou go? And she said, I flee from the face of my mistress Sarai. And the *Angel of the Lord* (Jehovah) said unto her, Return to thy mistress, and submit thyself under her hands. And the *Angel of the Lord* said unto her, I will multiply thy seed exceedingly, that it shall not be numbered for multitude. And the *Angel of the Lord* said unto her, Behold, thou art with child, and shalt bear a son, and shalt call his name Ishmael; because the LORD hath heard thy affliction. And he will be a wild man; his hand will be against every man, and every man's hand against him; and he shall dwell in the presence of all his brethren. And she called the name of the LORD (Jehovah) that spake unto her, Thou God seest me : for she said, Have I also here looked after him that seeth me?"—*Gen.* xvi. 7-13.

As the Angel here mentioned is called by Hagar, "Lord" (Heb. Jehovah), and as he addresses her in a style befitting only the Most High, promising to perform what He alone could do, and foretelling what He alone could know, the inference is not only fair, but inevitable, that an identity of some kind subsisted between Jehovah and the Angel. The precise nature of this relation will be clearly developed by and by.

"And Abraham stretched forth his hand, and took the knife to slay his son. And the *Angel of the Lord* called unto him out of heaven, and said, Abraham, Abraham. And he said, Here am I. And he said, Lay not thine hand upon the lad, neither do thou any thing unto him : for now I know that thou fearest God, seeing thou hast not withheld thy son, thine only son, from me. . . . And the *Angel of the Lord* called unto Abraham out of heaven the second time, and said, By myself have I sworn, saith the Lord, for because thou hast done this thing, and hast not withheld thy son, thine only son : That in blessing I will bless thee, and in multiplying I will multiply thy seed as the stars of the heaven, and as the sand which is upon the sea-shore; and thy seed shall possess the gate of his enemies; and in thy seed shall all the nations of the earth be blessed; because thou hast obeyed my voice."—*Gen.* xxii. 10-12, 15-18.

Here also it is obvious that the angel predicates of himself what can only strictly pertain to the supreme Jehovah. This is abundantly confirmed by Paul (Heb. vi. 13, 14), "For when God made promise to Abraham, because he could swear by no greater, he sware by himself, saying, Surely blessing I will bless thee, and multiplying I will multiply thee." If the angel sware by himself, and *could* swear by no greater, there must surely be some sense in which the angel is Jehovah. He is besides expressly called "God" by the Apostle.

"And Balaam rose up in the morning, and saddled his ass, and went with the princes of Moab. And God's anger was kindled because he went: and the *Angel of the Lord* stood in the way for an adversary against him. Now he was riding upon his ass, and his two servants were with him. And the ass saw the *Angel of the Lord* standing in the way, and his sword drawn in his hand : and the ass turned aside out of the way, and went into the field : and Balaam smote the ass, to turn her into the way. But the *Angel of the Lord* stood in a path of the vineyards, a wall being on this side, and a wall on that side. And when the ass saw the *Angel of the Lord*, she thrust herself unto the wall, and crushed Balaam's foot against the wall : and he smote her again. And the *Angel of the Lord* went further, and stood in a narrow place, where was no way to turn either to the right hand or to the left. And when the ass saw the *Angel of the Lord*, she fell down under Balaam; and Balaam's anger was kindled, and he smote the ass with a staff."—*Num.* xxii. 21-27.

This Angel is mentioned repeatedly in the subsequent verses, and in ver. 32-35 it is said—

"And the *Angel of the Lord* said unto him, Wherefore hast thou smitten thine ass these three times ? Behold, I went out to withstand thee, because thy way is perverse before me : and the ass saw me, and turned from me these three times : unless she had turned from me, surely now also I had slain thee, and saved her alive. And Balaam said unto the *Angel of the Lord*, I have sinned ; for I knew not that thou stoodest in the way against me : now therefore, if it displease thee, I will get me back again. And the *Angel of the Lord* said unto Balaam, Go with the men : but only the word that I shall speak unto thee, that thou shalt speak."

It is then the Angel of the Lord who speaks to Balaam, and dictates what he is to say to Balak. Yet it is clear that he regarded him as the Lord himself, for he says to the king of Moab, "The word that God putteth in my mouth, that shall I speak." Moreover, it is expressly said (ch. xxiii. 5), "And the Lord put a word in Balaam's mouth, and said, Return unto Balak, and thus shalt thou speak." So, also, ver. 16, "And the Lord met Balaam, and put a word in his mouth, and said," &c. The evidence, therefore, would seem to be decisive, that the titles, " Angel of the Lord," and " Lord," are here used as equivalent.

"And an *Angel* (or, *the Angel*) *of the Lord* came up from Gilgal to Bochim, and said, I made you to go up out of Egypt, and have brought you unto the land which I sware unto your fathers ; and I said, I will never break my covenant with you. And ye shall make no league with the inhabitants of this land ; ye shall throw down their altars : but ye have not obeyed my voice : why have ye done this ? Wherefore I also said, I will not drive them out from before you ; but they shall be as thorns in your sides, and their gods shall be a snare unto you."—*Judg.* ii. 1.

It was surely no other than Jehovah who brought the Israelites out of Egypt, who made a covenant with them, and to whom they were accountable for disobedience. These are acts and relations which could not be predicated of any creature. The Angel of the Lord must here denote the Lord himself. As to the circumstance of his being said to "come up from Gilgal," it is probably in allusion to the fact that in Gilgal near to Jericho this divine personage had recently appeared to Joshua as an armed warrior. That *he* was Jehovah cannot be doubted, because he suffered Joshua to worship him, and even commanded him to put off his shoes from his feet, inasmuch as the ground on which he stood was, by reason of *his* presence, holy. The evidence is cumulative of the truth of this construction.

"And there came an *Angel of the Lord*, and sat under an oak which was in Ophrah, that pertained unto Joash the Abi-ezrite: and his son Gideon threshed wheat by the wine-press to hide it from the Midianites. And the *Angel of the Lord* appeared unto him, and said unto him, The Lord is with thee, thou mighty man of valor. And Gideon said unto him, O my Lord, if the Lord be with us, why then is all this befallen us? and where be all his miracles which our fathers told us of, saying, Did not the Lord bring us up from Egypt? but now the Lord hath forsaken us, and delivered us into the hands of the Midianites. And the Lord looked upon him, and said, Go in this thy might, and thou shalt save Israel from the hand of the Midianites: have not I sent thee? And he said unto him, O my Lord, wherewith shall I save Israel? behold my family is poor in Manasseh, and I am the least in my father's house. And the Lord said unto him, Surely I will be with thee, and thou shalt smite the Midianites as one man. And he said unto him, If now I have found grace in thy sight, then show me a sign that thou talkest with me. Depart not hence, I pray thee, until I come unto thee, and bring forth my present, and set it before thee. And he said, I will tarry until thou come again. And Gideon went in, and made ready a kid, and unleavened cakes of an ephah of flour: the flesh he put in a basket, and he put the broth in a pot, and brought it out unto him under the oak, and presented it. And the *Angel of God* said unto him, Take the flesh and the unleavened cakes, and lay them upon this rock, and pour out the broth. And he did so. And when Gideon perceived that he was an *Angel of the Lord,* Gideon said, Alas, O Lord God! for because I have seen an *Angel of the Lord* face to face. And the Lord said unto him, Peace be unto thee: fear not: thou shalt not die. Then Gideon built an altar there unto the Lord, and called it Jehovah-Shalom; unto this day it is yet in Ophrah of the Abi-ezrites."—*Judges* vi. 11-24.

The language here employed leaves no room for doubt as to our main position. The "Angel of the Lord," called also, v. 20, the "Angel of God," is all along addressed by Gideon as the Lord (Jehovah), and in v. 14 is expressly called so. In v. 22 the more appropriate rendering would be, "When Gideon perceived that he was *the* Angel of the Lord," as the form of the expression in the original is precisely the same here as throughout the Pentateuch and the Prophets. There is therefore no ground for the wavering of our version between "*an* Angel" and "*the* Angel." It would have been altogether preferable to have adopted the uniform rendering "the Angel of the Lord."

In Judges xiii. 8–23, we have an account of a remarkable interview between "the Angel of the Lord" and Manoah and his wife, the parents of Samson. In the outset of the narrative he is termed "a man of God," a designation which he himself acknowledges, v. 11, but this is dropped in the sequel, and that of "Angel" alone employed. After reciting his answer to their interrogatories the story proceeds:

"And Manoah said unto the *Angel of the Lord,* I pray thee, let us detain thee until we shall have made ready a kid for thee. And the *Angel of the Lord* said unto Manoah, Though thou detain me, I will not eat of thy bread: and if thou wilt offer a burnt-offering, thou must offer it unto the Lord. For Manoah knew not that he was an *Angel of the Lord.* And Manoah said unto the *Angel of the Lord,* What is thy name, that when thy sayings come to pass we may do thee honor? And the *Angel of the Lord* said unto him, Why askest thou thus after my name, seeing it is secret? So Manoah took a kid, with a meat-offering, and offered it upon a rock unto the Lord; and *the Angel* did wondrously, and Manoah and his wife looked on. For it came to pass, when the flame went up toward heaven from off the altar, that the *Angel of the Lord* ascended in the flame of the altar, and Manoah and his wife looked on it and fell on their faces to the ground. But the *Angel of the Lord* did no more appear to Manoah and to his wife. Then Manoah knew that he was an *Angel of the Lord.* And Manoah said unto his wife, We shall surely die, because we have seen God."—*Judges* xiii. 8–23.

The words of the Angel to Manoah, "Why askest thou thus after my name, seeing it is secret," have the air of a rebuke for putting the question alluded to. But what offence could attach to a respectful and reverential interrogation of this kind? Why was the mere *secresy* of the name a reason for its not being asked. Was it not rather the reason why he *did* ask it? We admit, indeed, that if Manoah had been *previously* informed that the name was *ineffable*—that it was designed to be kept a profound secret—he would have been guilty of high presumption in demanding it. But we see no evidence of this in any part of the sacred text, and conclude therefore that the Angel made use of this interrogative form of speech merely in order to introduce, in the most suitable and impressive manner, the declaration that follows, constituting the real *point* of his reply: "It is secret;"—or rather, as in the margin, "It is wonderful," for so the original (פלאי, *pelai*) properly implies, and so it is expressly rendered, Is. ix. 6 "His name shall be called *Wonderful* (פלא, *pela*)"; i. e. his nature, his character shall *be* wonderful; properly implying that kind of wonder which is the natural effect of *miracles,* of *marvellous and superhuman works.** In *apparently* declining therefore to reveal his name he does in fact make known one of his most august and glorious titles, one which went far towards conveying an idea of the divine attributes of his nature, and one which was therefore eminently appropriate to the drift of Manoah's question. The implication probably is, "You have scarcely occasion to inquire as to my name (nature); for it is obvious from the words, promises, and actions already witnessed and yet further to be displayed, that *I am,* and am therefore *to be called, Pela, the Admirable One, the great Worker of Wonders,*

---

* There is some slight variation among commentators in the mode of rendering this term. Michaelis, Dathe, Boothroyd, and others follow our English version. Le Céne has *it must remain secret ;* the Genevese of 1805, *it is sublime.* De Wette has *wunderbar,* which does not differ from Luther's *wundersam, wondrous, admirable.* Michaelis remarks upon the original, that "it includes all these significations—*unknown, secret, enigmatical, mysterious, wonderful.* Manoah probably understood it thus,—*his name remains secret, he will not tell it, but is determined to remain unknown.* But in fact, it carries a further meaning; *his name is so mysterious that men cannot perfectly understand it ; it is unspeakable,* that is, he is God, whose nature and perfections surpass the comprehension of mortals."—*Anmerk. in loc.*

the Master of Miracles." The original (פלאי, *pelai*) has the *form* of a proper name, but the *force* of an appellative. Whether Manoah fully understood its entire import is perhaps to be doubted; but whether he did or not, the declaration is to us, considered in one point of view, immensely important; for by assuming a title which unquestionably belongs to the promised Messiah, he identifies himself with that divine personage, and consequently puts it beyond a doubt who it is that is meant by the term " Angel" or "Angel of the Lord," so frequently occurring in the Old Testament Scriptures, in connection with miraculous appearances and revelations.

In v. 19 it is said that " Manoah took a kid, with a meat-offering, and offered it upon a rock unto the Lord, and *the angel* did wondrously." As the words "the angel," are supplied by the translators, not being found in the original, and as "Lord" is the next immediately preceding subject, it might be as properly rendered, " and *he* (the Lord) did wondrously." The Heb. term for "did wondrously" is מפלא, *maphlia*, from the same root with פלא, *pela*, occurring above The term, therefore, corresponds with the name which he had before attributed to himself. Being *wonderful*, he put forth a *wonderful* manifestation.

The following passage from the prophet Isaiah presents us with another marked instance of parallel allusion:

"I will mention the loving-kindnesses of the Lord, and the praises of the Lord, according to all that the Lord hath bestowed on us, and the great goodness toward the house of Israel, which he hath bestowed on them according to his mercies, and according to the multitude of his loving kindnesses. For he said, Surely they are my people, children that will not lie : so he was their Saviour. In all their affliction he was afflicted, and the *Angel of his presence* saved them : in his love and in his pity he redeemed them, and he bare them and carried them all the days of old. But they rebelled, and vexed his Holy Spirit: therefore he was turned to be their enemy, and he fought against them."
—*Is.* lxiii. 7–10.

The personage here denominated the " Angel of his presence" is beyond all question the same with him who is frequently mentioned as having conducted the children of Israel through the wilderness, and as having often interposed to deliver and save them. We have given the above extract in full, as it contains a not very obscure allusion to the threefold phasis of the divine nature, indicated by the titles Jehovah, Angel of the Presence, and Holy Spirit, which are still one.

On bringing together the principal features in these remarkable citations, we find that the personage described claims an uncontrolled sovereignty over the affairs of man;—that he has the attribute of omniscience and omnipresence;—that he performs works to which omnipotence only is competent;—that he uses the sacred formula peculiar to Jehovah; he swears by Himself;—that he is the gracious Protector and Saviour, the Redeemer from evil, and the Author of the most desirable blessings;—that his favor is to be sought with the deepest solicitude;—that he is the object of religious invocation; —that he is in the most express manner, and repeatedly, declared to be Jehovah, God, the ineffable I am that I am;—and yet that notwithstanding all this, the mysterious Being in question is represented as, in some sense, *distinct* from the Lord himself and acting, as the term *Angel* imports, under some kind of divine mission.

What then is the inference from all this? Are there two Jehovahs? Reason and revelation at once reclaim against such a conclusion, and some solution must be found which shall recognize the distinction and still preserve the identity. Such a solution we believe to be afforded in the theological developments of Swedenborg, and upon this branch of our subject we shall enter in the sequel, which will disclose results of great importance.

Yours, &c.

LETTER II.

THE ANGEL JEHOVAH.

DEAR SIR,

In my former letter, the evidence was somewhat largely adduced of the fact of a remarkable usage by the sacred writers in regard to the term *Angel*, in connections where, at the same time, the real personage would still seem to have been Jehovah himself, as the predicates apply to him rather than to any created being. The Angel speaks in a style which is at once perceived to be appropriate to the Lord of Angels only. This is pre-eminently the case in a passage which was not cited in my former communication; I allude to the recorded divine appearance to Moses at the burning bush.

" Now Moses kept the flock of Jethro his father-in-law, the priest of Midian: and he led the flock to the back side of the desert, and came to the mountain of God, even to Horeb. And the *Angel of the Lord* appeared unto him in a flame of fire out of the midst of a bush; and he looked, and behold, the bush burned with fire, and the bush was not consumed. And Moses said, I will now turn aside, and see this great sight, why the bush is not burnt. And when the Lord saw that he turned aside to see, God called unto him out of the midst of the bush, and said, Moses, Moses! And he said, Here am I. And he said, Draw not nigh hither: put off thy shoes from off thy feet; for the place whereon thou standest is holy ground. Moreover he said, I am the God of thy father, the God of Abraham, the God of Isaac, and the God of Jacob. And Moses hid his face, for he was afraid to look upon God."—*Exod.* iii. 1-6.

Throughout the entire narrative it is plain that it is Jehovah himself who speaks in the person of the Angel, for he says, v. 6, "I am the God of thy father, the God of Abraham, the God of Isaac, and the God of Jacob;" and Moses is said to have hidden his face, because " he was afraid to look upon God." Again, when Moses inquired what answer he should return to his people, when they demanded of him in whose name he came to them—

The Angel Jehovah. 15

"God said unto Moses, I AM THAT I AM: And he said, Thus shalt thou say unto the children of Israel, I AM hath sent me unto you. And God said moreover unto Moses, Thus shalt thou say unto the children of Israel, The Lord God of your fathers, the God of Abraham, the God of Isaac, and the God of Jacob, hath sent me unto you: this is my name for ever, and this is my memorial unto all generations."—v. 14, 15.

This, be it observed, is spoken by Him who is called in the outset the "Angel of the Lord," for the same original term translated "appeared" is applied to each. We have seen, v. 2, that the Angel is said to have "appeared" to Moses, and in the ensuing context it is said—

"Go and gather the elders of Israel together, and say unto them, The Lord God of your fathers, the God of Abraham, of Isaac, and of Jacob, *appeared* unto me, saying, I have surely visited you, and seen that which is done to you in Egypt."—v. 16.

Nothing can be more unequivocal than this. The Angel that made himself manifest in the burning bush is expressly declared to be "the Lord God of Abraham, of Isaac, and of Jacob," and if this title do not designate the supreme Jehovah, we may well despair of finding any such title in the entire compass of Revelation. The momentous inferences that follow from this, will appear in due time; but at present I would offer a remark upon the nature of the *appearance* here predicated of the personage spoken of, and the remark will hold good in general of the divine and angelic *theophanies* or *manifestations* so frequently mentioned in the Scriptures. The phraseology doubtless implies a *visibility* of some kind, and, judging from the simple letter, we should probably suppose that the function merely of the natural or outward eye was involved in the *seeing* affirmed of the spectator. If the Lord *appeared* to Moses or the patriarchs, the spontaneous impression would be, that they *saw* him, and that they saw him just as they would have seen any other object that came within the range of their ocular vision. But our Saviour declares, in language that would seem incapable of mistake, that "no man hath seen God at any time;" and the Most High himself is equally explicit in his reply to Moses on a subsequent occasion, "there shall no man see me, and live." You are moreover well aware of the prevalent belief among the Jews, that the sight of the Divine Being would be followed by the instant extinction of life. Here, then, we have a problem to be solved, in the apparent conflict of two classes of texts, one of which affirms the visibility of Jehovah, and the other denies it. How shall we reconcile them? Does Moses utter the truth when he affirms of himself, of Aaron, of Nadab, and Abihu, and the seventy elders, that "they saw the God of Israel?" Does Isaiah declare the truth when he says, "Woe is me, for mine eyes have seen the King, the Lord of Hosts?" And is it equally true, on the other hand, that "the blessed and only Potentate, the King of kings, and Lord of lords," is He "whom no man hath seen or can see," as the apostle Paul unequivocally affirms? Surely some explanation is needed which shall relieve these passages of the air of direct contrariety in their literal teachings. Whence is it to be sought? Are we not inevitably shut up to the conclusion that the *kind* of seeing is not the same in the case in which it is denied, as in that in which it is affirmed ? Is not the predicated *seeing* in the one case that of the outward eye, and in the other that of the inward? How is it possible that spiritual objects can be perceived by any other than a spiritual eye? An angel is a spirit, and a spiritual organ only can behold a spiritual being. Of this, however, the beholder may not himself be conscious, as the outward and inward vision act in unity. When the servant of Elisha saw the mountain covered by horses and chariots of fire, it was not surely by the natural eye that he perceived them, for it is said that the Lord "opened his eyes" for the purpose, and no one can imagine that his outward eyes were previously closed. Yet I know of no reason to suppose that he was himself aware of seeing the spectacle by any other than the natural organs of vision. Still there was the opening of an inward eye, and the necessity for this which existed in his case, exists in every similar case. No object can be seen by the material eye which does not reflect the rays of the sun's light. But a spirit, being immaterial, cannot reflect these rays, and cannot therefore be seen by the operation of the ordinary laws of optics. It requires the couching, as it were, of the inward eye of the spirit, in order to produce this effect. When the women entered the vacated sepulchre of our Lord, on the morning of his resurrection, they at first saw nothing. A moment after, two angels in white stood before them. Why did they not see them on their first entrance? Obviously for the reason, that their internal organs of vision were yet sealed. As soon as the spiritual eye had its film removed, the spectacle of the angels appeared. So in the case of the risen Saviour himself, and so in *every* case of angelic or divine apparition. The external human eye is not competent to the perception of spiritual beings or spiritual objects.

I would here, however, observe that when I speak of a spiritual mode of vision by which an angel is perceived, I refer only to the perception had of the angel, and not of the Lord by whom the angel is employed. Jehovah, as viewed in himself, is forever incapable of being *seen* by any created being, except so far as *seeing* coincides with *knowing*. He may be said to be *seen* in representatives by those who are brought into a state of spiritual vision, as were the ancient prophets, and so far as an angel represented the Lord, so far those who saw the Angel saw the Lord.

"When man's interior sight is opened, which is the sight of his spirit, then there appear the things of another life, which cannot possibly be made visible to the sight of the body. The visions of the prophets were nothing else. There are in heaven, as was said above, continual representatives of the Lord and of his kingdom; and there also significatives; insomuch that nothing at all exists before the sight of the angels, which is not representative and significative. Hence are the representatives and significatives in the Word; for the Word is through heaven from the Lord."—*A. C.* 1619.

It was then the spiritual ocular sense that beheld the Angel, but the Lord *in* the Angel was *known*, not *seen*. Throughout the Word that species of *seeing* of which the Lord is the object is in fact of the same nature, psychologically viewed, with that intellectual perception which is understood by faith.

"That the sense of sight corresponds to the affection of understanding and of being wise, is because the sight of the body altogether corresponds to the sight of its spirit, thus to the understanding. For there are two lights, one which is of the world from the sun, the other which is of heaven from the Lord; in the light of the world there is nothing of intelligence, but in the light of heaven there is intelligence. Hence, so far as with man the things which are of the light of the world are illumined by those which are of the light of heaven, so far the man understands and is wise; thus so far as they correspond. Because the sight of the eye corresponds to the understanding, therefore also sight is attributed to the understanding and is called intellectual sight; also those things which man apperceives, are called the objects of that sight; and also in common speech it is said, that those things are *seen* when they are *understood;* and also light and illumination, and thence clearness, are predicated of the understanding, and on the other hand, shade and darkness, and thence obscurity. These and similar things have come into use with man in speaking, from the fact that they correspond; for his spirit is in the light of heaven, and his body in the light of the world, and his spirit is what lives in the body, and also what thinks; hence, many things, which are interior, have thus fallen into vocal expressions."—*A. C.* 4405, 4406.

On this head, I beg permission to introduce an extract from Swedenborg, which will not, I think, be found to contain any thing that requires an apology on the score of overtasking a rational credence.

"That *seeing*, in the internal sense, signifies faith from the Lord, is manifest from numberless passages in the Word, of which we shall adduce the following. Ezek. xii. 2, 'Son of man, Thou dwellest in the midst of a house of rebellion, who *have eyes to see,* but do *not see,* who have ears to hear, and do not hear.' Having eyes to see but not seeing, signifies that they were able to understand the truths of faith, but were not willing, and this by reason of evils, which are the house of rebellion, inducing a deceitful light on falses, and darkness on truths. In Matthew, 'Blessed are the pure in heart, for *they shall see God,*' v. 8 : where it is evident that to see God is to believe in Him, thus to see Him by faith, for they who are in faith, by faith see God, for God is in faith, and in that which constitutes true faith. Again, 'Blessed are your *eyes,* because *they see,* and your ears because they hear : Verily I say unto you, that many prophets and righteous men have desired to *see the things which ye see,* but have *not seen them,*' xiii. 13 to 17 ; John xii. 40. To see is to know and understand the things relating to faith in the Lord, thus it denotes faith ; for they were not blessed because they saw the Lord, and saw His miracles, but because they believed, as may appear from these words in John, 'I said unto you, that *ye also have seen Me, and believed not:* This is the will of Him Who sent Me, that every one who *seeth the Son,* and *believeth on Him,* should have eternal life ; not that any one hath *seen the Father,* except He Who is with the Father, He hath *seen the Father ;* verily, verily, I say unto you, whosoever *believeth* on Me hath eternal life,' vi. 36, 40, 46, 47. To see and not to believe is to know the truths of faith and not to receive them ; to see and to believe is to know and to receive ; no one having seen the Father except He Who is with the Father, denotes that Divine Good cannot be acknowledged except by Divine Truth. Hence the internal sense is, that no one can have heavenly good, unless he acknowledge the Lord. In like manner in the same evangelist, ' *No one hath seen God at any time,* the only-begotten Son, Who is in the bosom of the Father, He hath made Him manifest,' i. 18. And again, Jesus said, ' *Whoso seeth Me, seeth Him* Who sent Me ; I am come a light into the world,

2

that whosoever *believeth on Me* should not abide in darkness,' xii. 45, 46; where it is said plainly, that to see is to believe or to have faith. Again, 'Jesus said, If ye have known Me, ye have known My Father also, and from henceforth ye have known Him and *have seen Him;* whoso hath *seen Me, hath seen the Father,'* xiv. 7, 9. Again, 'The world cannot receive the *Spirit of Truth,* because it *seeth Him not,* neither knoweth Him : I will not leave you orphans, I come to you, yet a little while and the world *shall see no more,* but ye *shall see Me,* because I live ye shall live also,' xiv. 17, 18, 19 ; where to see denotes to have faith, for the Lord is seen only by faith, for faith is the eye of love, the Lord being seen of love by faith, and love is the life of faith, wherefore it is said, ' Ye shall see me ; because I live, ye shall live also.' Again, ' I say unto you, there be some of those standing here, who shall not taste death, until *they shall see the kingdom of God,'* ix. 27 ; Mark ix. 1 : to see the kingdom of God denotes to believe. From these and other passages it is evident, that to see, in the internal sense, denotes faith from the Lord, for there is no other faith, which is faith, but what comes from the Lord : this also enables man to see, that is, to believe ; but faith from self, or from man's proprium, is not faith, for it causes him to see falses as truths, and truths as falses, and if he sees truths as truths, still he does not see, because he does not believe, for he sees himself in them, and not the Lord. That to see is to have faith in the Lord, manifestly appears from what has been frequently said above concerning the light of heaven, namely, that being from the Lord it has with it intelligence and wisdom, consequently faith in Him, for faith in the Lord is contained within intelligence and wisdom, wherefore to see from that light, as the angels do, can signify nothing else but faith in the Lord. The Lord Himself also is in that light, because it proceeds from Him. It is this light also which shines bright in the consciences of those who have faith in the Lord, although man is ignorant of it while he lives in the body, for the light of the world then obscures that light."—*A. C.* 3863.

This, you will observe, is proffered as a true solution of the meaning of the inspired Word wherever mention is made of *seeing God.* In this case the sight even of the interior or spiritual sense is merged in intellection.* But in regard to the representing Angel, he could be seen, but only by means of the eyes of the spirit. This discrimination is important, and in view of what has been said we feel authorized to assume the position, that in no recorded instance of *theophany* or *angelophany* was the appearance made to the outward eye, but invariably to an interior or spiritual vision preternaturally developed for the occasion.

In the exposition of that part of the Mosaic history which relates to the vision granted to Moses and Aaron, Nadab and Abihu, and the elders of Israel, in which it is said that "they saw the God of Israel, and there was under his feet as it were a hand work of a sapphire stone, and the body of heaven in his clearness," Swedenborg remarks that they were then permitted to behold the heavenly patterns or representative types of the various holy things of the Jewish worship, and in regard to the mode of the vision with which they were then favored, he gives us the following information :

---

* " Hath appeared to me "—that it signifies presence, is manifest from the signification of appearing to any one, as denoting presence ; for by *appearing* or *being seen,* in the internal sense, is not signified being seen by the eyes, but by the thought ; thought itself causes presence, for the person thought of appears as if present before the internal sight. In the other life this is actually the case, for when any one is there thought of intensely, he is presented to view."—*A. C.* 6893.

"Such things cannot be seen by the eyes of man, whilst he is in the world, for those eyes are formed to apprehend terrestrial and corporeal things, thus things material. They are therefore so gross, that they cannot even apprehend by vision the interior things of nature, as may be sufficiently manifest from the optical glasses, with which they must be armed, in order to see those things only which are proximately of interior nature. In a word, they are most dull, and being of such a quality, the representatives which appear to spirits in the other life, cannot be at all seen by them; but if those representatives must appear, the lumen of the world must be taken away from the eyes, in which case the things which are in the light of heaven are seen; for there is a light of heaven, and there is a light of the world; the light of heaven is for the spirit of man, and the light of the world for his body; and the case herein is this: Those things which are in the light of heaven are in thick darkness, so long as man sees from the light of the world; and *vice versa*, those things which are in the light of the world are in thick darkness, when man sees from the light of heaven. Hence it is, that when the light of the world is taken away from the sight of the corporeal eye, the eyes of man's spirit are then opened, and those things are seen which are in the light of heaven, thus the representative forms, as was said above. From these considerations it may be known, whence it is that man at this day is in thick darkness concerning heavenly things, and some in darkness so great, that they do not even believe that life after death is given, thus they do not believe that themselves are to live for ever. For man at this day is so much immersed in the body, thus in things corporeal, terrestrial and worldly, and hence in so gross a light of the world, that heavenly things are altogether thick darkness to him, and therefore the sight of his spirit cannot be enlightened. From these considerations it is now evident, that the eyes of the spirit were those, with which Moses saw the form of the tent in Mount Sinai."—*A. C.* 9577.

Such then is the nature of the vision by which spiritual and heavenly things are discerned, and as angels are thus and no otherwise seen, so when the Lord appeared under the angelic form, he was seen as other angels are seen, by the eye of the spirit and not by the eye of the body.

The only other hypothesis is that of the miraculous assumption, for the time, of a material body; that is to say, that the angel ceases *pro tem.* to be an angel and becomes a man—a supposition implying an infraction of divine order so gross and revolting to our conceptions that we cannot entertain it for a moment. If, moreover, a departure from the ordinary course of things is to be hypothecated at all, how much more reasonable to suppose that it should be in accordance with the laws of order than in opposition to them. Although it is true that the faculty of interior or spiritual vision is not enjoyed in the normal condition of man in the present life, yet every one has the innate capability of its development from the general laws of his being, since after death he comes into the immediate exercise of the power, by means of which he at once perceives spirits in their true nature. But the clothing a disembodied spirit with a material form is instantaneously seen to involve a violation of the fixed order of things and to embarrass our conceptions beyond measure. And what is gained by it? A certain effect is to be produced—viz. the vision of an immaterial being. This effect, on the one hypothesis, is produced by a process which merely anticipates, for a little while, the operation of a universal law of our being, and, on the other, by the direct contravention of such a law. If then the resulting effect is in the two cases the same, which is the most probable supposition as to the *modus operandi?* You can take your choice of the suppositions. For myself I hesitate not for a moment to adopt the idea of the opening of an interior, spiritual eye, which so acts in conjunction with the external, that the percipient is not aware but that his vision is altogether normal, and that he sees the angel as he sees any other object which addresses itself to his sense of sight.*

Regarding it then as a point established that the *appearances* of the angel mentioned were in no case made to the outward organ of vision, I proceed to the consideration of the legitimate inferences yielded by the general subject. A solution is to be sought of the grounds on which the titles "Jehovah" and "Angel of Jehovah" are interchangeably employed in the sacred record—a fact of which no possible doubt can remain after the abundant testimony I have adduced. This solution I give in the language of Swedenborg. That he professes to have come to the knowledge of the truth on this head in consequence of a special illumination, is certain. At the same time, this is not the point to which your assent is, in the outset, demanded. I leave you at full liberty to enjoy your own opinion on this score. The question submitted to your decision is, whether what he affirms does not approve itself as intrinsically true, independent of the medium through which he declares it to have been received. Upon this you are competent to pronounce. If you find it to stand the test of your severest judgment, and yet is such a view of the subject as was never before announced to the world, and such as cannot well be accounted for on any other supposition than that of its being the product of a special divine enlightenment, I do not see that you can refuse to admit his claim as so far made good. But of this I leave you to judge. I wish nothing to be forced upon you but what forces itself.

"The Angel of Jehovah is sometimes mentioned in the Word, and everywhere, when in a good sense, represents and signifies some essential appertaining to the Lord, and proceeding from him; but what is represented and signified may appear from the series. There were angels who were sent to men, and who also spake by the prophets, but what they spake was not from the angels, but by them: for their state then was, that they knew no otherwise than that they were Jehovah, that is, the Lord: nevertheless, when they had done speaking, they presently returned into their former state, and spake as from themselves. This was the case with the angels who spake the Word of the Lord; which has been given me to know by much experience of a similar kind at this day in the other life; concerning which, by the divine mercy of the Lord, we shall speak hereafter. This is the reason that the angels were sometimes called Jehovah; as was evidently the case with the angel who appeared to Moses in the bush, of whom it is thus written, 'The angel of Jehovah appeared unto him in a flame of fire out of the midst of the bush.—And when

---

* "When spiritual beings touch and *see* spiritual things the effect is exactly the same to the sense, as when natural beings touch and *see* natural things, and therefore when man first becomes a spirit, he is not aware of his decease, and believes that he is still in the body which he had when he was in the world. A human spirit also enjoys every sense, both external and internal, which he enjoyed in the world. He sees as before. He hears and speaks as before. He smells and tastes as before, and when he is touched he feels as before."—*H. & H.* 461.

Jehovah saw that he turned aside to see, God called unto him out of the midst of the bush.—God said unto Moses, I am that I am.—And God said moreover unto Moses, Thus shalt thou say unto the children of Israel, Jehovah God of your fathers hath sent me unto you' (Exod. iii. 2, 4, 14, 15); from which words it is evident, that it was an angel who appeared to Moses as a flame in the bush, and that he spake as Jehovah, because the Lord, or Jehovah spake by him. For, in order that man may be spoken to by vocal expressions, which are articulate sounds, in the ultimates of nature, the Lord uses the ministry of angels, by filling them with the divine, and by laying asleep what is of their own proprium, so that they know no otherwise than that they are Jehovah: thus the divine of Jehovah, which is in the supremes, descends into the lowest of nature, in which man is as to sight and hearing. Hence it may appear how the angels spake by the prophets, viz. that the Lord himself spake, although by angels, and that the angels did not speak at all from themselves. That the Word is from the Lord, appears from many passages; as in Matthew: 'That it might be fulfilled which was spoken of the Lord by the prophet, saying, Behold, a virgin shall bear in the womb, and shall bring forth a son' (i. 22, 23): besides other passages. Because the Lord speaks by angels when he speaks with man, it is hence that he is throughout the Word called an angel; and then by an angel is signified, as was said, some essential appertaining to the Lord, and proceeding from the Lord."—*A. C.* 1925.

We have in the above what we conceive to be the true key to the mystery of the divino-angelic theophanies recorded in the Scriptures. The interiors of the angel were so infilled and occupied by an influx from the Divine, that his own powers were in abeyance, his consciousness suspended, and he became, for the time being, a mere organ of Jehovah, through which he conveyed his will and made known his counsels. There is nothing, I think, incredible in this, although there is much more to be said in explanation, as will appear in due time. In fact, the same thing holds good occasionally in regard to human agents who are employed as the Lord's messengers, and, therefore, speak in his name. Thus Deut. xxxi. 23, "And he (Moses) gave Joshua, the son of Nun, a charge and said, Be strong and of a good courage; for thou shalt bring the children of Israel unto the land which I sware unto them; and I will be with thee." Moses here merges himself in the Divine Prompter of his words. Not unlike this is the case of the prophet who is spoken of as doing what he announces in the name of the Lord. Jer. i. 10, 11, "Behold, I have put my words in thy mouth. See, I have this day set thee over the nations, and over the kingdoms, to root out, and to pull down, and to destroy, and to throw down, to build, and to plant." Numerous additional instances of this usage could be adduced, but adequate proof of the *principle* is all that is at present requisite. The interior grounds, the rationale, of the grand fact itself, I shall endeavor to unfold in subsequent letters; but ere we can with advantage enter upon this ground, it will be expedient to develop at some length the doctrine of the Lord's DIVINE HUMANITY, to which accordingly I shall devote my next.

I would simply remark in conclusion, that from the considerations above adduced, it will appear to be of little consequence whether the original be rendered *Angel of Jehovah* or *Angel-Jehovah*, which I have adopted as the heading of my letter. Grammatical usage is probably somewhat more in favor of the former rendering, although, as Dr. J. Pye Smith remarks, the correctness of the latter cannot be absolutely disproved. Swedenborg's explanation of the fundamental truth involved, shows that the appellation is intrinsically proper.

Yours, &c.

LETTER III.

THE DIVINE HUMANITY.

DEAR SIR,

In order to a just appreciation of the closing extract given in my last from Swedenborg and of numerous others to follow, it will be requisite to present more distinctly his leading doctrine of the Divine nature, in which the principles of Love and Wisdom are made to comprehend the sum of all the perfections usually ascribed to Jehovah. As Heat and Light may be said to comprise all the properties of the sun, so the Divine Love and the Divine Wisdom embrace within themselves all the moral and intellectual elements which the mind conceives of as constituting the infinite and uncreated source of all being. What are ordinarily termed Holiness, Justice, Mercy, Benevolence, &c., are merely the different modifications or phases of Love. Omniscience, Omnipresence, and Omnipotence, refer themselves to the head of Wisdom, for which we may substitute Truth, just as we may speak of Good or Goodness in the place of Love, for Good is the correlate of Love, as Truth is of Wisdom. This holds as well in regard to man as to God, since man, in the grand constituents of his nature, is an image of God. Assuming these then as the paramount principles in the nature of Jehovah, we shall have little difficulty in admitting that the Divine Love is to the Divine Wisdom what the *Esse* of any thing is to its *Existere*, or the *substance* to the *form;* for Thought in all intelligent beings is the *form* of Affection. But the *Esse* of all existence is its Life; the Divine Life, therefore, is the Divine Love, and all human life is, in the last analysis, identical with love. That the truth of this proposition may not strike you at once, is very possible; yet I am persuaded that it will eventually force itself upon your conviction. How otherwise will you account for the effect produced even upon the physical system by the shock of disappointment falling upon a dominant and all-absorbing love? What an utter prostration of all the faculties and functions of the body oftentimes ensues. But the life of the body is in the life of the spirit, and the spirit is the seat of love, or rather its very essence is love.

In assuming that Love is the *Esse* of all being, whether Divine, angelic, or human, we necessarily preclude the idea that it is a *quality* pertaining to some unknown substance or substratum, as sweetness is the quality of sugar. It is itself the primary substance and substratum. As in regard to Heat, it is impossible for the mind, in its research into the nature of this element, to reach the conception of any primordial substance, short of the Divine substance itself, of which it is a quality, or to say that Heat proceeds *from something hot* (for how came it hot except by heat previously applied?), so in respect to Love, we must at length inevitably rest in the conclusion, that there is nothing that *lies back of it*—nothing of which it is to be predicated as a quality. It is fundamental and primary in every idea of intelligent being. In God it is underived, self-subsisting, and eternal. In angels and men it is derived by incessant influx from its infinite source. And as the love is the life of every thing that lives, Life itself is not creatable, because Love is not. Throughout the universe of dependent being, whether angelic, human, animal, or vegetable, there is no *created life*. It is perpetual influx, from the self-existing fountain of life in the Deity, into adapted receptive organs. In Him we live, move, and have our being.

Such, then, if our position be sound, is God—infinite Love and infinite Wisdom, or, what is equivalent, infinite Goodness and infinite Truth. In this character he is to be viewed as subsisting from eternity, and it is a character predicable strictly of *one* being, in whom no distinction can exist that will admit of being expressed by a term indicative of a divided personality. Love and Wisdom, or Affection and Intellect, or Will and Understanding, enter essentially into the very elemental conception of an intelligent person, whether create or uncreate, and the duality involved in the idea of these principles offers no more disturbance to the impression of absolute unity of being, than does the fact of man's possession of Love and Intellect interfere with the conviction of his being still but one person and not two. As easily could we imagine that the unity of the sun was destroyed by reason of its two-fold emanation of light and heat, as that the Divine Love and Wisdom could be the basis of a bi-personal distinction. If now we add to this the idea of *action, operation, proceeding energy,* we complete our conception of a trinal Deity without at the same time mentally dividing him into three. There is indeed a triplicity of aspects in which he is presented to the mind, and one too founded upon a real three-fold distinction, in the constituent principles of his nature, but not one that can, with any propriety, be laid as the foundation of a *tri-personal* distinction. The terms Father, Son, and Holy Ghost, denote not three *persons*, but three *essentials of one person*.

All this, I think, is somewhat easy of apprehension, and what many Trinitarians would perhaps admit, so long as their thoughts remained centred in the contemplation of the abstract and absolute Godhead, apart from all reference to Christ as "God manifested in the flesh." But no sooner does the idea of the Lord's incarnation form itself in the mind, than a vague conception of some mysterious Trinity of *persons* ensues, to the *second* of which the assumption of our nature is attributed. But the view already given of the necessary and essential unity of the Divine Being, we hold to be absolutely imperative on our belief, and to be utterly exclusive of any theory of the Godhead which involves the idea of three *persons* subsisting from eternity. Whatever be the true character of Christ as the Redeemer of men—whatever the Divinity predicated of Him—it *must* be such as to consist entirely with the unity above asserted. This lies at the foundation of every correct view of the nature of the Deity, as truly as the axioms lie at the foundation of every course of mathematical reasoning. The denial of it is the denial of a first principle, which does violence to intuition. Nor can this conviction be shaken by the most multitudinous array of Scriptural passages *apparently* declaring the contrary, for so overwhelming is the evidence from inspiration and reason on this head, that we *know* the position cannot be contravened by anything contained in holy writ when *rightly understood*. While, therefore, we readily concede and strenuously maintain the fact of a threefold distinction in the Divine nature, indicated in its reference to the economy of redemption by the terms Father, Son, and Holy Spirit, we at the same time reject, with equal assurance, that form of the doctrine which makes what is termed the second *person* of the sacred three, in contradistinction from the other two, to have come into the conditions of humanity. The true doctrine we hold to be, that the one, undivided, and absolute Jehovah took upon him our nature and accomplished redemption in our behalf. This we affirm to be, upon the authority of Revelation, not only true in itself, but *the* great and paramount truth of the Christian system, without the sincere recognition of which there is no genuine faith in the God of the Scriptures. This I shall hope to show still more distinctly in the sequel.

The ground I have thus far assumed will necessarily govern the tenor of the whole discussion upon which I have entered. The ultimate scope at which I aim is to determine the true character of Christ's work in the scheme of human redemption, and this can never be done without first discovering his true character in himself, and the relation which he sustains to the Supreme Deity. The knowledge of what Christ was *prior to* the incarnation is indispensably requisite to a knowledge of what he was and did *in* his incarnation. That he was from eternity divine, you have no hesitation to admit. But if he was divine he was God, and if God, the supreme God ; for the terms are of identical import. Again, the supreme God is Jehovah, and God incarnate is Jehovah incarnate, which necessitates *with you* the admission, that Jesus and Jehovah are one and the same. The Unitarian of course denies this, because he denies the competency of the Old Testament to determine the point for Christians, who are shut up, in their view, exclusively to the teachings of the New Testament in relation to every thing touching the person and work of the Saviour. I would not, however, imply by this, that the view of Christ for which I am contending is not sustained in the writings of the Evangelists and Apostles. On the contrary, I am fully persuaded, and shall hope to show, that the testimony of the two Covenants is perfectly univocal on this head, and that the Unitarian must be cast before his own tribunal ; but, as I remarked in the outset, 1 propose to found my argument primarily on the Old Testament

Scriptures, by which the language of the New on this subject is throughout controlled.

Maintaining, then, on adequate grounds, that Jesus Christ prior to his incarnation was the veritable and only Jehovah, it remains to be ascertained, if possible, what view can be gained of his nature which will make it conceivable that in this character he should have assumed the earthly humanity of the sons of men. This is the grand problem to be solved. This is the master mystery, the unfolding of which discloses the true economy of redemption and converts faith into knowledge. And here it is that we are constrained to avow our grateful thanks to the God of all grace for the illumination vouchsafed to his servant Swedenborg, in consequence of which a flood of light has been thrown upon the deepest arcana pertaining to the Divine Being and the universe of creatures. We, who have studied the purport of these sublime revelations and compared them with the fairest deductions of our own minds, can scarcely desire any information on the subjects treated of which has not been granted. Still I am well aware that what is from this source authority with me, on the themes in question, cannot be supposed to be authority with you in your present state of mind, and I shall therefore endeavor to present the matter in such a light that the conclusions reached may stand before you independent of any estimate that either you or I may have formed of Swedenborg as a professed messenger from Heaven. Indeed, it is because we perceive that what he has announced is intrinsically true in itself that we so firmly believe he was commissioned to announce it. Our credence is given to the truthfulness of the messenger from our conviction of the truth of the message; while at the same time we refuse to admit that the intelligence which thus recognizes the truth of the message was competent to have reached it apart from the medium of the messenger. Human reason may put the seal of its sanction on a multitude of truths which it could never have discovered by its own powers.

That "God is a spirit" is one of the most emphatic declarations of holy writ, and equally clear is its teaching that man was made in the image of God. It is reasonable, therefore, to look for the leading points of this similitude in the spiritual nature of man. On the same grounds we are authorised to suppose that the divine image will be more clearly recognised in the disembodied than in the embodied man, especially when a *moral* conformity to his divine prototype exists within him. The essential constituents of humanity are more in the spirit than in the body, inasmuch as the body is an effect of which the spirit is the proximate cause. Yet as every effect is potentially *in* its cause, we infer that there is that in the human spirit which is normally represented in the human body; the body is the exponent of the spirit, so far as that which is natural and material can effigy that which is spiritual; in a word, that the body *corresponds* to the spirit, which is but another form of saying, that the body is what it is from the influx of the elaborating spirit into it. The hidden potencies of the spirit develop themselves in sensible manifestation in the structure and functions of the corporeal fabric. I am unable to see why it is not a fair deduction from this, that if man is created in the image of God, and what we term his essential humanity—made visible to the senses in his bodily frame—is virtually and elementally comprised in his spiritual entity, that this very humanity is a part of the divine image—that is, that there is a sense in which the true human principle pertains to the divine exemplar after which man was formed. Indeed, how can it be otherwise? Does not man derive his distinctive nature from the possession of Understanding and Affection? Are not these the very principles and attributes which constitute him man? Take these away and what of humanity is left to your conception? If you say, the body, still there would be no human body if there were no human spirit to form it, and what possible idea can you have of a human spirit to which Will or Affection and Understanding were wanting? But the Will and Understanding in man are the finite counterparts to the infinite Love and Wisdom of his Maker. It is in these faculties that the image of God is reflected, and yet these are the very groundwork of his humanity. How then is it possible to avoid the conclusion that there is in God a Divine Humanity? That these terms may, at first blush, strike you as utterly incompatible with each other, is very possible, but the sequel, I trust, will dispel the air of paradox which invests the position. That your conception on this head may also be embarrassed by the consideration of *form*, is by no means unlikely, but I beg you, nevertheless, to ponder well the proposition and see whether it can be by any possibility avoided. If it do not involve an essential truth, pray what *is* the truth in regard to the inspired declaration that man was made in the image of God? Does not image imply resemblance? If a child is said to be an image of his father, do we not necessarily convey the idea of that in the child which reflects the father, as the impression on wax reflects the seal that stamped it? If you say that this is merely external, relating only to the aspect of the father, I entreat you to carry your thoughts a little further, and inquire whether the external similitude is not due to an internal cause, or, in other words, whether the soul of the child, derived from the father, has not moulded the countenance to the paternal image? If so, it can by no means be maintained that the likeness is merely external. The outer man is evermore the creation of the inner man, and the father, in his distinguishing attributes, is reproduced in the child. Shall we hesitate to say, then, that man is man because God is Man? The relation is that of a type to an archetype—of a copy to a pattern. *Man could not possibly be an image of God, were not God an exemplar of man.*

But God, you say, is infinite, and man is finite. How can the finite represent the infinite? But this is a question which you are as much concerned to answer as I am. We are both estopped in our interrogation by the unequivocal averment that man was made in the Divine image. You have to determine the sense in which this holds as well as myself. My position, however, involves no difficulty; the difficulty pressing on yours is, I conceive, insuperable. But of this more as we proceed.

As to the fact of God's existing in the human form, one thing may with all confidence be asserted. Love and Wisdom cannot subsist, or be conceived of, apart from a subject in whom they inhere. "No intelligent person," says Swedenborg, "can deny in himself that in God are love and wisdom, mercy and clemency, and good and truth itself, for they are from Him; and as he cannot deny that these things are in God, neither can he deny that God is man; for none of these things can exist abstractedly from man; man is their subject, and to separate them from their subject is to say that they do not exist. Think of wisdom, and suppose it out of a man; is it anything?" Indeed the idea of Love and Wisdom existing out of a personal subject is as absurd as to suppose that the heart and lungs can exist and act apart from a body which they actuate. Can anything more completely baffle all rational conception?

We are shut up, therefore, as we believe to the inevitable conclusion that God is Very Man—the Infinite Man—comprising within Himself all the distinguishing attributes of our human nature, and thus affording an adequate ground for man to be made in his veritable image.* But as we have already seen that Christ is God, therefore the infinite humanity of Jehovah must be the humanity of Jesus, or, in other words, our Lord Jesus Christ must have possessed from eternity a Divine Human principle, and this admitted it is comparatively easy to conceive that this Divine Human may have clothed itself with the ultimates of our *human* Humanity, so to speak, in order to come down to our level and to reach us by its vivifying influx of spiritual life. For the same reason, we can more readily apprehend the grand truth which we are endeavoring to establish, that the manifestations of Jehovah were made to the fathers from the earliest periods under a human form, for this was the appropriate form, inasmuch as the Lord from his very nature exists in that form. Of this I shall hope to adduce still more abundant proof in the progress of the discussion.

Yours, &c.

---

* " I will relate what must needs seem wonderful: every man, in the idea of his spirit, sees God as a man, even he who in the idea of his body sees Him like a cloud, a mist, air, or ether, even he who has denied that God is a man : man is in the idea of his spirit when he thinks abstractedly, and in the idea of his body when he thinks not abstractedly. That every man in the idea of his spirit sees God as a man, has been made evident to me from men after death, who are then in the ideas of spirit; for men after death become spirits, in which case, it is impossible for them to think of God otherwise than as of a man."— *A. E.* 1115.

LETTER IV.

THE DIVINE HUMANITY.

DEAR SIR,

In the preceding series of letters we have found ourselves conducted, by a course of independent reasoning, to substantially the same result with that which forms the grand theme of Swedenborg's disclosures respecting the nature of our Lord prior to the incarnation. We have seen that a Divine Human principle pertains essentially to Jehovah, and is actually involved in every just conception of his being.* We do not say, however, that this result, announced by Swedenborg, could ever have been attained so as to be set forth clearly and distinctly, if his illumination had not led the way and put us upon the right track of inquiry. But it is important to hold the assurance, that his discoveries of divine things do find a response in the oracles of our own minds, and that thus they may be, as it were, rationally verified. I shall, therefore, henceforward feel under no embarrassment in quoting his language whenever occasion shall render it expedient. The views advanced by such a man, on such a subject, cannot but be entitled to the gravest consideration.

Our position, be it recollected, is, that a Divine Humanity exists in Jehovah as the very condition of his being, and the only adequate idea we can form on this subject results from mentally transferring to Him the distinctive attributes of our own humanity, and supposing Him to possess them in an infinite degree. If it be objected that our humanity exists in a finite *form*, and that we cannot conceive of an infinite human *form*, I would submit whether the same difficulty does not press upon the conception of infinite Wisdom and infinite Love, which, being substance, must necessarily have a form. These attributes you admit are, in us, an image in miniature of the same attributes in Jehovah. But in Him they exist in infinite measure. How then can the finite be an image of the infinite? Yet you do not whisper the least dissent from the divine declaration that *such is the fact*. You will perceive, therefore, that until this fact is in some way explained so as to subvert our main position, we cannot be expected

---

* " All the angels who are in the heavens never perceive the Divine under any other form than the human; and what is wonderful, those who are in the superior heavens cannot think otherwise concerning the Divine. They are brought into that necessity of thinking from the Divine itself which flows in, and also from the form of heaven, according to which their thoughts extend themselves around: for every thought which the angels have has extension into heaven, and according to that extension they have intelligence and wisdom. Hence it is, that all there acknowledge the Lord, because the Divine Human is given only in Him. These things have not only been told me by the angels, but it has also been given me to perceive them, when elevated into the interior sphere of heaven. Hence it is manifest, that the wiser the angels are, the more clearly they perceive this; and hence it is, that the Lord appears to them: for the Lord appears in a divine angelic form, which is the human, to those who acknowledge and believe in a visible Divine, but not those who acknowledge and believe in an invisible Divine; for the former can see their Divine, but the latter cannot."—*H. & H.* 79.

to recede from our ground, simply from the urgency of an objection which presses as heavily upon your argument as upon ours. It is certain that man was created in the image of God—it is certain that this image consists in the possession of wisdom and love—it is certain that these principles in Jehovah are infinite and yet must inhere in a person, and that person must be both a substance and a form, as a substance without a form, or a form without a substance, is a nonentity. But an infinite substance must have an infinite form, and the conception labors no more in regard to the one than to the other. Our difficulties on this subject arise solely from our subjection, in this world, to the influence of the ideas of time and space. Let these be abstracted, and let us apprehend the real truth, that God has no relation to space—no other at least, than that he is "in all space without space, and in all time without time,"—and we shall be enabled to rise to a higher and juster conception of the divine nature. We shall then feel the force of our author's language in the following paragraph:

"That God is Man, can hardly be comprehended by those who judge all things from the sensual things of the external man: for the sensual man cannot think otherwise of the Divine than from the world and from the things which are there; thus not otherwise of the Divine and Spiritual Man, than as of a corporeal and natural one. He concludes thence, that if God were man, He would be in size as the universe: and if He ruled heaven and earth, it would be done by means of many, according to the manner of kings in the world. If it should be said to him, that in heaven there is not extension of space as there is in the world, he would not at all comprehend it; for he who thinks from nature and its light alone, never thinks otherwise than from an extense, such as is before the eyes. But they are exceedingly deceived, when they think in like manner concerning heaven; the extense which is there is not as the extense in the world."—*H. & H.* 85.

You see then the conclusion to which we are brought, and which we perceive no way of avoiding but by a direct denial of the inspired declaration, that man was made in the image of God, or by an equally direct assertion, that as to the constituents of that image we neither know nor can know anything. This, however, is itself no slight assumption—to claim to know how much or how little can be known —to define the exact limits of the human powers, and to prescribe the *ne plus ultra* of their attainments. As we have seen the futility of this claim in a thousand instances in the history of the past—as the boundaries once set to the human mind have been repeatedly broken through—so we have no distrust of its continued advances in time to come. By the ampler unfoldings of nature, we believe the Deity is for ever to be more and more fully disclosed to the intelligence of his creatures, and by the laws of interpretation a more distinct and definite conception gained of the import of the terms employed by revelation to set forth his being and perfections. If he addresses men in human language, we see no reason to doubt that that language is capable of an explication which shall incessantly bring it nearer and nearer to the grasp of our faculties, and that in proportion as this is done we shall see the God of the Universe becoming more perceptibly one with the God of the Bible, which is but to say that the highest Rationalism shall eventually harmonize with the highest Revelation-ism. That this result is even now actually realized in the system of Swedenborg, we are doubtless much more ready to assert than you are to admit; but our assertion is made upon the basis of a profound examination of the whole scheme, while the denials of our opponents are put forth upon a presumption that dispenses with inquiry. This we affirm, because we never meet with objections that take the least cognizance of the fundamental grounds of our belief. They invariably skim the surface without striking into the sub-soil of the *principles* of the system.

From the conclusion hitherto reached, that a Divine Humanity pertains to Jehovah, the mind is undoubtedly greatly relieved on the score of the *theophanies* made to the patriarchs and prophets. We see an adequate ground for these appearances having been made under the human form, and we are naturally prompted to recognise in them, though spiritually perceived, a significant foreshadowing of that subsequent manifestation which was made in the *ultimates* of humanity, that is to say, in a body of flesh and blood.* Still I can easily conceive that you are not yet prepared to apprehend the precise mode in which the asserted angelic agency is involved in these manifestations of Jehovah. Why, you ask, was any medium of communication necessary? Why was it not competent to omnipotence to bring down the requisite revelation *directly* to the human faculties? —a question to which I acknowledge the difficulty of offering a reply that shall be satisfactory to a state of mind not at present in accordance with the vein of Swedenborg's spiritual announcements. To one that is, the difficulty is comparatively slight. In attempting, however, an answer, I must revert to the distinction above stated of Love and Wisdom in the Divine nature, on which the true solution entirely depends. This distinction must be regarded as extremely marked in itself, though the two principles, both in God and man, really form *a one*. Love, constituting as it does the *esse* of being, can never be directly manifested. Though in reality the inmost element of the being of man and angel, yet neither man nor angel can ever come to the interior *sight* of the love which constitutes their life, as they can in regard to their thought, which is the form or *existere* of love. There is obviously a sense in which a man may be said to *see* his thoughts. But love is made known only by *feeling*. It reveals itself by the sense of itself. So also in regard to the Divine Love. It is by influx *in* every thing that lives, but it is in it latently, as heat is in the sun's light in the season of spring, yet it is for ever incapable of *immediate* manifestation. So far then as this element of the Divine nature is concerned, it is utterly inaccessible to the vision of any created being, and no language affirming

---

* "The Israelitish Church worshiped Jehovah, who in himself is the invisible God, but under a human form, which Jehovah God put on by means of an angel, and in which form he was seen by Abraham, Sarah, Moses, Hagar, Gideon, Joshua, and sometimes by the prophets, *which human form was representative of the Lord who was to come ;* therefore, all and every thing in that Church was made representative also."—*T. C. R.* 786.

visibility, in any sense, of Jehovah, can possibly be understood as relating to his essential Love, or what may be termed the fundamental ground of his being. "That," says our author, "which proceeds from His Divine *Esse* without a medium, reaches not man, for His Divine *Esse* is invisible, and being invisible comes not within the reach of thought." So far, therefore, as *manifestation* is predicated of Him, it must always be conceived of as referring to his Wisdom or Truth alone, which is the appropriate *form* of his Love, just as a man's intellect is the *form* of his affection.

I am well aware of the stone of stumbling which must necessarily lie in your way from the application of the term *form* to subjects of a purely intellectual or spiritual nature. Yet how can it be avoided when treating of *substance?* Are not the two inseparably united? Can there be a substance without a form? and if a spiritual substance, must it not have a spiritual form? Is there, in fact, any real impropriety or incongruity in saying that a man's thought is the *form* of his affection?—for surely we understand very easily what is meant when it is said that a man's dominant affection controls and *moulds* his thought, albeit this would be termed a metaphorical expression. We cannot, therefore, dispense with the term, even in speaking of the Deity himself, in whom Wisdom or Truth is the *form* of Love, the two constituting in unison the basis of the similitude which renders man an image of God.

If, then, it be conceded that we may speak of the Divine Truth as the form of the Divine Love or Good, the question comes before us as to the relation which subsists between the Divine Truth and the Divine Humanity previously established; the determining of which will necessarily guide our researches as to the nature of the *theophanies* we are now considering.

The grand point of inquiry is to ascertain how the idea of God, as a personal being, can come to the human mind, seeing that he is infinite and man is finite, and seeing too that the Divine *Esse* or Love cannot, in the nature of things, become a subject of *immediate* manifestation. Whatever of the Divine is made directly manifest to the intellectual perception of creatures, must pertain, not to his Love, but to his Wisdom or Truth. This is a fact of great moment in the discussion—that it is the Divine *Existere* and not the Divine *Esse* which becomes cognizable to the interior vision both of men and angels, just as a man in this world becomes visible to another by means of his body, which is his *existere*, though his soul, which is his *esse*, and *in* his body. But we do not *see* the soul; we see only the body, and the *man* is manifested in the body. Now apply this to the Lord himself, in whom the Divine Wisdom or Truth, which is his *existere*, is to the Divine Love, which is his *esse*, what the body is to the soul, or the form to the substance. How can this Divine Truth manifest itself, in its personality, to the mind of man, so as to concentrate upon it his affections, and by an intelligent apprehension effect a saving conjunction with itself? Must it not come before him in a *form?* And yet this form must be finited to be brought within the reach of his finite faculties? He is incapable of perceiving an infinite form. Here then is the exigency—to conceive how the infinite Divine Truth can present itself in a form to the mental perception of a man. We have, however, the advantage, having previously established the fact that Jehovah is essentially Man, or that there is in Him a Divine Human from eternity. The only difficulty is in conceiving how this Humanity, which is infinite, can make itself cognizable to an intelligence which is finite.*

In the solution of this difficulty we must necessarily elevate our thoughts to a contemplation of Jehovah as the self-existent and eternal fountain of the efflux of Love, Life, and Light to the universe of angels and men. In all ideas of communication to men from this boundless source of being, we must conceive of him as *flowing down* through heaven into the minds which are formed to be receptive of his Wisdom and Love. But when we speak of the Lord's *descending by influx*, we are carefully to exclude all ideas of mere *local transition*. We are dealing wholly with spiritual conceptions, from which time and space are to be entirely banished. So likewise as to heaven—the true conception will be at once destroyed if we think of it as *a place* spatially defined. Heaven is the aggregate states of all heavenly minds, and these states are formed by the pervading presence of the elements of Love and Wisdom. It is the Divine of the Lord which constitutes heaven. "The angels taken together, are called heaven, because they constitute it; but still it is the Divine proceeding from the Lord which flows in with the angels, and which is received by them, which makes heaven in general and in particular. The Divine proceeding from the Lord is the good of love and the truth of faith; as far, therefore, as they receive good and truth from the Lord, so far they are angels, and so far they are heaven." "Heaven in general with all, and in particular with each, is a reception of the influx which is from the Divine Essence." Thus teaches Swedenborg, and if revelation does not expressly *say* as much, it must assuredly *mean* it, and "the meaning of the Word *is* the Word." The true sense of the Scriptures can be no other than that sense which is according to truth.

For the Lord, therefore, to *descend* through heaven, is for his Divine Truth and Good to flow through the interiors of angelic spirits downward to the natural plane of men on earth. But these angels are all men, and, viewed collectively, they are as one Grand Man before the Lord, for the heavenly form is the human form.† This

---

* "That Jehovah appearing denotes the appearing of the Lord's Divine in his Human, is evident from this, that his Divine cannot appear to any man, nor even to any angel, except by the Divine Human; and *the Divine Human is nothing but the Divine Truth which proceeds from himself.*"—*A. C.* 6945.

† "That heaven in the whole complex resembles one man, is an arcanum not yet known in the world; but in the heavens it is very well known." "The angels indeed do not appear in the whole complex in such a form, for the whole heaven does not fall into the view of any angel; but they sometimes see remote societies, which consist of many thousands of angels, as one in such a form; and from a society, as from a part, they conclude as to the whole, which is heaven. For in the most perfect form, the wholes are as the parts, and the parts as the wholes; the distinction is only as between similar things greater and less. Hence they say the whole heaven is such in the sight of the Lord, because the Divine forms the inmost and supreme of all things."—*H. & H.* 59, 62.

results from the plastic power of the Lord's Divine Human principle which continually tends to produce images of itself. The Divine is in the Grand Man of heaven as the soul is in the body; and as the soul manifests itself through the medium of the body, so the Lord, before he appeared in flesh, manifested himself through the medium of the angelic heaven.* He did this from necessity, for in no other way could he approach man so as to impart to him an intelligible idea of his personal mode of existence. "Before the Lord's advent into the world, whenever Jehovah appeared, it was in the form of an angel; for when he passed through heaven He clothed Himself with that form, which is the human form; the whole heaven from the Divine *Esse* there being as one man."—*A. C.* 10,579. The human mind might indeed have otherwise formed a vague *quasi* idea of Jehovah as a boundless, formless spirit—a kind of illimitable ether—but this is not the true conception of the true God, inasmuch as it is one that is devoid of all conjunctive virtue. Of this, however, I shall have more to say hereafter.

It was then by an angelic medium that the Lord made himself known in the early ages to his people. He inflowed into an angel and filled him with his presence and in his form revealed his own form, as far as it was possible to do it. The angel was his representative for the time being, and on this ground an identity of person is often predicated of the Lord and the angel in the sacred record. This is very clearly indicated in the following passage:

"The reason why the Divine Human is called the Angel of Jehovah, is because Jehovah, before the coming of the Lord, when He passed through heaven, appeared in a human form as an angel: for the whole angelic heaven resembles one man, which is called the Grand Man: wherefore when the Divine itself passed through the angelic heaven, He appeared in a human form as an angel before those with whom He spake: this was the Divine Human of Jehovah before the coming of the Lord: the Lord's Human, when made Divine, is the same thing, for the Lord is Jehovah Himself in the Divine Human. That the Lord, as to the Divine Human, is called an angel, is further evident from several passages in the New Testament, where the Lord says that He was *sent* by the Father; and *to be sent* signifies to *proceed*, and *sent*, in the Hebrew tongue, signifies *an angel*. That the Lord calls Himself *the Sent*, may be seen, Matt. x. 40; xv. 24; Mark ix. 37; Luke iv. 43; ix. 48, x. 16; John iii. 17, 34; iv. 34; v. 23, 24, 36, 37, 38; vi. 29, 39, 40, 44, 57; vii. 16, 18, 28,

* "The infinite *Existere*, in which is the infinite *Esse*, they (the most Ancient Church) perceived as a Divine Man, by reason that they knew that the infinite *Existere* was brought forth from the infinite *Esse* through heaven; and as heaven is the Grand Man, therefore they could not have any other idea or perception concerning the infinite *Existere* from the infinite *Esse*, than concerning a Divine Man, for whatever passes through heaven as through the Grand Man from the infinite *Esse*, this has with it an image thereof in all and single things."—*A. C.* 4687.

"The Lord spake with John through heaven, and through heaven he also spake with the prophets, and through heaven he speaks with every one to whom he does speak: and this by reason that the angelic heaven is in common as one man, whose life and soul the Lord is, wherefore all that the Lord speaks, he speaks through heaven, just as the soul and mind of man speaks through his body—for there is an influx of the Lord through heaven, just as there is an influx of the soul through the body; the body indeed speaks and acts, and also feels something from influx, but still the body does nothing from itself as of itself, but is acted upon; that such is the nature of speech, yea, of all influx of the Lord through heaven into men, has been given to me to know from much experience."—*A. R.* 943.

29; viii. 16, 18, 29, 42; ix. 4; x. 36; xi. 41, 42; xii. 44, 45, 49; xiii. 20; xiv. 24; xvi. 5, 7; xvii. 3 to 8, 18, 21 to 23, 25."—*A. C.* 6831.

"The Infinite itself, which is above all the heavens, and above the inmosts with man, cannot be manifested except by the Divine Human, which exists with the Lord alone. The communication of the infinite with the finite is not possible in any other way: which is also the reason that when Jehovah appeared to the men of the Most Ancient Church, and afterwards to those of the Ancient Church after the flood, and also in succeeding times to Abraham and the prophets, he was manifested to them *as a man*. Hence it may appear that the Infinite Esse never could have been manifested to man, except by the Human Essence, consequently by the Lord."—*A. C.* 1990.

It was in the finite person of the angel that his own infinite person was, as it were, reflected, and thus brought down to the perception of the finite faculties of man, and all this from the intrinsic necessity of the case. A divine manifestation to finite man was in no other way possible. This can by no means be deemed incredible when it is considered, that even in this world the human spirit, which pervades and animates the whole material man, may sometimes display itself, in its entire present *state*, by the medium of a single member of the body—by a cast of the countenance, a glance of the eye, a curl of the lip, or a wave of the hand. The face alone, we well know, will often mirror the whole actings of the soul under the predominance of a powerful emotion or passion, and even in its repose we see depicted the ruling character of the man. "The face," says Swedenborg, "is the external representation of the interiors, for the face is so formed that the interiors may appear in it, as in a representative mirror, and another may thence know what the person's mind is towards him, so that when he speaks he manifests the mind's meaning as well by the speech as by the face." Nothing more than this is necessary to afford a solution of the title מלאך פני, *malak panai, angel of the face* (or *faces*), usually rendered *angel of the presence*, because the affection of a being is made *present* in his face. The plural form *faces* occurs in the original to denote the varieties of affection which impress themselves upon the countenance. The divine *faces*, however, imply no *absolute* variation in the divine affections, but simply the effect produced by the state of reception in the beholder, which always modifies the manifestation made to him. That this should be Swedenborg's interpretation was of course to be expected. "The Divine Esse has never appeared in any visible form (*in facie*), although his Divine Human has so appeared, and by that, and, as it were, in that, the Divine Love has appeared." "The Lord in respect to the Divine Human is called the *Angel of the faces* of Jehovah, because the Divine Human is the Divine Esse in a visible appearance, that is, in a form."

I would here remark that I see nothing in the nature of the subject or in the exigencies of the Scriptural testimony to necessitate the idea of any *particular* angel—any one angel by *pre-eminence*—as having been uniformly employed on these occasions, notwithstanding the apparently specificating force of the article *the*—"*the* angel of the Lord." Considering the infinite interval which separates the highest conceivable creature from the Creator, it is plain that no angelic intelligence could possess in himself, a dignity that should peculiarly entitle him to this honor; and as the end to be attained by the assumption of the angelic medium could, to human view, be as well secured by the intermediate agency of one of this class of beings as of another, we are at a loss to perceive the grounds of the supposition to which I am now adverting. The grand fact assumed is simply that of the presence of an angel-personator in the Divine *theophanies*. So far as I can see, nothing depended upon the selection for the office of one being of this order rather than another.

We are now prepared for the presentation more *in extenso* of Swedenborg's grand announcement on this theme of the Lord's *theophany* through an angelic medium. In his explanation of Ex. xxiii. 23, " my Angel shall go before thee," he thus writes ;—

" The reason why the Lord as to the Divine Human [principle] is meant by an angel is, because the several angels, who appeared before the Lord's coming into the world, were Jehovah Himself in a human form, or in the form of an angel; which is very manifest from this consideration, that the angels who appeared were called Jehovah. Jehovah Himself in the human form, or what is the same thing, in the form of an angel, was the Lord. His Divine Human [principle] appeared at that time as an angel, of whom the Lord Himself speaks in John ' Jesus said, Abraham exulted to see My day, and he saw, and rejoiced. Verily, verily, I say unto thee, before Abraham was, I am,' viii. 56, 58. And again, ' Glorify thou Me, O Father, with Thyself, with the glory which I had with Thee before the world was,' xvii. 5. That Jehovah otherwise could not appear, is also manifest from the Lord's words in John, ' Ye have not heard at any time the voice of the Father, nor seen His appearance,' v. 37. And again, ' Not that any one has seen the Father, except He who is with the Father, He hath seen the Father,' vi. 46. From these passages it may be known what the Lord was from eternity. The reason why it pleased the Lord to be born a man, was that he might actually put on the Human [principle], and might make this Divine, to save the human race. Know, therefore, that the Lord is Jehovah Himself, or the Father, in a human form, which also the Lord Himself teaches in John, ' I and the Father are one,' x. 30. Again, ' Jesus said, henceforth ye have known and seen the Father. He who hath seen Me hath seen the Father. Believe Me that I am in the Father and the Father in Me,' xiv. 7, 9, 11. And again, · All Mine are Thine, and all Thine are Mine,' xvii. 10. This great mystery is described in John in these words, ' In the beginning was the Word, and the Word was with God, and God was the Word; the same that was in the beginning with God. All things were made by Him, and without Him was not anything made which was made. And the Word was made flesh, and dwelt amongst us, and we have seen His glory, the glory as of the only-begotten of the Father. No one hath seen God at any time, the only-begotten Son, who is in the bosom of the Father, He hath brought Him forth to view,' i. 1, 2, 3, 14, 18. The Word is the Divine Truth, which has been revealed to men, and since this could not be revealed except from Jehovah as a man, that is, except from Jehovah in the human form, thus from the Lord, therefore it is said, ' In the beginning was the Word, and the Word was with God, and God was the Word.' It is a known thing in the Church, that by the Word is meant the Lord, wherefore this is openly said,' ' The Word was made flesh, and dwelt amongst us, and we have seen His glory, the glory as of the only-begotten of the Father.' That the Divine Truth could not be revealed to men, except from Jehovah in the human form, is also clearly said, 'No one hath seen God at any time, the only-begotten Son, who is in the bosom of the Father, He hath brought Him forth to view.' From these considerations it is evident, that the Lord from eternity was Jehovah, or the Father in a human form but not yet in the flesh, for an angel has not flesh. And whereas Jehovah or the Father willed to put on all the human [principle], for the sake of the salvation of the human race, therefore also He assumed flesh, wherefore it is said 'God was the Word, and the Word was made flesh.' And in Luke, 'See ye My hands and My feet, that it is I myself, handle Me and see, for a spirit hath not flesh and bones as ye see Me have,' xxiv. 39. The Lord by these words taught, that He was no longer Jehovah under the form of an angel, but that He was Jehovah-Man; which also is meant by these words of the Lord, 'I came forth from the Father, and am come into the world, again I leave the world, and go to the Father,' John xvi. 28."—*A. C* 9315.

From all this, taken in connection with the train of the foregoing remark, it would seem difficult to avoid the conclusion, not only that Christ is the supreme Jehovah, but that he is Jehovah in unity, to the entire and absolute exclusion of any such *hypostases* or *subsistents* in the Divine Nature as are usually understood by the term *persons*. What possible ground can there be for such *hypostases?* If the Divine Love and Divine Wisdom as already explained, together with the Divine *procedere,* i. e. act, energy, operation of the united two, comprise the totality of the Divine nature, and form the complement of one Divine Person, what basis remains on which to build the theory of the three distinct persons of the Trinity? What is the idea which shall answer to the language of the popular creeds on this subject?* Is there any intelligible meaning to the words Father, Son, and Holy Ghost, so long as they are made the representatives of three distinct personalities in Jehovah? We have already found the Trinity complete in one person; why, then, seek for it in three? If you say that by *persons* is not meant *persons,* but unknown *somewhats*—certain mysterious *distinctions* in the Deity to which the word *persons* is applied for want of a better—still I would beg you to task your intellect to the utmost, and see if you can conceive of any other distinctions than those which I have designated as the three *essentials* of the Godhead; yet these three constitute, of necessity, but one person.† I know, indeed, that it is common to speak of the Son of God as the second person of the Holy Trinity, and also to refer the ancient *theophanies* before spoken of to him. But the Scriptures never speak of them in this manner. They give no warrant for this peculiar attribution. They recognize only the one, absolute, undivided Jehovah as the true subject of these manifestations. They never intimate that the Angel was Christ in any other sense than that in which the alone Jehovah was Christ, and even he could not properly be then so denominated, because the *anointing* on which the title is founded did not take place till after

---

* "What means this, that the Divine is distinguished into three persons? Where is this to be found in the Word? What means this, that the Divine was born from eternity? But that the Divine is one, or one person, or one man, this is intelligible, as also that the Divine should have been from eternity: But they are to be excused for thus teaching who have known nothing of the style of the Word, that a spiritual sense pertains to every expression."—*De Dom. et de Athan. Symb.* p. 1.

† "A trine or triune God is not one God, so long as this trine or triunity exists in three persons; but he in whom a trine or triunity exists in one person, is one person, is one God, and that God is the Lord; enter into whatever intricacies of thought you please, yet will you never be able to extricate yourself and make out that God is one, unless he is also one in person."—*A. R.* 490.

he was made flesh: nor was he, except prophetically, termed Son prior to that event. The *Son of God* was born in time, and not begotten from eternity, as I shall produce ample ground for asserting as I proceed. All such expressions, in such relations, are *proleptical*, and even the titles *Jesus* and *Christ*, strictly considered, are now retrospective, as the character indicated by them has merged itself, by reason of the glorification, in that of the alone Jehovah or Lord. Again, then, I ask, what are the grounds of the tripersonal theory of the Godhead? Where are its sanctions to be found? You surely will not refer me to those passages of Holy Writ which assert a triplicity in the Divine Nature; for the establishment and elucidation of this is the main feature of Swedenborg's doctrine, and what I have all along assumed as the primary truth of revelation. It amounts to nothing to tell me that you are taught by the Bible to acknowledge God under the threefold character of Father, Son, and Holy Ghost. I should be very sorry indeed if you were not; but I am brought no nearer by this confession to an apprehension of three coequal and coeternal persons in the Godhead. And yet this is the very point to which, as an opponent of Swedenborg, you have put your faith, your logic and your exegetic in pledge. If you make not this apparent on adequate grounds, you accomplish nothing to the purpose. The question is not concerning a revealed fact—in this we are both agreed—but concerning the manner in which this fact is to be understood. What is the absolute truth couched under the inspired words? If you still insist upon a veritable trinity of persons, are you not bound to show that your position can stand in entire consistency with the declaration of the Divine unity contained in the following passages: "Hear, O Israel, the Lord our God is ONE Lord." "There is none good but ONE, that is, God." "ONE is your Father, which is in heaven." "There is none other God but ONE." "God is ONE." "There is ONE God, and there is no other but He." In that day Jehovah shall be King over all the earth: in that day there shall be ONE Jehovah, and his name ONE;" this last passage plainly implying the advent of a period when the very views promulgated by the New Church on this head shall be universal.

You will not fail to perceive the central point of my position on the whole subject: that that Divine Essence which clothed itself with a material humanity in the person of Jesus of Nazareth, was no other then the one, exclusive, absolute, and eternal Jehovah. It is a position which utterly ignores, not only the fact, but the very possibility, of any such tripersonal mode of existence in the Deity as shall constitute a ground for ascribing the assumption of flesh and blood to the *second* of these persons in contradistinction from the other two. I hesitate not to affirm that such a view of the Divine nature is not only repugnant to the clearest voice of reason, but to the most explicit teaching of the Word. Where do you find any thing to warrant it? No passages can be cited from the Old Testament bearing more directly on the question than those which I have already adduced, and these as we have seen, both admit and demand another mode of interpretation. In the Angel Jehovah we can recognize no manifestation but that of Jehovah himself in his indivisible unity. We see not the slightest intimation of any second *hypostasis* or person of whom the *theophany* is predicated. And if this be the purport of the Old Testament, must not that of the New accord with it? If then the tripersonal theory be attempted to be sustained by Scripture, it must doubtless be on the ground of *inference*. It is to be *inferred* that, as a Trinity is expressly taught under the threefold appellation of Father, Son, and Holy Ghost, therefore these terms must imply the distinction of three pesons. But this inference not only conflicts with the inspired declaration of the absolute unity of Jehovah, but is rendered useless by our previous ascertainment of the fact, that a distinction of three Essentials in the Godhead most perfectly consists with the idea of one person; thus answering all the demands of the acknowledged doctrine of the Trinity, without doing the least violence to the genuine conception of the Unity. The question then is as to the priority of claim between an interpretation which thus recognizes a Trinity entirely consistent with Divine Unity, and one which is wholly at war with it: for this is clearly the alternative. I cannot doubt, indeed, that you will deny the existence of such a conflict, although I confess myself wholly baffled in the attempt to see how it is to be avoided. On this head you will resolutely fall back upon the buttress of the literal averments of Scripture and the devout acknowledgement of *mystery* which frowns rebuke upon the prying researches of the human mind. Such a posture of spirit the man of the New Church contemplates merely as a strange psychological curiosity. He finds no demand made upon him to give an implicit credence to inspired enunciations which he cannot receive without admitting both sides of a contradictory proposition. He cannot concede, in one breath, that Jesus Christ is the supreme and only Jehovah, and in the next grant that he is but the second *hypostasis* of a nature which the intuitions of his own mind, in response to the voice of revelation, declare can admit of but one. That there *are* inferences, and those too of transcendent moment, affecting the whole scheme of Christian doctrine, to be drawn from the scriptural language in regard to the true Trinity of Jehovah, it will be my object to evince in the sequel.

At present I must be permitted to adduce from Swedenborg another paragraph fraught with most important bearings upon the general subject:

" 'Behold I send an angel before thee ;' that hereby is signified the Lord as to the Divine Human [principle], appears from the signification of sending, when concerning the Lord, as denoting to proceed ; in this case, to cause to proceed ; and from the signification of angel, as denoting Him who proceeds, for angel in the original tongue signifies sent. Hence is the derivation of that expression ; and by sent is signified proceeding, as may be manifest from the passages quoted from the Word, n. 6831. Hence it is evident that by the angel of Jehovah is meant the Lord, as to the Divine Human [principle], for this proceeds from Jehovah as a Father. Jehovah as a Father is the Divine Good of the Divine Love, which is the very Esse ; and the proceeding [principle] from the Father is the Divine Truth from that Divine Good, thus the Divine Existere from the Divine Esse ; this is here signified by angel. In like

The Divine Humanity.

manner in Isaiah, ' *The angel of His faces* shall liberate them by reason of His love, and His indulgence; *He redeemed* them, and took them, and carried them all the days of eternity,' lxiii. 9. And in Malachi, ' Behold the Lord, whom ye seek, shall suddenly come to His temple, and *the angel of the covenant* whom ye desire,' iii. 1, 2 ; to the temple of the Lord is to His Human [principle]; that this is His temple, the Lord Himself teaches in Matthew, chap. xxvi. 61 ; and in John, chap. ii. 19, 21, 22. In the Church it is said, that out of three who are named, Father, Son, and Holy Spirit, there exists one Divine [being or principle], which is also called one God; and that from the Father proceeds the Son, and from the Father by the Son proceeds the Holy Spirit; but what it is to proceed or to go forth is as yet unknown. The ideas of the angels on this subject differ altogether from the ideas of the men of the Church who have thought about it; the reason is, because the ideas of the men of the Church are founded upon three, but of the angels upon one. The reason why the ideas of the men of the Church are founded upon three is, because they distinguish the Divine [being or principle] into three persons, and attribute to each special and particular offices. Hence it is that they can indeed say, that God is One, but in no case think otherwise than that there are Three, who by union, which they call mystical, are One ; but thus indeed they may be able to think that there is one Divine [being or principle], but not that there is one God ; for in thought the Father is God, the Son God, and the Holy Spirit God; one Divine [being or principle] is one by consent, and is thus unanimous, but one God is altogether one. What is the quality of the idea, or what is the quality of the thought, which the man of the Church has concerning one God, appears manifestly in the other life, for every one brings along with him the ideas of his thought; their idea or thought is, that there are three gods, but that they dare not say gods but God ; a few also make one of three by union, for they think in one way of the Father, in another way of the Son, and in another of the Holy Spirit; hence it has been made evident, what is the quality of the faith which the Church has concerning the most essential of all things, which is the Divine [being or principle] Itself; and whereas the thoughts which are of faith, and the affections which are of love, conjoin and separate all in the other life, therefore they who have been born out of the Church, and have believed in one God, fly away from those who are within the Church, saying that they do not believe in one God, but in three gods, and that they who do not believe in one God under a human form, believe in no God, inasmuch as their thought pours itself forth without determination into the universe, and thus sinks into nature, which they thereby acknowledge in the place of God. When it is asked what they mean by proceeding, when they say the Son proceeds from the Father, and the Holy Spirit from the Father by the Son, they reply that proceeding is an expression of union, and that it involves that mystery; but the idea of thought on the subject, when it was explored, was no other than of a mere expression, and not of any thing. But the ideas of the angels concerning the Divine [being or principle], concerning the trine [*trinum*], and concerning proceeding, differ altogether from the ideas of the men of the Church, by reason, as was said above, that the ideas of thought of the angels are founded upon one, whereas the ideas of the thought of the men of the Church are founded upon three; the angels think, and what they think believe, that there is one God, and He the Lord, and that His Human [principle] is the Divine Itself in form, and that the Holy [principle] proceeding from Him is the Holy Spirit; thus that there is a trine [*trinum*], but still one. This is presented to the apprehension by the idea concerning the angels in Heaven ; an angel appears there in a human form ; but still there are three things appertaining to him, which make one— there is his internal, which does not appear before the eyes, there is the external which appears, and there is the sphere of the life of his affections and thoughts, which diffuses itself from him to a distance ; these three [things or principles] make one angel. But angels are finite and created, whereas the Lord is infinite and increate ; and inasmuch as no idea can be had concerning the infinite by any man, nor even by any angel, except from things finite, therefore it is allowed to present such an example, in order to illustrate that there is a trine in one. and that there is One God, and that He is the Lord, and no other."—*A. C.* 9303.

You may possibly have doubts as to what is said about the difference of angelic and human ideas on this profound subject, and say that you have no sufficient evidence of the fact; but if the thing asserted is intrinsically true, the thoughts of the angels are undoubtedly in accordance with it, and the intrinsic truth of what they are said to think is certainly in itself some evidence that they do think it, and consequently that Swedenborg's assertion on the subject is also true. But, after all, the grand question is rather what you and I *ought* to think on this theme, than what the angels *do* think, although there is every likelihood that if we think as we ought, we shall think as they do. If there is any truth of stupendous concern to mortal man, it is that which we are now considering. The scriptural idea of God enters into the inmost vitalities of Christian faith, and it is vain to think of enjoying him in heaven so long as the idea of his nature and perfections does not conform to the essential verity, *for the true idea of God, with its appropriate affection, is the very medium of conjunction with him, and this conjunction is the essential element of heavenly bliss.** "The reason," says Swedenborg, "why there is no appropriation of good with those who do not acknowledge the Lord is, because for man to acknowledge his God is the first principle of religion, and with Christians to acknowledge the Lord is the first principle of the Church, for without acknowledgment there is no communication given, consequently no faith, thus no love; hence the primary tenet of doctrine in the Christian Church is, that without the Lord there is no salvation. Hence it is manifestly evident, that those who do not acknowledge the Lord cannot have faith, thus neither can they have love to God, consequently neither can

---

* "Inasmuch as the church at this day does not know that conjunction with the Lord makes heaven, and that conjunction is effected by the acknowledgment that He is the God of heaven and earth, and at the same time by a life conformable to his commandments, therefore it may be expedient to say something on this subject: he who is utterly unacquainted with the subject may possibly ask, what signifies conjunction? How can acknowledgment and life occasion conjunction? What need is there of such acknowledgment and life? May not every one be saved by a bare act of mercy? What occasion then for any other medium of salvation but faith alone? Is not God merciful and omnipotent? But let such an one know, that in the spiritual world all presence is occasioned by knowledge and acknowledgment, and all conjunction by affection which is of love; for spaces there are nothing else but appearances according to similarity of mind, that is, of affections and their derivative thoughts; wherefore, when any one knows another, either from fame or report, or from intercourse with him, or from conversation, or from relationship, when he thinks of him from an idea of that knowledge, the other becomes present, although to all appearances he were a thousand furlongs distant; and if any one also loves another whom he knows, he dwells with him in one society, and if he loves him intimately, in one house; this is the state of all throughout the whole spiritual world, and this state of all derives its origin from hence, that the Lord is present to every one according to love; faith and the consequent presence of the Lord is given by means of knowledges of truths derived from the Word, especially concerning the Lord himself there; but love and consequent conjunction is given by a life according to His commandments, for the Lord says, 'He that hath my commandments and keepeth them, he it is that loveth Me, and I will love him, and make my abode with him,' John xiv. 21."—*A. E.* 1340.

they be saved, which the Lord also teaches openly in John : ' He that believeth in the Son, hath eternal life; but he that believeth not the Son shall not see life, but the wrath of God abideth in him.'" And again, "The reason why they who do not from faith acknowledge the Lord, have not eternal life, is because the whole heaven is in that acknowledgment; for the Lord is the Lord of heaven and earth ; wherefore to those who do not acknowledge Him, heaven is closed ; and he who does not acknowledge in the world, that is, who is within the Church, does not acknowledge in the other life ; such is the state of man after death." The acknowledgment here insisted on is not a bare verbal assent to a proposition which conveys no definite meaning to the mind. It is an acknowledgment founded on a distinct intellectual perception of the truth acknowledged. Nothing short of this is entitled to the name.

You will understand, also, that in these passages, and in Swedenborg's writings generally, the title "Lord" is the equivalent of "Jehovah," and is the peculiar and distinctive appellation of Jesus Christ, than whom neither he nor his adherents know any other Jehovah, or Lord, in the universe. Swedenborg has placed the following sentence at the very threshold of his great work, the *Arcana Cœlestia*, and the remark is of the utmost importance in the perusal of every part of his writings:—" In the following work, by the LORD is solely meant Jesus Christ, the Saviour of the world, who is called the LORD without other names. He is acknowledged and adored as the LORD in the universal heaven, because he has all power in heaven and earth. He also commanded his disciples so to call him when he said, ' Ye call me LORD, and ye say well, for so I am.' And after his resurrection his disciples called him LORD. Throughout all heaven they know no other Father but the LORD, because he and the Father are one." This term in Swedenborg's writings is always to be understood as the equivalent of *Jehovah.** In the New Church, therefore, is to be seen the incipient fulfilment of the prediction before adverted to: " In that day there shall be one LORD (Jehovah), and his name one." The propriety of this title in reference to Christ I shall consider more at length hereafter. The use of it in this relation is in fact bringing forward into the Christian Church, under its last form, the distinguishing appellation of Jehovah, the God of the Old Testament, the exclusive and supreme object of worship, who alone is to be recognized in the person of Jesus Christ the Saviour. The introduction of this name as the familiar title of Jesus, when apprehended in its full import, is the signal of a complete revolution in the entire scheme of Christian doctrine built upon the assumption of a threefold distinction of persons, the second of whom makes an atonement to the first. No such theory of atonement can possibly stand when once it is seen that the Jehovah of the Jew is identically one with the Jesus of the Christian ; for one Divine Person cannot make an atone-

---

* Without the above explanation, the title of the first chapter of the treatise concerning Heaven and Hell would seem to announce a most obvious truism, viz., " That the Lord is the God of Heaven." This assumes a new phase when it is understood as asserting that Jesus Christ is the God of heaven.

ment to himself. This result, however, I do not ask you to receive, till you become convinced that it is inevitable. I announce it here that you may have a more vigilant eye on the successive evolutions of the argument whose object it is to establish it. And I may remark, also, by the way, that it is easy to perceive how insuperable is the obstacle in the way of the Jewish mind in general to the adoption of Christianity, so long as it holds forth to them a view of the Divine Being so utterly at war with all the conceptions of the Deity which they have formed from their own Scriptures. I do not say that they would readily embrace even the true doctrine of the incarnation of their own Jehovah, but they must necessarily be vastly more scandalized by the dogma which presents him under a threefold *hypostasis*. A Trinity of Essentials in one person they might possibly be led to concede; but a Trinity of persons, I believe, never; and who can blame them? As to any special display of divine influence in their behalf, so far as this point is concerned, we can of course have no hope of it, if the tenet itself is false, and that it is so we have the same evidence that we have that the doctrine of the Divine Unity is true; for the two we hold to be in diametrical and everlasting antagonism with each other.

Yours, &c.

LETTER V.

JEHOVAH JESUS.

DEAR SIR,

If the tenor of my remarks in the preceding series of Letters shall have approved itself as resting upon a stable basis, we have obtained an important clew, not only to the true character of the Saviour, as being no other than the one only Jehovah, but also to the correct interpretation of those numerous passages in the Old Testament which speak of Him as having been made *visible* to holy men of that dispensation. If I have at all succeeded in my attempted solution of the *theophanies* of the former economy, the conclusion reached cannot well be any other than that they were really manifestations of the Supreme Jehovah in his undivided person, and made through the medium of an angel, because they could not possibly be made in any other way. "The Divine itself," says Swedenborg, "is far above the heavens, not only the Divine good itself, but also the Divine truth itself, which proceeds immediately from the Divine good; the reason why those principles are far above heaven, is because the Divine itself is infinite, and the infinite cannot be conjoined with finites, thus not with the angels in the heavens, *except by the putting on of some finite first, and thus by accommodation to reception.*"

On the ground of what I have now advanced upon the general subject, you will see what we are taught by Swedenborg to believe concerning the relation which the ancient *theophanies* bear to the person of Christ. They were manifestations of Him only so far as he was identically one and the same with Jehovah himself, regarding this as the title of the Supreme Godhead. For ourselves, we are free to say that our minds utterly fail to grasp the idea of the *appearance* of any Divine personage termed the "Son of God," who made himself, by anticipation, visible to the patriarchs, prophets, and holy men of the early ages. We know of no "Son of God," but him who was born, as to his natural humanity, of the virgin mother, and who became a Son simply by being thus born.

But I may here be met by the position, that the Old Testament does in fact contain intimations respecting the "Son of God" which abundantly warrant the inference of such a distinction of persons as I am now endeavoring to show unfounded. Justice to the argument requires me to advert to these passages. The result, I think, will show that something far more decisive is demanded by the exigencies of the theory against which I contend.

The first and most prominent text adduced by Trinitarians is Ps ii. 7,—"Thou art my Son; this day have I begotten thee." In regard to this we fully accord with Swedenborg's interpretation. "In this passage is not meant a Son born from eternity, but the Son that was born in time; for it is a propetical Psalm, relating to the Lord who was to come, and therefore it is called the statute which Jehovah declared unto David; wherefore it is written before in the same Psalm, 'I have anointed my King over Zion' (v. 6); and it follows, 'I will give him the nations for an inheritance' (v. 8), and of consequence the expression, *this day*, does not mean from eternity, but in time; for with Jehovah the future is present. By the Son is meant the Lord as to his humanity." Are you prepared to deny this to be the true sense of the language of the Psalmist?

Another passage subsidized by theologians to the same purpose is Prov. xxx. 4,—"Who hath ascended up into heaven or descended? Who hath gathered the wind in his fists? Who hath bound the waters in a garment? Who hath established the ends of the earth? What is his name, and what is his *Son's* name, if thou canst tell?" It is here supposed that these questions are affirmative of the wisdom and power of God, whose Son is here mentioned; but this is doubtless a mistake. The questions relate to man, and imply a strong denial that any man can do these things. In the foregoing verses Agur confesses his ignorance, and in this verse he declares that neither he nor any other man else can perform or explain the works of God. "What is his name or his son's name?" i. e. what is the man's name who hath done or can do these things? or what is the name of his son? Negative interrogations of this kind are frequent in the Scriptures.

Again, we are referred to Dan. iv. 25, where Nebuchadnezzar is said to have seen "one like THE SON OF GOD." This is adduced in evidence of Christ's being a Son abstract from humanity. But it would be strange if we were required to found our faith on the testimony of a heathen king, a polytheist, who was then compelling men to idolatry, and who a little while after was driven from among men for his pride and contempt of the true God. To suppose that he knew the Son of God—that he knew him to be such *abstract* from *humanity*, and yet called him a *man* whose form was *like* the Son of God— and farther, that he should afterwards call this same man an *angel* sent by God, as if he knew that this coequal Son of God was also his servant or messenger—all this is so unnatural and so unsupported by the whole history, as to be altogether incredible. Besides, you cannot be ignorant that it is generally conceded by the learned, that the proper reading is, "like *a son of the gods.*"* It is therefore far more probable that by this expression he meant an *angel*, as he expressly terms him (v. 28), and if he intended a divine person, it was only according to the heathen mythology which abounded in begotten gods who were considered as subordinate divinities, and as coming down in the likeness of men, as the Lycaonians thought Paul and Barnabas were.

Besides the above I know of no other text in the Old Testament which lends any support to the idea of the eternal Sonship of Christ. Nothing in fact can be adduced to prove him to have been a *Son* before he came in the flesh, but will, by the same course of argument, prove him also to have been *Jesus Christ* before that period, which is manifestly contrary to the tenor of the New Testament. Nothing can be more explicit than the announcement of Gabriel to Mary,—" Behold, thou shalt conceive and bear a Son, and shall call his name Jesus. He shall be great, and shall be called THE SON OF THE MOST HIGH. But Mary said to the angel, How shall this be since I know not man? And the angel answered and said to her, THE HOLY SPIRIT SHALL COME UPON THEE, AND THE POWER OF THE HIGHEST SHALL OVERSHADOW THEE; wherefore also THAT HOLY THING that is born of thee, shall be called THE SON OF GOD."† As then we find no evidence of the existence of a Son of God from eternity, we see no ground for the opinion that such a Son was manifested in the ancient *theophanies*, which is the same as saying that they were not manifestations of what is termed the *second person* of the Trinity. They were manifestations of Jehovah, and if that term does not in itself con-

---

* " It is greatly to be lamented, that so very an important mistranslation should remain in the English Bible to mislead the simple. Printed too, as it is, with the word " Son" commenced with a capital letter, none who are destitute of other means of information can avoid supposing, that there was a proper Son of God then existing; while no shadow of ground really exists for such an imagination."—*Noble's Appeal*, p. 367.

† " It is not known in the church, but that the Son of God is another person of the Godhead, distinct from the person of the Father. Thence is the faith concerning a Son of God born from eternity. Because this is universally received, and is concerning God, there is given no power or liberty of thinking about it, from any understanding, not even of thinking what it is to be born from eternity ; for whosoever thinks about it from the understanding, will surely say with himself, ' This is above my apprehension, but still I say it, because others say it, and I believe it, because others believe it.' But they may know, that there is no Son from eternity. but that the Lord is from eternity. When it is known what the Lord is, and what the Son is, one can also think from the understanding concerning the triune God, and not before."—*Doct. of the Lord*, 19.

vcy the idea of such a threefold distinction, we must seek for the evidence of it elsewhere, and if you know where it is to be found, I should be grateful for having it pointed out.

Is it said that we are forced to recognize it in the peculiar use of the term "Word" (Logos), evidently applied to Christ in his ante-incarnate state who was "in the beginning with God, and was God?" Yet here, if I mistake not, it will be easy to show that the Scriptures are still conversant with the same Divine Personage, who has before been brought to our view under the appellation of Jehovah, and who was manifested, in the earlier ages of the world, and to the Jews, under the form of an angel. As the subject is one of deep interest to the theologian I shall pursue it somewhat in detail.

You are well aware of the remarkable fact that the Chaldee Targumists or Pharaphrasts, who were all Jews, wherever, in our version, there is any intimation of the visible display of the Divine glory or power, are accustomed to make use of the term "Shekinah," which signifies *dwelling* or *habitation*, from the Hebrew שכן, *shâkan, to dwell or inhabit*. The derivative *Shekinah* is used more particularly of the divine presence, glory, or majesty, or of the Divine itself when said to be present to men, or converse with them, or to vouchsafe to them his sensible and gracious aid. Accordingly the following, among hundreds of other passages, are rendered by the Chaldee Targums of Onkelos and Jonathan conformably to this import of the term;— Ps. lxxiv. 2, "Remember thy congregation which thou hast purchased of old; this mount Zion wherein *thou hast dwelt.*" Chal. "Wherein thou hast made thy *Shekinah* to dwell." Num. x. 36, "Return, O Lord, unto the many thousands of Israel." Chal. "Return now, O Word of the Lord, to thy people Israel, make the glory of thy *Shekinah* to dwell among them, and have mercy on the thousands of Israel." Num. xi. 20, "Ye have despised the Lord which is among you." Chal. "Ye have despised the Word of the Lord whose *Shekinah* dwelleth among you." Hag. i. 8, "Go up to the mountain, and bring wood, and build the house, and I will take pleasure in it, and will be *glorified*, saith the Lord." Chal. "And I will make my *Shekinah* to dwell in glory." Ps. lxxxv. 10, "His salvation is nigh them that fear him, that *glory* may dwell in our land." This is distinctly explained by Aben Ezra as meaning that the *Shekinah* may be established in the land. It would be easy to multiply passages to the same effect ad libitum, for even the voluminous citations of Buxtorf do not embrace a tithe of the examples of the usage which may be drawn from the Pentateuch alone. It is the ordinary phraseology of the Chaldee Paraphrases wherever in our version we meet with any intimation of a visible display of the divine glory. Indeed the terms "Glory" and "Shekinah" are evidently recognized by the Targumists as convertible terms.

While this then is the current phraseology of these ancient Jewish paraphrases in regard to the visible manifestations of Jehovah, and to whom *as visible* (though not to the outward eye), and as dwelling or *Shekinizing* between the Cherubim, the whole worship of the Jewish Church was directed, it is a fact equally worthy of notice, that the Divine Personage thus manifested is termed by them *Mimra da-Yehovah*, *the Word of the Lord*, of which "Logos" is the Greek representative. As the Shekinah was the medium of the divine presence and of the declaration of the divine will, and as a voice inwardly audible frequently accompanied the manifestation, it was not unnatural that the title "Word of the Lord," or, by way of eminence, "The Word," should come to be habitually applied in this connexion. As words, either written or spoken, are the established vehicle for conveying the thoughts and feelings of one human being to another, so it is easy to conceive that the denomination "Word" should have been appropriated to what was deemed a medium of imparting the divine thoughts and counsels to men. The Shekinah and the Mimra, therefore, are in Jewish diction terms employed in most intimate connexion with those ancient divine manifestations which I have indicated by the term *theophanies*. I shall hope to show in the sequel that the ideas which, in their minds, were couched under these appellations were in all probability extremely inadequate when tried by the fundamental truth involved, yet as the usage itself is a fact of some moment in its relations to the general subject, I shall adduce, in tabellated form, a sufficient number of instances to illustrate it clearly.

Hebrew.	Chaldee.
Gen. iii. 8. And they heard the voice of the Lord God walking in the midst of the garden.	And they heard the voice of *the Word of the Lord* walking in the garden.
Ch. xxviii. 20, 21. And Jacob vowed a vow, saying, If God will be with me, and keep me, &c., then shall the Lord be my God.	And Jacob vowed a vow to the *Word*, saying, If *the Word of the Lord* will be my help, &c., then shall the Lord be my God.
Ch. xxxv. 9. And God appeared unto Jacob again when he came out of Padan-aram; and blessed him.	And *the Word of the Lord* appeared to Jacob a second time, when he was coming from Padan-Aram; and blessed him.
Ex. xvi. 8. Your murmurings are not against us, but against the Lord.	Your murmurings are not against us, but against *the Word of the Lord*.
Ch. xix. 17. And Moses brought forth the people out of the camp to meet with God.	And Moses brought forth the people out of the camp to meet with *the Word of the Lord*.
Ch. xxx. 6. Where I will meet with thee.	Where I will appoint for thee *my Word*.
Lev. xxvi. 11, 12. And I will set my tabernacle among you; and my soul shall not abhor you. And I will walk among you and be your God.	And I will set my tabernacle among you; and *my Word* shall not reject you. And I will cause my *Shekinah* to dwell among you, and be to you a God.
Num. xi. 20. Because that ye have despised the Lord which is among you.	Because ye have contemptuously rejected *the Word of the Lord*, whose *Shekinah* dwelleth among you.

Jehovah Jesus.

HEBREW.	CHALDEE.
Ch. xiv. 9. Only rebel not ye against the Lord.	But rebel not ye against *the Word of the Lord.*
Ch. xxiii. 4. And God met Balaam.	And *the Word from before the Lord* met Balaam.
Deut. i. 30. The Lord your God which goeth before you, he shall fight for you.	*The Word of the Lord thy God,* who is thy leader, shall fight for you.
Ch. i. 32, 33. Yet in this thing ye did not believe the Lord your God, who went in the way before you, to search you out a place to pitch your tents in, in fire by night, to show you the way ye should go, and in a cloud by day.	And in this thing ye did not believe in *the Word of the Lord your God,* who went as a leader before you, &c.
Ch. xiii. 18. When thou shalt hearken to the voice of the Lord thy God.	If thou shalt be obedient to *the Word of the Lord thy God.*

We have here, if I mistake not, indubitable evidence that the term "Logos" or "Word," which in Chaldee or Rabbinical usage is most intimately related to the "*Shekinah,*" is in fact a designation of the very Personage whose recorded *theophanies* in the Old Testament were made through the medium of an angel, and on grounds which I have previously endeavored to explain. But I have utterly failed in my attempted elucidations of the subject, if I have not succeeded in showing that this Personage is indeed no other than the one only Jehovah, the Supreme God, the Creater of the universe, and the exclusive object of all religious worship. What can more unequivocally establish this than the title given to Christ by the Seer of Patmos?—"And his name is called the WORD OF GOD.—And he hath on his vesture and on his thigh, a name written, KING OF KINGS AND LORD OF LORDS." Who is "King of Kings and Lord of Lords" but Jehovah himself? Consequently, if Christ is the Word, and the Word is Jehovah, the inference as to his sole and absolute Divinity is unquestionable, and all ground for recognizing any allusion to a tri-personal Trinity in this title vanishes from under our feet. As no such distinction is implied in the term Jehovah, so none is implied in the term Word.

Still I feel that, on the position which I assume, you are authorized to demand somewhat of a detailed explication of the language of the Evangelist in respect to the Divine Word. This I proceed to give, planting it, of course, on the basis of Swedenborg's theology. I have already remarked that the principles of Love and Wisdom comprise the all of Deity. The Divine Love is the Divine *Esse,* the Divine Wisdom the Divine *Existere.* So far as manifestation is concerned, this is always predicated of the latter and never of the former, because the *Esse* is always *invisibly* latent in the *Existere.* When we speak, therefore, of the Divine Humanity we necessarily centre our thoughts upon the *Existere* of Jehovah, which is Wisdom or Truth, and from this, the idea of the human principle is inseparable. The "Word" is but another name for the Divine Truth, predicated especially of the Son, as Divine Good is predicated especially of the Father, and as the Divine Proceeding is predicated of the Holy Spirit. But I will here make Swedenborg the expounder of his own doctrine, the truth of which is to be determined by an appeal to Scripture, in its genuine sense, and not to alleged visions.

"From these words, 'In the beginning,' &c., it is manifest that the *Lord* is from eternity *God*, and that He is that *Lord* who was born in the world; for it is said, The Word was with God, and God was the Word; as also, that without Him was nothing made that was made; and afterwards, that the Word became flesh, and they saw Him. That the Lord is called the Word, is little understood in the church; but He is called the Word, because the Word signifies divine truth, or divine wisdom; and the Lord is divine Truth itself, or divine Wisdom itself; wherefore also He is called Light, concerning which also it is said, that it came into the world. Because divine wisdom and divine love make one, and in the Lord were one from eternity, therefore also it is said, 'In Him was life, and the life was the light of men.' Life is divine love, and light is divine wisdom. This one is what is meant by 'In the beginning the Word was with God, and God was the Word.' *With* God is *in* God, for wisdom is in love, and love in wisdom. Likewise in another place in John, 'Glorify Thou Me, Father, with thyself, with the glory which I had with thee before the world was,' (xviii. 5). *With* Thyself is *in* Thyself. Wherefore also it is said, that God was the Word; and elsewhere, that the Lord is in the Father, and the Father in Him; as also, that the Father and He are one. Now, because the Word is the divine Wisdom of divine Love, it follows that it is *Jehovah* himself, thus the Lord, by whom all things were made that are made; for all things were created by divine Wisdom, from divine Love." —*Doct. of the Lord*, 1.

"How the Lord is the Word, is understood by few, for they think that the Lord can indeed enlighten and teach man by the Word, and yet that he cannot hence be called the Word: but let them know that every man is his own love, and thence his own good and his own truth, man not being a man from any other source, and nothing else appertaining to him being man. From this consideration that man is his own good and his own truth, angels and spirits are also men; for every good and truth proceeding from the Lord is in its form a man: but the Lord is divine good itself and divine truth itself; thus He is the man himself, from whom every man is a man."—*Swed. apud Clowes on John*, p. 11.

That by the Word in this relation is meant the Lord's Divine Humanity, is evident from its being said that " the Word became flesh and dwelt among us." This is a point which, I venture to think, I have established in a former letter. The Divine Humanity existing from eternity in " first principles," descended, in the incarnation, into "last principles," or " ultimates," or, as we may properly say, the Alpha descended into the Omega. He thus became an earthly man among earthly men, and became visible to the outward eye, as he had been visible, in the angelic form, to the spiritual eye. This is doubtless what is meant by the Apostle in saying that though he was " in the form of God, and thought it not robbery to be equal with God," yet "he made himself of no reputation, and took upon him the form of a servant," &c. The " form of God" is the Divine

Humanity in its first principles, as it exists in the Divine nature from eternity. But nothing in the data on which our reasoning is founded requires the recognition of a triad of persons to make the Scriptural testimony intelligible or consistent. The Word is still the Lord, or Jehovah, in the indivisible unity of his nature, and he is the eternal Word, not because he is identical with an eternal Son, but because he is identical with the eternal Jehovah.

But has not the title "Word" some relation to the written Word? Undoubtedly it has. "Since truth is meant by the Word, by the Word is meant all revelation, thus likewise the Word itself or Holy Scripture." This relation I cannot better present than in the language of Swedenborg. "He who understands these words, 'In the beginning,' &c., in their interior sense, may see that the Divine Truth itself in the Word which was formerly in this world, which likewise is in our Word at this day, is meant by the Word which was in the beginning with God and which was God; but not the Word regarded merely as to the words and letters of the languages in which it is written, but as seen in its essence and life, which is from within in the senses or meaning of its words and letters; from this life does the Word vivify the affections of that man's will who reads it devoutly; and from the light of its life it illuminates the thought of his understanding; therefore it is said in John, 'In him (the Word) was life, and the life was the light of man;' this constitutes the Word, because the Word is from the Lord, and concerning the Lord, and thus *is* the Lord. *All thought, speech, and writing derives its essence and life from him who thinks, speaks, and writes; the man with all that he is being therein; but in the Word the Lord alone is.*"

You will probably find yourself compelled to demur to this explicit declaration of identity between the revealed Word and its Divine Author, but farther reflection will scarcely fail to bring you to the admission of the fact. The grounds of the position I have stated in a somewhat formal manner in a former production ("Statement of Reasons," &c.), and as the language suits my present purpose you will allow me to quote it: "He (Swedenborg) declares, that the Word is not only *from* the Lord, but *is* the Lord, just as any written or spoken communication of a man *is a form of the man himself.* A man's vocal speech is an emanation from the man himself; he is essentially *in* his utterance; and the case is not altered by its being embodied in written language. A letter addressed by one person to another, is as truly a going forth of his spirit, in the form of words, as if the communication were made by spirit coming in contact with spirit in the spiritual world. The Divine Word is the divine voice speaking to man, and the Divine voice is as much a form of the Divine being as a man's voice is a form of his being. But the human voice is effected by the medium of the undulations of the atmosphere, which of course cannot hold in respect to the Deity. The aerial sound, however, in man's case, is nothing more than a vehicle for conveying the thought and affection of the speaker's mind, and cannot be needed for the communication of spirits disembodied. They then communicate by impressing *themselves* upon each other. Now

God is a spirit, and in our present corporeal state he comes into communion with our spirits through the medium of written speech, but this speech is *Himself*, in his essential Love and Truth, and whatever is in Himself is in his speech, that is, in his Word, just as Swedenborg remarks in a passage already quoted, that 'every thought, speech, and writing derives its essence and life from him who thinks, speaks, and writes, the whole man with his quality being in those things; but in the Word is the Lord alone.' The Word of God therefore is the *living* Divine Truth, and is at any one moment just as really the *present* utterance, expression, or emanation of the Divine Being, as when flowing into the minds of the sacred penmen by whom it was indited, as they were *moved* (φερομενοι, *acted, borne, or carried away*) by the Holy Ghost. But if the Divine Word is the Divine Lord, it is impossible to conceive that his inmost affections and thoughts—in a word, his essential Divinity—should not be in it, and consequently that there should not be a depth of import entirely transcending the sense of the outward letter."—P. 118.

In another paragraph of his writings, Swedenborg, in speaking of this passage in John, says; "Inasmuch as this has been understood in no other way than to mean, that God taught man by the Word; therefore it has been explained by an expression of elevation, which involves that the Lord is not the Word itself: the reason is, because it was not known, that by the Word is meant the divine truth of the divine good, or, what is the same thing, the divine wisdom of the divine love. In what manner the Lord is the divine truth of the divine good, shall here also be briefly shown: every man is not a man from his face and body, but from the good of his love, and from the truths of his wisdom; and whereas man is a man from these principles, every man likewise is his own truth and his own good, or his own love and his own wisdom, and without these he is not a man; but the Lord is good itself and truth itself, or, what is the same thing, love itself and wisdom itself; and these are the Word, which 'in the beginning was with God, and which was God, and which was made flesh.'"—*Div. Prov.* 172. The evident intimation in this passage is, that as the most proper light in which to view man is in his *first principles* as constituted of love and wisdom, and apart from his bodily being, so also in regard to the Lord himself, we are to elevate our thoughts to what he is in his essential nature, that is, as infinite Love and infinite Wisdom; and not only so, but we are always to conceive of him as *acting according to the principles of his nature*.* Hence it is impossible to form any adequate idea of

---

* The following extract from De Guays' "Letters to a Man of the World," presents a striking view of the analogy between the Word of God and the word of man, considered as a creative agency.

"Man having been created in the image of God, every thing which exists in man, so far as he remains in the order of his creation, must be the image of something which exists in God; so there must be a kind of analogy between the word of Man and the Word of God. Let us see if this analogy confirms what has been said concerning the Word of God. We have said that the Word in its principle, or the Logos, created the universe, that is to say, all that God has made. Is it the same with the word of man relatively to

the process of creation, unless it be regarded as the normal operation of these principles. But Love and Wisdom must necessarily operate by emanation or influx, so that when it is said, in the present connexion, "that all things were made by him, and without him was not any thing made that was made," we are to recognize the legitimate operation of the Divine Truth or Wisdom ultimating itself, by its own laws, in the material universe. Accordingly Swedenborg says,

" Scarce any one knows at this day that there is any power in truth, for it is only supposed that it is only a word spoken by some one who is in power, which on that account must be done, consequently the truth is only as breathing from the mouth, and as sound in the ear; when yet truth and good are the principles of all things in both worlds, the spiritual and the natural, by which principles the universe was created, and by which the universe is preserved; and likewise by which man was made; wherefore those two principles are all in all. That the universe was created by Divine Truth is plainly said in John, 'In the beginning was the Word, and the Word was with God, all things were made by Him.' And in David, ' By the Word of Jehovah were the heavens made,' Ps. xxxiii. 6 ; by the Word in both cases is meant the divine truth. Inasmuch as the universe was created by Divine Truth, therefore also the universe is preserved by it; for as subsistence is perpetual existence, so preservation is perpetual creation."—*T. C. R.* 224.

This is confirmed by the fact that the original word, εγενετο, *egeneto, were made*, does not properly signify *created* in its ordinary acceptation, but *became* —" all things *became* by him,"—and I am fully prepared to accede to the views of Professor Lewis in his "Platonic Theology," where he clearly intimates, in his elaborate discussion of the distinctive sense of the verbs Eιμι, *to be*, and Γινομαι, *to become*, that the true sense of creation comes very near to that of *generation* (γενεσις, *genesis*), or *becoming*.* We claim, therefore, to be occupying the soundest philosophical ground when we maintain that what is termed *creation* on the part of Jehovah is a process of *emanation* from himself, who is the first, absolute, only, self-existing substance. Matter is the elaboration of spirit, or, in other words, spirit has the potency of clothing itself in material forms. The most solid substances on our globe are the result of the combination of gases; the gases, therefore, must be conceived as of prior formation; but

---

all that man does? By the Word or Logos creating we understand the Divine Wisdom of God acting from the Divine Love or Will of God. Man's word, analogous to the Logos, is, then, the understanding acting from the will, or what is the same thing, thought acting from affection. Now it is evident that all that man does is done by his thought from his affection ; every work of man is then produced by his word Thus considered, the word of man is not only that which he expresses, whether by sounds and articulations, or by the physiognomy of the countenance and gestures, but moreover all that which is produced by him ; so that this word of man is the man himself, as the Word (Logos) is God Himself; for will and thought are man, as Love Itself and Wisdom Itself are God."—*Letters, &c.*, 2d *Series, Letter* 3d.

* This distinction is very clearly marked in our Lord's declaration, John viii. 58, " Before Abraham *was* (γενεσθαι) *I am* (ειμι) ;" i. e. before Abraham *became*. The same word is applied to our Lord himself as the Son of God, Gal. iv. 4, " God sent forth his Son *made* (γενομενον) of a woman ;" i. e. who *became* by a woman. It is in several cases thus translated in our version.

they are themselves the product of solar heat and light, and the heat and light of the natural sun are the effect of spiritual heat and light, and these are the Divine Love and Wisdom. To this then we come at last. We hold it to be impossible, on just grounds, to avoid the conclusion, that every thing created is from a spiritual origin, that is to say *developed* from the Love and Wisdom of Jehovah; and this process never ceases, because these principles ever energize. The creation of the universe is as truly going on at this moment as it was millions of ages ago, for the Divine Love and Wisdom can never intermit their activities.* It doubtless seems to our limited view, as if the work of *creation* were finished, and *preservation* alone could now be attributed to the Most High. But subsistence is perpetual existence, and perpetual existence is perpetual creation.† If we could suppose an individual of our race to have been introduced upon the globe myriads of centuries ago, in some of the immensely remote geological periods, and to have lived out the common measure of human life at the present day, he would doubtless have had as strong an impression of the *completed* state of the terrestial creations as we now have. Yet the work was then going on, as it is still going on, by incessant changes and new combinations. Every thing is in the process of *becoming* by virtue of the same laws which were operative from the outset. But the cycles are so vast—the sweep so boundless—the evolutions so slow—that the process to us seems to have become stationary.

I return in my next, to the general subject.

Yours, &c.

---

* "Were what is spiritual to be separated from what is natural, that which is natural would be annihilated. All things derive their origin in this mode. Every thing, both in general and in particular, is from the Lord. From Him is the celestial principle; by the celestial from Him exists the spiritual principle; by the spiritual the natural; and by the natural the corporeal and sensual principles; and as each thus exists from the Lord, so also does it subsist, for, as is acknowledged, subsistence is perpetual existence. They who conceive otherwise of the existence and origin of all things, as do the worshipers of nature, who derive them all from her, have adopted such fatal principles, that the phantasies of the beasts of the forest may be said to possess more of truth; yet there are many such persons who seem to themselves to excel the rest of mankind in wisdom."—*A. C.* 775.

† "The case is with influx, as with existence and subsistence; nothing exists from itself, but from what is prior to itself, thus finally all things from the First, that is, from that which is, which is *Esse* and *Existere* from Itself; and also from the Same all things subsist, for the case is with subsistence as with existence, inasmuch as to subsist is perpetually to exist."—*A. C.* 6040.

LETTER VI

JEHOVAH JESUS.

DEAR SIR,

The result of our investigations thus far has been, to establish the conclusion that all evidence is wanting which shall go to prove the existence of any such divided personality in the Godhead as is supposed on the tri-personal theory. The Divine appearances under the old economy were appearances of the absolute Jehovah himself, under the form of angel. That these appearances were preludes or anticipations of the Lord's advent in the flesh, is undoubtedly true, but not of his advent in any other character than that of the supreme and unipersonal Jehovah. It becomes then a point of importance to establish the identity of Jesus of Nazareth with the Jehovah of the Old Testament, and the most obvious mode of doing this is to show that the title "Lord," so frequently bestowed upon Christ by the New Testament writers, is an express confirmation of this identity. I would not imply by this that such a process of proof is absolutely indispensable to my argument, for it in fact follows by necessary consequence from all that I have hitherto said, if there is any reason to believe that such a personage as Christ is announced in the Old Testament. Still, as the evidence is ample, I proceed to adduce it. In assuming this position, however, I would not be understood to deny that the term "Lord" is often used even in reference to Christ, in a lower sense, as an honorary compellation equivalent to "Sir" or "Master,"—a usage for the most part easily determinable from the context. But it is, in my view, equally beyond dispute, that in a multitude of passages the title in question is most unequivocally bestowed upon the Saviour in such a way as to compel the inference that he can be no other than the Jehovah of Moses and the Prophets. As the settlement of a *principle* is the object aimed at, it will not be necessary to multiply instances to a great extent. What is proved of a few will probably be admitted to be *proveable* of a great many more of the same class. I present the examples in parallel columns.

Old Testament.	New Testament.
Mal. iii. 1. Behold, I will send my messenger, and he shall prepare the way before me: and the Lord (Jehovah), whom ye seek, shall suddenly come to his temple, even the messenger of the covenant, whom ye delight in: behold, he shall come, saith the Lord of hosts.	Mark i. 1–3. As it is written in the prophets, Behold, I send my messenger before thy face, which shall prepare thy way before thee; the voice of one crying in the wilderness, Prepare ye the way of the Lord, make his paths straight.
Mal. iii. 1. Behold, I will send my messenger, and he shall prepare the way before me.	Luke i. 76. And thou, child, shalt be called the Prophet of the Highest, for thou shalt go before the face of the Lord to prepare his ways.

Letters to a Trinitarian.—Letter VI.

OLD TESTAMENT.	NEW TESTAMENT.
Is. xl. 3. The voice of him that crieth in the wilderness, Prepare ye the way of the Lord (Jehovah), make straight in the desert a highway for our God.	Matt. iii. 3. For this is he that was spoken of by the prophet Esaias, saying, The voice of one crying in the wilderness, Prepare ye the way of the Lord, make his paths straight.
Is. xliv. 6. Thus saith the Lord (Jehovah), the King of Israel, and his Redeemer the Lord (Jehovah) of hosts; I am the first, and I am the last; and besides me there is no God.	Rev. xxii. 13. I (Jesus) am Alpha and Omega, the beginning and the end, the first and the last.
Is. vi. 5. Then said I, Wo is me! for I am undone; because I am a man of unclean lips, and I dwell in the midst of a people of unclean lips; for mine eyes have seen the King, the Lord (Jehovah) of hosts.	John xii. 41. These things said Esaias, when he saw his (Christ's) glory, and spake of him.
Jer. xxiii. 6. In his days Judah shall be saved, and Israel shall dwell safely: and this is his name whereby he shall be called, the Lord (Jehovah) our Righteousness.	1 Cor. i. 30. But of him are ye in Christ Jesus, who of God is made unto us wisdom, and righteousness, and sanctification, and redemption:
Jer. ix. 24. But let him that glorieth glory in this, that he understandeth and knoweth me, that I am the Lord (Jehovah), which exercise lovingkindness, judgment, and righteousness, in the earth: for in these things I delight, saith the Lord (Jehovah).	v. 31. That, according as it is written, He that glorieth, let him glory in the Lord.
Zech. xii. 4. In that day saith the Lord (Jehovah), v. 10, they shall look on me whom they have pierced.	John xiv. 37. They shall look on him (Christ) whom they have pierced.
Is. xl. 10. Behold the Lord (Jehovah) God will come—his reward is with him.	Rev. xii. 12. Behold, I (Jesus) come quickly, and my reward is with me. v. 20. Even so, come, Lord Jesus.
Is. xliii. 3, 11. For I am the LORD thy God, the Holy One of Israel, thy Saviour: I gave Egypt for thy ransom, Ethiopia and Seba for thee. I, even I, am the LORD (Jehovah); and besides me there is no Saviour. Is. xlv. 21. A just God and a Saviour; there is none beside me.	1 Pet. iii. 18. But grow in grace, and in the knowledge of our Lord and Saviour Jesus Christ. Luke ii. 11. For unto you is born this day, in the city of David, a Saviour, which is Christ the Lord.
Hos. i. 7. I will have mercy on the house of Judah, and will save them by the Lord (Jehovah) their God.	Luke ii. 11. For unto you is born this day, in the city of David, a Saviour, which is Christ the Lord.

Jehovah Jesus.

OLD TESTAMENT.	NEW TESTAMENT.
Ps. cii. 25. Of old hast thou laid the foundations of the earth: and the heavens are the work of thy hands.	Heb i. 10. Thou, Lord, in the beginning hast laid the foundation of the earth; and the heavens are the works of thy hands.
Is. xlv. 23. I have sworn by myself, the word is gone out of my mouth in righteousness, and shall not return. That unto Me every knee shall bow, and every tongue shall swear.	Rom. xiv. 11, 12. For we shall all stand before the judgment seat of Christ. For it is written, As I live, saith the Lord, every knee shall bow to me.
Ps. xxiv. 8. Who is the King of Glory? the Lord (Jehovah) strong and mighty, the Lord (Jehovah) mighty in battle.	1 Cor. ii. 8. Which none of the princes of this world know; for had they known it, they would not have crucified the Lord of glory.
Deut. x. 17. For the Lord (Jehovah) your God is God of gods, and Lord of lords, a mighty and a terrible.	Rev. xvii. 14. These shall make war with the Lamb, and the Lamb shall overcome them; for he is Lord of lords, and King of kings.

What remains from this array of testimony but a cordial resting in the conclusion announced by the apostle, Phil. 2, 9–11, "Wherefore God also hath highly exalted him, and given him a name which is above every name: that at the name of Jesus every knee should bow, of things in heaven, and things in earth, and things under the earth; and that every tongue should confess that JESUS CHRIST is LORD, to the glory of God the Father" (i. e. Jehovah).

I am not aware that in the above citations there is any one as to which there can be any reasonable doubt that the reference is distinctly to Jesus Christ, "the only Lord God, and (i. e. *even*) our Lord Jesus Christ." Several of them are expressly explained of him by the sacred writers as the Personage to whom the title properly pertains, and by parity of reasoning numerous others obviously demand the same interpretation. If I am warranted in assigning to them this reference, the conclusion that naturally yields itself is, that in these passages, at least, the Saviour of men is distinguished by an appellation the highest that can be applied to the Supreme Deity, and which is, in fact, usually denominated his *incommunicable* name. The dignity of the Godhead knows no more august appellation than that of Jehovah, and yet nothing short of a torturing criticism can deny the attribution of this title to the Saviour of the world, or refuse to recognize in him the being justly denominated JEHOVAH JESUS. And to the present point of the discussion I have reserved the reference to a passage which is perhaps entitled to carry with it more weight than any of the preceding. I allude to Rev. i. 8, "I am Alpha and Omega, the beginning and the ending, saith the Lord, which is, and which was, and which is to come, the Almighty,"— evidently the language of Christ, as the same declaration occurs Rev.

xxii., where there can be no doubt as to the speaker. The word Κυριος, *Kurios, Lord,* here represents the Hebrew יהוה, *Yehovah* which is compounded of the *past, present,* and *future* tense of the verb היה, *hayah, to be,* of which the following words—" which is, and which was, and which is to come"—are plainly a definition, while the last epithet "Almighty" (παντοκρατωρ), answers obviously to צבאות, *tezbaoth, hosts,* of which it is the usual rendering in the Septuagint. The two terms, therefore, " Lord of Hosts," are distinctly defined. There is the less doubt of this from the fact, that in the parallel passages, Is. xliv. 6, this title is expressly given;—" Thus saith the Lord the King of Israel, and his Redeemer, *the Lord of hosts;* I am the first, and I am the last; and besides me there is no God." Now if this is an assertion of the exclusive Deity of the speaker, as is evident from the language, and yet the same character is expressly claimed for Jesus the Saviour, can more than one inference possibly be drawn? The entire clause, therefore, is an explanation, for the Greek reader, of the Hebrew יהוה צבאות, *Yehovah tzebaoth,* or *Lord of hosts,* with the unequivocal intimation that this title belongs to Jesus Christ. By being *the Lord,* he is of necessity *the Lord of hosts,* as the titles are of equivalent import. It would seem difficult, then, to indicate any thing as wanting to establish completely the point for which I contend, viz. the absolute identity of Jehovah and Jesus.

I will here adduce a passage from Swedenborg by way, not of simple authoritative declaration, but of confirmation, as I venture to regard the truth affirmed as sufficiently established from other sources.

"In the word of the New Testament, with the Evangelists and in the Apocalypse, *Jehovah* is nowhere named, but for *Jehovah* it is said *Lord,* and this from hidden causes, of which we shall speak presently. That in the Word of the New Testament it is said *Lord* instead of *Jehovah,* may appear evident with Mark: 'Jesus said the first (primary) of all the commandments is, Hear O Israel, the *Lord* our God is one *Lord,* therefore thou shalt love the *Lord* thy God with all thy heart, and with all thy soul, and with all thy thought, and with all thy strength,' Mark xii. 29, 30; which is thus expressed in Moses; 'Hear O Israel, *Jehovah* our God is one *Jehovah,* and thou shalt love *Jehovah* thy God with all thy heart, and with all thy soul, and with all thy strength,' Deut. vi. 4, 5; where it is manifest that it is said Lord for Jehovah. In like manner in John: 'Behold a throne was set in heaven, and one sat on the throne; and round about the throne were four animals full of eyes before and behind, each had for himself six wings round about, and within full of eyes; and they said Holy, holy, holy, *Lord* God Omnipotent,' Apoc. iv. 2. 6, 8; which is thus expressed in Isaiah: 'I saw the *Lord* sitting on a throne high and lifted up; the seraphim were standing above it, each had six wings; and one cried to another, Holy, holy, holy, *Jehovah Zebaoth,*' vi. 1, 3, 5. 8; there it is said *Lord* for *Jehovah,* or *Lord God Omnipotent* for *Jehovah Zebaoth;* that the four animals are seraphim or cherubim, is plain from Ezekiel, chap. i. 5, 13, 14, 15, 19; chap. x. 15. That in the New Testament the *Lord* is *Jehovah,* appears also from several other passages, as in Luke: 'The angel of the *Lord* appeared to Zacharias,' i. 11; the angel of the *Lord* for the angel of *Jehovah.* In the same evangelist, the angel said to Zacharias concerning his son: 'Many of the sons of Israel shall he turn to the *Lord* their God,' i. 16; to the *Lord* their God, for to *Jehovah* God. Again, the angel said to Mary concerning Jesus: 'He shall be great, and shall be called the Son of the Highest, and the *Lord* God shall give unto him the throne of David,' i. 32; the *Lord* God for *Jehovah* God. Again:

Jehovah Jesus. 57

'Mary said, my soul doth magnify the *Lord*, and my spirit hath exalted itself on God my Saviour,' i. 46, 47; where the *Lord* also is for *Jehovah*. Again: 'Zacharias prophesied, saying, Blessed be the *Lord* God of Israel,' i. 68; where the *Lord* God is for *Jehovah* God. Again; 'The angel of the *Lord* stood near them (the shepherds), and the glory of the *Lord* shone round about them,' ii. 9; the angel of the *Lord* and the glory of the Lord, for the angel of *Jehovah* and the glory of *Jehovah*. In Matthew : ' Blessed is he that cometh in the name of the *Lord*,' xxi. 9; chap. xxiii. 39; Luke xiii. 34; John xii. 13 ; in the name of the *Lord*, for in the name of *Jehovah:* besides many other passages, as Luke i. 28; chap. ii. 15, 22, 23, 24, 29, 38, 39; chap. v. 17; Mark xii. 9, 11. Amongst the hidden causes that they called Jehovah Lord, were also, that if it had been declared at that time, that the Lord was the Jehovah so often mentioned in the Old Testament, it would not have been received, because it would not have been believed ; and further, because the Lord was not made Jehovah as to his human also, until he had in every respect united the Divine Essence to the human, and the human to the Divine; the plenary unition was effected after in the last temptation, which was that of the cross, wherefore the disciples after the resurrection always called him *Lord,* John xx. 2, 13, 15, 18, 20. 25 ; chap. xxi. 7, 12. 15, 16, 17, 20 ; Mark xvi. 19, 20 ; and Thomas said, ' My *Lord* and my God,' John xx. 28; and inasmuch as the Lord was the *Jehovah*, who is so often mentioned in the Old Testament, therefore also he said to the disciples, 'Ye call me Master and *Lord*, and ye say right, for I am,' John xiii. 13. 14, 16; by which words is signified that he was *Jehovah* God. That the Lord was *Jehovah*, is understood also by the words of the angel to the shepherds, ' Unto you is born to-day a Saviour, who is Christ the *Lord*.' Luke ii. 11; where Christ is for the Messiah, the Anointed, the King, and *Lord* for *Jehovah*. They who examine the Word without much attention, cannot know this, believing that our Saviour, like others, was called *Lord* merely from respect and veneration, when yet he was so called from this, that he was *Jehovah*."---*A. C.* 2921.

From this it appears that the common rendering of *Jehovah* in the Old Testament is by *Lord* in the New, and this usuage is obviously derived from the Septuagint where Κυριος, *Kurios, Lord*, is employed in numberless instances for יהוה, *Yehovah*. Thus, for instance, as a sample of multitudes of similar cases, Ps. lxxiii. 18, "Thou, whose name alone is Jehovah, art the Most High in all the earth." Ex. vi. 9, "I appeared unto Abraham, unto Isaac, and unto Jacob, by the name of God Almighty (Shaddai) ; but by my name Jehovah was I not known to them." In these passages the original for *Jehovah* is rendered in the Septuagint by *Lord*, and as the New Testament writers followed this version, they undoubtedly by this title understood the proper name of God, *Jehovah*. Moreover, it is made very clear both by Pearson (*Creed*, p. 234) and Hengstenberg (*Christology*, vol. 1. p. 161-187), that the ancient Jews attributed the name *Jehovah* to their expected Messiah. Thus the former adduces the following remarkable testimony from Rabbinical sources;--"The Scripture calleth the name of Messias, *Jehovah our righteousness.*" "God calleth the Messias by his own name, and his name is *Jehovah.*" "What is the name of the Messias? R. Abba said, *Jehovah* is his name." But it is well known that the Jews worshiped but one God in one person, and if Jesus Christ was the true Messiah, they at least could never have regarded him as the second of a trinity of persons, for by the term *Jehovah* they could never have understood any other than the one Supreme Deity.

The result of the whole, if I am not mistaken, is, that the title "Lord" (Kurios), though like its Hebrew counterpart *Adon, Adonai,* often used as a mere term of civil respect, has, in the New Testament usage, when spoken of the Saviour, the dominant import of *supreme divinity.* The *Lord* Jesus Christ is Jesus Christ the true and only *Jehovah,* and as Jehovah is one without distinction of persons, so not the slightest trace of any such distinction can be properly recognised in any thing that is revealed of the character and offices of Christ.

As to the objection to this view founded upon his economical relations to the great scheme of redemption, in which he speaks of himself, and is represented by the sacred writers, as sent by the Father—as doing the Father's will and not his own—as inferior to the Father—as praying to him—as receiving glory and honor from him—all this will form the subject of future communications, in which I shall endeavor to show its entire consistency with everything hitherto advanced in respect to the absolute unity and unapproached supremacy of his nature.

To one grand result of the whole discussion I cannot but here advert. You will readily perceive that the same train of evidence which makes the Jehovah of the Old Testament the Jesus of the New, makes, of course, the Jesus of the New the Jehovah of the Old. It therefore establishes a perfect identity of Divine person and unity of worship, in the true Church, from Adam down to the present day. The very same Being, in his immutable grandeur, is presented to our contemplation in every period of the Divine dispensations, so that by christianizing the heathenism of Pope's—"Jehovah, Jove, or Lord," and reading it "Jehovah, Jesus, Lord,"—we recognize under the triple denomination the one God whose worship hallowed the garden of Eden, and the temple of Jerusalem, and still consecrates the true churches of Christendom. We have at once also a satisfactory clew to all such passages as the following:—" Esteeming the reproach of *Christ* greater riches than the treasures in Egypt."—" The rock that followed them was *Christ.*" " Neither let us tempt *Christ* as some of them tempted, and were destroyed by serpents." This title is indeed proleptically employed, but after the evidence above adduced there would seem to be no room to doubt the identity of the person. It was clearly he who was "to come forth from Judah, a Ruler of Israel ; *whose goings forth have been from of old, from everlasting ;*" i. e. as we believe to be the true import of the words, whose *manifestations*—whose prelusory *theophanies*—have been from of old, from the earliest periods of recorded time.

Our Lord and Saviour Jesus Christ has been therefore the manifested God from the remotest ages of human history. This one and immutable God, devoid of all personal distinction, is the august I AM, or self-existent Deity, who was before Abraham, and who revealed himself to Moses at the burning bush, proclaiming the name of Jehovah as his "memorial for ever." That this being is identically the same with the Jesus of the New Testament, the predicted Messiah of the Jews, is the grand paramount truth of the inspired oracles, the denial of which leaves those divine documents shorn of their essential glory and the hopes of human redemption a very mockery. Who remains to accomplish it, when the language affirming a God made flesh, though no more expressive language ascertains the existence of a God at all, is frittered away in forced and jejune explanations aiming to obliterate the idea of *theanthropism* from the minds of men?* We can indeed find some apology for this extreme of the humantarian, in the equally gross error of the tripersonal, dogma, revolting no less to Scripture than to reason, but we scruple not to say that the reaction from that violent position has transcended its legitimate limit, and that the mind of Unitarian Christendom must oscillate backward to the point where it is met by the sublime annunciation of Unity and Trinity *in one person*, and that Person "the Word made flesh and dwelling among us." This, we are persuaded, is the common ground on which the Unitarian and the Trinitarian must eventually meet; and as there must be mutual recession, so there must be mutual concession. The Trinitarian now claims what the Unitarian can never admit, and what he ought not to admit—the doctrine of three persons. The Unitarian now denies what the Trinitarian can never forego, and what he is entitled to insist upon— the supreme and absolute divinity of Jesus Christ. *The fatal error of Trinitarians has been to argue the Divinity of Christ on grounds that supposed a Trinity of Persons; that of Unitarians, to maintain the Unity of the Godhead in the denial of the Divinity of Jesus.* Alas! for the almost infinite mischiefs wrought to the entire scheme of Christianity by the use of the word "persons." It is this unhappy term, more than any thing else, which has thrown these two portions of Christendom into such direct antagonism with each other. We cannot, however, but deem it matter of felicitation that a way is opened, through the sublime developments of the New Church, for the making of the twain one. Swedenborg has shown how the two systems may harmonize their respective truths, and that in such a way as at the same time to secure, in the most eminent degree, all the practical interests of the *Christian life*, and it would be a weakness unworthy of both parties to suffer the mere force of prejudice against his name to neutralize the promptings to a union so devoutly to be wished.

I close my letter with an extract from this illuminated teacher of the last ages.

"Because the Lord, by the passion of the cross, fully glorified his Human, that is, united it to his Divine, and thus made his Human Divine, it follows, that He is Jehovah and God, also as to both. Wherefore in the Word, in many places, He is called Jehovah, God, and the Holy One of Israel, the Redeemer,

---

* "The Divine itself, the Divine Human, and the Holy Proceeding, are the same as the Lord, and the Lord the same as Jehovah. There are none who separate this Trine which is in One, but they who say that they acknowledge One Supreme Being (*Ens*), the Creator of the universe, which thing is forgiven those who are without the Church; but they who are within the Church and say thus, do not in fact acknowledge any God, whatever they may profess or suppose; still less do they acknowledge the Lord."—*A. C.* 2156.

Saviour, and Former. . . . . From these passages it may be seen, that the Divine of the Lord, which is called the Father, and here Jehovah and God, and the Divine Human which is called the Son, and here Redeemer and Saviour, also Former, that is, Reformer and Regenerator, are not two but one; for not only is it said, Jehovah God and the Holy One of Israel, the Redeemer and Saviour; but also it is said, Jehovah the Redeemer and Saviour; yet also it is said, 'I am Jehovah, and beside Me there is no Saviour.' From which it manifestly appears, that the Divine and Human in the Lord are one person, and that the Human is also Divine; for the Redeemer and Saviour of the world is no other than the Lord as to the Divine Human, which is called the Son: for redemption and salvation constitute the proper attribute of his Human, which is called merit and righteousness; for his Human endured temptations and the passion of the cross, and thus by the Human He redeemed and saved. Now because, after the union of the Human with the Divine in Himself, which was like that of the soul and body in man, there were no longer two but one person, according to the doctrine of the Christian world, therefore the Lord, as to both, is Jehovah and God; wherefore it is sometimes said, Jehovah and the Holy one of Israel, the Redeemer and Saviour, at other times, Jehovah the Redeemer and Saviour, as may be seen from the passages above quoted. It is said, the Saviour Christ; Luke ii. 10, 11; John iv. 42. God and the God of Israel, the Saviour and Redeemer; Luke i. 47; Isaiah xiv. 14, 15; liv. 5; Psalm lxxviii. 45. Jehovah the Holy One of Israel, the Saviour and Redeemer; Isaiah xli. 14; xliii. 3, 11, 14, 15; xlviii. 17; xlix. 7; liv. 5. Jehovah, the Saviour, Redeemer, and Former; xliv. 6; xlvii. 4; xlix. 26; liv. 8; lxiii. 16; Jeremiah l. 34; Psalm lxxviii. 35; cxxx. 7. 8; 2 Samuel xxii. 2, 3. Jehovah, God, the Redeemer and Saviour, and besides Me there is no other; Isaiah xliii. 11; xliv. 6; xlv. 14, 15, 21, 22; Hosea xiii. 4."—*Doct. of the Lord*. 34.

"That God and Man in the Lord, according to the doctrine, are not two, but one person, and altogether one, as the soul and body are one, appears clearly from many things which He said; as, that the Father and He are one; that all things of the Father are his, and all his the Father's; that He is in the Father, and the Father in Him; that all things are given into his hand; that He has all power; that He is the God of heaven and earth; that whosoever believes in Him has eternal life; and further, that the Divine and Human ascended into heaven, and that, as to both, He sits at the right hand of God, that is, that He is Almighty; and many more things which were adduced above from the Word, concerning his Divine Human, which all testify that *God is one as well in person as in Essence, in whom is a Trinity, and that that God is the Lord.* The reason why these things concerning the Lord are now for the first time made publicly known, is, because it is foretold in the Revelation, xxi. and xxii. that a new church should be instituted by the Lord, at the end of the former, in which this should be the primary thing. This church is what is there meant by the New Jerusalem, into which none can enter, but those who acknowledge the Lord alone as God of heaven and earth. And this I can aver, that the universal heaven acknowledges the Lord alone; and that whosoever does not acknowledge Him, is not admitted into heaven; for heaven is heaven from the Lord. This acknowledgment itself from love and faith, causes all there to be in the Lord, and the Lord in them, as the Lord himself teaches in John: 'In that day ye shall know, that I am in my Father, and ye in Me, and I in you,' xiv. 20. And again: 'Abide in Me, and I in you. I am the vine, ye are the branches; he that abideth in Me and I in him, the same bringeth forth much fruit; for without Me ye cannot do any thing. If a man abide not in Me, he is cast out;' xv. 4-6; xvii. 22, 23. That this was not seen from the Word before, is, because, if it had been seen, still it would not have been received."—*Ib.* 60, 61.

Yours, &c.

LETTER VII.

THE INCARNATION.

DEAR SIR,

The results already reached in the foregoing discussion, though highly momentous in themselves, still leave many important phases of the subject unconsidered. The conclusion announced—I trust on legitimate and unimpeachable grounds—that Jesus of Nazareth is the Jehovah of the Old Testament, the Lord of the universe, the one only and true God, in whom is concentrated a Trinity of Essentials indicated by the terms Father, Son, and Holy Ghost, is doubtless, if sound, the fundamental fact of the revelations contained in the Bible; and yet it is a conclusion which must stand in perfect consistency with every other truth relating to his person and work, as the author and accomplisher of redemption. To this department of the subject, I now address myself, and I feel impelled to offer a general remark in regard to such a course of reasoning as that in which I have been thus far engaged, viz., that if, on the whole, fairly and legitimately conducted, and the mind recognizes the truth of the result, we are authorized to abide by it. We are not required to forego our conclusions simply because we do not clearly perceive, at the present moment, how they may be made to consist with other results which seem to be of equal validity and yet of adverse bearing. Such an apparent conflict of issues ought doubtless to enforce the most rigid requisition of evidence in support of a conclusion that seems satisfactory, though, to our own minds, coming short of demonstration; but if upon the whole we see no way of avoiding it, and that if there be any yielding, it must be on the other side; then we say that the true course is to adhere firmly to what is firmly established, and to rest in the assurance that the seemingly opposite view may, when more fully apprehended, be seen entirely to harmonize with it. If, for instance, the process of proof in regard to the absolute identity of Jehovah and Jesus is fairly beyond question, then a moral compulsion rests upon us to interpret those passages of the Word, which seem to hold a different language, in a sense consistent with that unity of Divine essence and person which we have previously certified to our own minds. I am well aware of the difficulty that you will doubtless find, in the outset, in your attempts to solve the apparent problem which our main position sets before you. The grand ideal which you have formed of the design and genius of the Christian system, involves as an essential element, a certain *disjunction* and *duality* of the Father and the Son, which is virtually annulled in the view that I have now presented, so that you feel that its adoption would be not so much a modification, as a total subversion, of all your most cherished theories in regard to the redemption and salvation of men. You perceive at a glance, that the established dogma of *vicarious atonement* sinks at once out of sight when the position is admitted, that Jesus Christ is as truly the Father as the Son, which of course he must be if he is the veritable Jehovah, and which, in the sequel, I shall show still more clearly that he is. This result, if admitted, cannot fail to give a violent shock to your pre-conceptions, and it would not be strange, if under the first effects of the concussion, your faith should so " reel like a drunken man" that you should find yourself for a time *desperabund*, and ready to renounce the hope of *ever* attaining the truth on the most momentous of all themes. But cooler reflection will restore the equilibrium of reason and religion. It is impossible for any honest mind to remain in an attitude of permanent rebellion against a clear and irresistible induction drawn from both the spirit and the letter of the Holy Oracles. In the present case, I will venture to say that you will find every attempt abortive to array before yourself a *stronger* body of evidence in support of the common doctrine of atonement than I have above presented of the supreme and exclusive Godhead of Jesus Christ, and as surely as this is received as true, so surely will that doctrine be renounced as false, for the two cannot possibly stand together. If the Deity exists in one person he cannot, in that person, as I have already remarked, make an atonement to himself.

What remains then but to attempt to show, that all the sublime ends of redemption may be more fully attained, and the Divine perfections be far more gloriously displayed, on the ground which I have assumed than upon that which is made the basis of the current theology of the church? This is what I have ventured to propose to myself in the sequel of these letters. Whether I shall do justice to the theme, or even to my own imperfect views of it, I am not a little in doubt. But that there is a great truth in relation to the subject, which is intrinsically *capable* of presentation, I am altogether satisfied, nor ought I perhaps to despair of exhibiting it in an intelligible form, if I have succeeded thus far in stating the preliminary argument out of which the ultimate results legitimately grow.

The aim of my preceding elucidations has been to evince that our adorable Lord and Saviour, being Jehovah in unity, exists, in his very nature, in a Divine Humanity, the manifestation of which, prior to the advent in the flesh, could only be rendered possible by the assumption of an angel as a medium. The angel thus employed was not necessarily any particular angel with whom the Divine Being was more permanently connected than with any other individual of the angelic order. The Divine influx merely *infilled* the created angel, who thus became, as it were, a body to that measure of the essence of Jehovah which for the time pervaded it as a soul, and appeared and spake through it. The ontological grounds of this I have already developed, and a secondary reason for renewing the mention of it here, is, to introduce a remarkable passage from Watts' "Glory of Christ as God-Man," which—with the abatement of his idea respecting the angel as the *pre-existing human soul* of Jesus, and therefore *permanently* united with the Supreme Divinity, and also with the understanding that by the term angel is meant a real created angel temporarily assumed—exhibits a most striking approximation to the truth as it regards the real relation subsisting between the visible angel and the informing Deity. He is replying to an objection which he thus states;—" Though it should be allowed that God was present with this angel, and resided in him, and spake by him, yet is this sufficient to make a *personal union* between God and the angel? or is it ground enough to say that *God and the angel were one complex person?*" This objection he proceeds to answer.

" The most common and the most familiar idea that we have of a *complex person* is human nature or man, who is made up of a soul and body. Let us now consider whether most of those mutual relations or communications between soul and body which render man a *complex person* are not found in this glorious *person* composed of the great God and this angel. Has the body of a man a *nearer relation* to his soul than any other body in the world? So had this angel a nearer relation to God than any other creature whatsoever. Is the soul said to *inhabit* the body, or *reside* in it constantly during the whole term of life? So did God constantly reside in this glorious angel. Does the soul *influence* the body to its chief human actions? So did God influence this angel. Is the body the *constant and immediate instrument* of the soul, whereby it speaks and acts and conveys its mind to men? Such was this angel to the Great God who dwelt in him. Is the body *obedient* to the volitions of the indwelling soul? Much more is this angel to the indwelling God. Is the soul immediately *conscious* of many of the motions of the body? Much more is God immediately conscious of every motion, action and occurrence that relates to this angel? Are the *properties* and *actions* of the body sometimes *attributed* to the soul, and the *properties* and *actions* of the soul sometimes to the body in the common language of men? So in the language of Scripture the names, title, and properties of the great God are attributed to this angel; the appearances, speeches, voice, words, motions, and actions of this angel are attributed to God. And if *man* upon these accounts be called a *complex person*, made up of *soul and body*, for the same reason we may suppose that the *Great God* and this angel *of his presence* make up a *complex person* also; and this is called a personal union."—*Watts on Glory of Christ*, p. 67, 68.

This, as I have remarked, is a wonderful approximation to the truth according to the New Church view of the subject, and the man of that church can hardly refrain from imagining to himself the cordial delight with which such a spirit would have welcomed revelations so well calculated to clear up the mysteries of the Divine nature with which his mind was evidently deeply oppressed. All that is necessary to bring this view into a very strict accordance with the truth, is to consider the angel as an angel, and to divest the relation set forth of the *permanency* which he attributes to it.

It was Jehovah, then, in his Divine Humanity, who appeared in the ancient *theophanies*, and these appearances were pre-intimations of his subsequent coming in the ultimates of our earthly humanity.

The temporary intermediation of an angel, who was of course a man, gave a kind of sensible demonstration of the fact, but the procedure was all along in "first principles," and it was reserved for the "fulness of times," to realise the actual result of the Lord's advent in the flesh. In the consideration of this stupendous event, our attention is naturally drawn to two distinct branches of the subject; (1) The *mode* of its accomplishment; (2) The *ends* to be answered by it; on both which I shall be constrained to be somewhat full. I shall count also upon your indulgence for the rather copious extracts from Swedenborg.

In entering upon an attempted explanation of the *mode* of the incarnation, I would fain shield myself from the charge of rudely invading the region of mystery. The apostolic declaration, "Great is the mystery of godliness; God manifest in flesh," will naturally rise up to your mind, and perhaps throw around it a sphere of repellency towards the least approach to a solution of the deep arcana which environ the subject. But I may plead as a sanction to the attempt the fact, which *you* cordially admit, that such an incarnation has actually taken place. I am not arguing the antecedent possibility or probability of such an amazing occurrence. It has already passed into the category of things transpired. It stands emblazoned as the paramount fact of all human, if not of all Divine, history. Its occurrence is the glory of earth, and the wonder of heaven. The only question in regard to it, is, whether there be any presumption—any unlawful prying into things hidden from mortal ken—in humbly endeavoring to bring our knowledge, such as it is, of the Divine nature, to bear on the nature of the great fact, with the view to learn how far the mode of it may be brought within the compass of our intelligence. I do not see that this is by any means forbidden, especially as after all our researches there will remain an immense residuum of absolute verity which will be for ever incomprehensible to our finite faculties. Yet we come, I think, to the inquiry with signal advantages if what we have already remarked as to the constitution of the Divine nature be conceded to be true. The cardinal tenet of the New Church, that Jesus is Jehovah, that Jehovah is one, and that a Divine Humanity is involved in the very essence of his being, prepares us to yield a more facile credence to the asserted fact of this eternal Humanity's having become incarnate in time, or, in other words, of its having "passed from first principles to last." Our conceptions of the subject are, moreover, somewhat aided by the views above advanced respecting the emanation-theory of creation, according to which we learn that the Divine influx in its descent continually tends to clothe itself in material embodiments, giving form and expression to the spiritual principle from which they are derived. Still, a measureless remove must for ever separate all other manifestations of the Divine agency from that which we are called to contemplate in the incarnation of Jehovah; and we only refer to them as casting some collateral gleams of light upon a subject inevitably obscure to us, under whatever aspect it be viewed.

For myself, I am unable to perceive what advance can be made towards a correct apprehension of the theme before us, except by divesting ourselves entirely, at the outset, of the prevalent idea of a Trinity of persons. This idea is an effectual closure of the mind against all access to the light of truth. The inference—for, as I have shown, it is nothing more—that it was the *second person* of the Godhead who assumed our nature, completely vacates all just and Scriptural conceptions of the wondrous fact.* If there is any intelligible sense in the inspired declarations as to what is to be believed on this subject, it is that Jehovah himself, in the unity of his person, condescended to become incarnate, and in so doing did not more assume our nature than *ultimate* his own, for our nature is human, because his is infinitely so.† But what is the true idea which is to be formed of Jehovah? Let our illumined author speak in reply.

"That by God and Jehovah in the Word was understood the Lord, was not known to the Jewish church, neither is it known at this day to the Christian church: that the Christian church has not known this, is because it has distinguished the Divine into three persons.: whereas the ancient church, which was after the flood, and especially the most ancient church, which was before the flood, by Jehovah and God understood no other than the Lord, and indeed the Lord as to the Divine Human. They had knowledge also concerning the Divine Itself which is the Lord, and which He calls his Father; but concerning that Divine Itself which is in the Lord, they were not able to think, but concerning the Divine Human, consequently they could not be conjoined to another Divine, for conjunction is effected by thought which is of the understanding, and by affection which is of the will, thus by faith and by love; for when the Divine itself is thought of, the thought falls as into a boundless universe, and so is dissipated, whereby is no conjunction; but it is otherwise when the Divine itself is thought of as the Divine Human. They knew also, that unless they were conjoined with the Divine, they could not be saved: on this account the Divine Human was what the ancient churches adored, and Jehovah also manifested Himself with them in the Divine Human; and the Divine Human was the Divine itself in heaven, for heaven constitutes one man, which

---

* "It is believed that God, the Creator of the universe, begat a Son from eternity, and that this Son descended and assumed the Human, to redeem and save men; but this is erroneous, and falls of itself to the ground, while it is considered that God is one, and that it is more than fabulous in the eye of reason, that the one God should have begotten a Son from eternity, and also that God the Father, together with the Son and the Holy Ghost, each of whom singly is God, should be one God. This fabulous representation is entirely dissipated, while it is demonstrated from the Word, that Jehovah God himself descended, and became MAN, and also Redeemer."—*T. C. R.* 82.

† "The reason that the Lord's internal man, which is Jehovah, is called a man, is, because no one is a man but Jehovah alone. For 'man' signifies, in the genuine sense, that Esse from which man originates. The very Esse from which man originates is Divine, consequently, is celestial and spiritual; without this Divine celestial and spiritual, there is nothing human in man, but only a sort of animal nature, such as the beasts have. It is from the Esse of Jehovah, or of the Lord, that every man is a man; and it is hence also that he is called a man. The celestial which constitutes him a man, is that he should love the Lord, and love the neighbor: thus he is a man, because he is an image of the Lord, and because he has that celestial from the Lord; otherwise he is a wild beast. The same may further appear from this, that Jehovah, or the Lord, appeared to the patriarchs of the most ancient church as a man; as he did afterwards to Abraham, and likewise to the prophets; wherefore also the Lord deigned, when there was no longer any man upon earth, or nothing celestial and spiritual remaining with man, to assume the human nature by being born as another man, and to make it Divine; whereby also he is the only man. Moreover, the universal heaven presents before the Lord the image of a man, because it presents Him; hence heaven is called the Grand Man, on this account especially, because the Lord is all in all therein."—*A. C.* 1894.

is called the Grand Man, and which has been treated of heretofore at the close of the chapters. This Divine in heaven is no other than the Divine itself, but in heaven as a divine man; it is this man which the Lord took upon Him, and made Divine in Himself, and united to the Divine itself, as it had been united from eternity, for from eternity there was oneness; and this because the human race could not otherwise be saved; for it could no longer suffice that the Divine itself through heaven, thus through the Divine Human there, could flow into human minds; wherefore the Divine itself willed to unite to itself the Divine Human actually by the human assumed in the world; the latter and the former is the Lord."—*A. C.* 5663.

If this be well founded, the Divine nature does not present to our conceptions an *absolute simple*, but a *complex*, the elements of which are the Divine itself in its own super-celestial *esse*, or the infinite Love, and the Divine Wisdom or Truth, related to the former as Intellect ever is to Affection, which is the relation of the *existere* to the *esse*. The Divine Wisdom is the *form* of the Divine Love, and this *form* is what is more especially to be understood by the Divine Humanity existing in "first principles," or as the Alpha, which, in the incarnation, assumed to itself the Omega; for when our Lord says of himself, " I am the Alpha and the Omega, the first and the last," it is obvious that he has no respect to time, as he is without beginning of days or end of years. In this character of the Divine Humanity from everlasting, our Lord was the Word, or the Truth, as I have already shown, and this "Word was made flesh," i. e., became incarnate.* The Word or Wisdom of Jehovah, indicated by the Son, could be made manifest, but not the Divine Love, answering to the Father. "That Jehovah's appearing denotes the Lord's Divine in his Human, is evident from this, that his Divine cannot appear to any man, nor even to, any angel, except by the Divine Human; and the Divine Human is nothing but the Divine Truth which proceeds from Himself." This *proceeding* of the Divine Truth from the Divine Good or Love, is what is otherwise expressed by the word *sent*, and the idea of *sent* is intimately related to *angel*, which, as we have seen, denotes the medium of manifestation prior to the advent in the flesh. The bearing of this will appear more clearly in the sequel, when we shall show that the Father's sending the Son into the world implies, in a consistent sense, the *sending himself into the world*. But preliminary to this it is necessary to lay down the great law of generation which is perpetually involved in all Swedenborg's expositions of this profound subject.

---

* " Who does not know that the Lord was conceived from God the Father, and who cannot thence understand, that God the Father who is Jehovah, took upon him Humanity in the world, and consequently that the Humanity is the Humanity of God the Father, and thus that God the Father and He are one, as the soul and the body are one? Can any one therefore approach the soul of a man, and descend from thence into the body? Is not his humanity to be approached? And is not his soul addressed hereby at the same time? I am aware it will be thought, How can Jehovah the Father, who is the Creator of the universe, come down and assume Humanity? But let these think also, How can the Son from eternity, who is equal to the Father, and also the Creator of the universe, do this? Does it not amount to the same thing? It is said the Father and the Son from eternity, but there is no Son from eternity; it is the Divine Humanity called the Son, that was sent into the world."—*A. R.* 743.

"To the above I shall add this arcanum, that the soul, which is from the father, is the very man, and that the body, which is from the mother, is not man in itself, but from the soul; the body is only a covering of the soul, composed of such things as are of the natural world.—Since the soul of man is the very man, and is spiritual from its origin, it is manifest whence it is that the mind, soul, disposition, inclination, and affection of the love of the father dwells in his offspring, and returns and renders itself conspicuous from generation to generation. Thence it is, that many families, yea, nations, are known from their first father; there is a general image in the face of each descendant, which manifests itself; and this image is not changed, except by the spiritual things of the church. The reason that a general image of Jacob and Judah still remains in their posterity, by which they may be distinguished from others, is, because they have hitherto adhered firmly to their religious principles; for there is in the seed of every one from which he is conceived, a graft or offset of the father's soul, in its fulness, within a certain covering from the elements of nature, by which the body is formed in the womb of the mother; which may be made according to the likeness of the father, or according to the likeness of the mother, the image of the father still remaining within it, which continually endeavors to bring itself forth, and if it cannot do it in the first generation, it effects it the following. The reason that the image of the father is in its fulness in the seed is, because, as was said, the soul is spiritual from its origin, and what is spiritual has nothing in common with space; wherefore it is similar to itself in a small, as well as in a large compass."—*T. C. R.* 103.

I have here given this law in full by reason of its vast importance in the present investigation, and though the principle involved comes fairly within the province of physiology, and may be said to demand proof, yet I scruple not to build upon it, not only because Swedenborg asserts it, after having given me reasons to warrant the most implicit reliance on his testimony, but because the presumptions in its favor amount very nearly, in my judgment, to positive proof. It cannot, I think, be doubted that there is, on the part of the father, a *descent* of the soul in its "first principles" to the ultimates of the body in the propagation of a human being, and that the office of the mother is to furnish the investment of the seminal principle or germ. Accordingly Swedenborg remarks, in illustration of the asserted fact, " that the soul is from the father, and its clothing from the mother, may be illustrated by things analogous in the vegetable kingdom. In this kingdom the earth or ground is the common mother, which, in itself, as in a womb, receives and clothes seeds; yea, as it were, conceives, bears, brings forth, and educates them as a mother her offspring from the father."—*C. L.* 206. The position is at any rate boldly assumed by Swedenborg in the face of all physiological science, and may be considered as a virtual challenge to the schools to dispute its soundness. As the truth of the principle is so essential to a just view of the whole doctrine of the incarnation as given by him, we are perfectly sure he would never have hazarded the enunciation but upon the most indisputable grounds.*

---

* Notwithstanding the general proclivity of Commentators to deny the reference of Jer. xxxi. 22; "The Lord hath created (i. e. shall create) a new thing in the earth, a woman shall compass a man," to the miraculous conception. I am for myself satisfied that no preferable explanation has ever been given. This original תסובב, *tesobëb*, properly signifies to *surround, environ, encompass, encircle,* and Michaelis renders and interprets

But how does this law specifically apply in the case of our Lord? Here again we are furnished with an answer.

"That Jehovah himself descended and assumed the Human, is very evident in Luke, where are these words : 'Mary said to the angel, How shall this be done, since I know not a man ? To whom the angel replied, The Holy Spirit shall come upon thee, and the virtue of the Most High shall overshadow thee ; whence the Holy Thing that is born of thee, shall be called the Son of God,' i. 34, 35. And in Matthew: 'The angel said to Joseph, the bridegroom of Mary, in a dream, that which is born in her is of the Holy Spirit; and Joseph knew her not, until she brought forth a Son, and called his name Jesus,' i. 20, 25. That by the Holy Spirit is meant the Divine which proceeds from Jehovah, will be seen in the third chapter of this work. Who does not know that the child has the soul and life from the father, and that the body is from the soul ? What, therefore, is said more plainly than that the Lord had his soul and life from Jehovah God; and, because the Divine cannot be divided, that the Divine itself was his soul and life ? Wherefore the Lord so often called Jehovah God his Father, and Jehovah God called Him his Son. What, then, can be heard more ludicrous than that the soul of our Lord was from the mother Mary, as both the Roman Catholics and the Reformed at this day dream, not having as yet been awakened by the Word."—*T. C. R.* 82.

Elsewhere he remarks;

"The Lord in the Word is called Jehovah as to Divine good, for Divine good is the very Divine, and the Lord is called the Son of God as to Divine truth, for Divine truth proceeds from Divine good, as a son from a father, and also is said to be born."—*A. C.* 7499.

This is according to the universal law, that all thought or intellect is the product of affection. In God, angel, and man, the *genesis* of Truth is from Good. But we are called to advance farther in the direction upon which we have entered. The common doctrine of the incarnation, if subjected to a rigid analysis, will undoubtedly resolve itself into the teaching of no higher a fact than this, viz., that the manhood of Jesus, both soul and body, was, as it were, externally *assumed* by God—was *appended* or *adjoined* to Deity—so that the union between the Divine and the human in our Lord, amounted to a mere *adjunction* of one nature to the other. This, however, as we conceive, comes very far short of the truth, for on this ground we are unable to perceive how the indwelling of Jehovah in Jesus differed, except in degree, from that which may be predicated of Moses, or David, or Daniel, or Paul, with each of whom there was doubtless a very special presence of the Divine Being endowing them for their work.* If Jesus Christ possessed a human soul, or *inmost*, from his

---

it—*circumdabit*, i. e. *in utero habebit*. So also Pocock, Hulsius, Schmidt, and many others among the earlier Christian Commentators. This interpretation, like many others, seems to have been yielded out of a kind of complaisance to the objections of Jews and other Anti-Messianists of the school of Grotius, who have been followed by the mass of modern German critics. The import of the passage according to Pocock is, that the Lord would create a new thing in the unprecedented fact of a woman's *encompassing* a man— a man *par eminence*—contrary to the ordinary laws of generation. And what is this but a veiled announcement of the great fact of the miraculous conception ?

* "The unition of the Divine Essence with the Human, is not to be understood as of two who are distinct from each other, and only conjoined by love as a father with a son,

mother, are you prepared to define in what sense he can be affirmed to have been essentially Divine? It will not, I conceive, avail to have recourse on this point to the convenient plea of mystery, for the proposition is a very plain one, and must be susceptible of a sense not difficult to be grasped, so far as the averment of the fact is concerned. We see, in regard to the ancient *theophanies*, that the assumption of an angel leaves the impression very distinct of the paramount presence and operation of Jehovah himself acting in and through him. The Divine person may be said to be translucent through the angelic humanity. In like manner, in the Lord's incarnation on earth, it is necessary that the Deity should be equally conspicuous, at least to the eye of the mind, in the terrestrial man with whom he is conjoined, for the natural body which he here assumed stands, in fact, in a very similar relation to the indwelling Divinity, as did the spiritual body of the mediating angel to the essential Godhead which temporarily informed it. But let it once be assumed that he received a human soul—understanding by that term an *inmost essence*—by nativity of the mother, and such a distinct Divine inhabitation becomes impossible, and nothing more than the bare *adjunction* of Deity can be recognized. Upon this ground, therefore, our Lord stands shorn of his essential glory, and his human principle will inevitably be thought of as the human principle of any other man, while his Divinity, though brought in contact with his humanity, will be viewed altogether apart from it, and ideally merged in that of the infinite Godhead, which is usually understood by the term Father. This is a virtual surrender of the great truth in question, and they to whom it is imputable have small cause to enter the lists with the Unitarians. Let once the humanity of our Lord be mentally *disjoined* from his Divinity, and "Ichabod" is written upon the pillars of the church. On this subject I will give place to higher authority.

"Another point which the Athanasian doctrine teaches, is, that in the Lord there are two essences, the Divine and the Human; and in that doctrine the idea is clear that the Lord has a Divine principle and a Human, or that the Lord is God and man; but the idea is obscure that the Divine principle of the Lord is in the Human, as the soul is in the body. Inasmuch as a clear idea prevails over an obscure idea, therefore most people, both simple and learned, think of the Lord as of a common man, like unto themselves. and in such case, they do not think at the same time of his Divine principle; if they think of the Divine principle, then they separate it in their idea from the Human, and thereby also infringe the unity of person. If they are asked, where is his Divine principle? they reply, from their idea, In heaven with the

---

when the father loves the son, and the son the father, or when a brother loves a brother, or a friend a friend; but it is a real unition into one, so that they are not two but one, as the Lord also teaches in several places."—*A. C.* 3737.

"With respect to the union of the Lord's Divine Essence with his Human, and of the Human with the Divine, this is infinitely transcendant; for the Lord's internal was Jehovah Himself, thus life itself; whereas man's internal is not the Lord: thus neither life, but a recipient of life. There was *union* of the Lord with Jehovah, but there is no *union* of man with Lord, but *conjunction*. The Lord from his own proper power united himself with Jehovah, wherefore also he was made righteousness; but man's conjunction is never effected by his own power, but by the Lord's, so that the Lord joins man to himself."—*A. C.* 2005.

Father; the reason why they so reply and so perceive, is, because they find a repugnance to think that the Human principle is Divine, and thus together with its Divine principle in heaven, not aware, that whilst in thought they thus separate the Divine principle of the Lord from his Human, they not only think contrary to their own doctrine, which teaches that the Divine principle of the Lord is in His Human, as the soul in the body, also, that there is unity of person, that is, that they are one person, but also they charge that doctrine undeservedly with contradiction or fallacy, in supposing that the Human principle of the Lord, together with the rational soul, was from the mother alone, when yet every man is rational by virtue of the soul, which is from the father. But that such thought has place, and such a separation, follows also from the idea of three Gods, from which idea it results, that His Divine principle in the Human is from the Divine of the Father, who is the first person, when yet it is His own proper Divine principle, which descended from heaven and assumed the Human. If man does not rightly perceive this, he may possibly be led to suppose, that his begetting Father was not one Divine principle but threefold, which yet cannot be received with any faith. In a word, they who separate the Divine principle from His Human, and do not think that the Divine is in His Human as the soul in the body, and that they are one person, may fall into erroneous ideas concerning the Lord, even into an idea as of a man separated from a soul; wherefore take heed to yourselves lest you think of the Lord as of a man like yourself, but rather think of the Lord as of a man who is God. Attend, my reader! when you are perusing these pages, you may be led to suppose, that you have never, in thought, separated the Divine principle of the Lord from His Human, thus neither the Human from the Divine; but, I beseech you, consult your thought, when you have determined it to the Lord, whether you have ever considered that the Divine principle of the Lord is in His Human as the soul in the body? Rather have you not thought, yea, if you are now willing to make the inquiry, do not you at present think of His Human principle separately, and of His Divine principle separately? And when you think of His human principle, do not you conceive it to be like the human principle of another man, and when of His Divine principle, do not you conceive in it your idea, to be with the Father? I have questioned great numbers on this subject, even the rulers of the church, and they have all replied that it is so; and when I have said, that yet it is a tenet taught in the Athanasian creed, which is the very doctrine of their church concerning God and concerning the Lord, that the Divine principle of the Lord is in His Human as the soul in the body, they have replied, that they did not know this: and when I have recited these words of the doctrine, 'Our Lord Jesus Christ, the Son of God, although He be God and man, yet there are not two but one Christ; one altogether by unity of person; since as the reasonable soul and body are one man, so God and man is one Christ;" they were then silent and confessed afterwards, that they had not noted these words, being indignant at themselves for having so hastily, and with so careless an eye, examined their own doctrine."—*A. E.* 1104.

To the same effect, he observes in another place, that "they who think of the Lord's Humanity and not at the same time of his Divinity, will on no account admit the phrase "Divine Humanity; for they think separately of his Humanity, and separately of his Divinity, which is like thinking of a man separately from his soul or life, which, however, is not to think of a man at all; still less is it an adequate way of thinking of the Lord."

We have here, then, if we mistake not, the grand cardinal truth of all Divine revelation—"God (i. e. Jehovah) manifest in the flesh;" not God merely *adjoined* to the soul and body of a human being like ourselves, but the true God truly *incarnated* in a tenement of flesh and blood received, not by ordinary generation, but by ordinary nativity, from the virgin womb of Mary. "That the Lord had Divinity and Humanity, Divinity from Jehovah the Father, and Humanity from the virgin Mary, is well known. Hence it is, that he was God and Man, and that he had a Divine Essence and a Human nature, the Divine Essence from the Father, and the Human nature from the Mother; and hence he was equal to the Father with respect to the Divinity, and less than the Father with respect to the Humanity. And further, *this Human Nature was not transmuted into the Divine Essence, neither commixed with it; for the Human Nature cannot be transmuted into the Divine Essence nor can it be commixed therewith.* Nevertheless, by our doctrine we maintain that the Divinity assumed a Humanity, that is, united itself to it, as the soul is united to its body, so that they are not two, but one person."

This we believe to be the true DOCTRINE OF THE LORD, or the doctrine *respecting* the Lord, and of such transcendant importance do we regard it, that we scruple not to subscribe with all our hearts to Swedenborg's declaration, that "the essential of all doctrines is to acknowledge the Divine Human of the Lord." Nay, we are expressly taught by him that the cordial recognition of this doctrine is that which really constitutes the Lord's Second Coming. "By the Lord's advent is not understood His advent in person, but that he will then reveal Himself in the Word, that He is Jehovah, the Lord of heaven and earth, and that He alone is to be adored by all who will be in His new church, which is meant by the New Jerusalem; for which end also He hath now opened the internal or spiritual sense of the Word, in which sense the Lord is everywhere treated of: this also is what is understood by His coming in the clouds of heaven with glory. Inasmuch as He Himself is the Word, as He is called in John, therefore the revelation of Himself in the Word is His advent." He comes in the revelation of His own essential glory as God-Man, Jehovah Jesus, Creator, Redeemer and Regenerator—a revelation made in connexion with the establishment of the Church of the New Jerusalem, as it is in this Church only that the doctrine in question is received in its genuine purport. "That there is in the Lord a threefold principle, namely, the Divinity Itself, the Divine Humanity, and the Divine Proceeding, is an arcanum from heaven and is revealed for the benefit of those who shall have a place in the Holy Jerusalem."—*H. D.* 997. For the inferential bearings of this averment upon the theological views or the moral state of others, we are not responsible, as we plant ourselves simply upon the instrinsic truth of the position, and if any truth has a train of just and inevitable consequences, we cannot reject the truth simply because we cannot dispose of the consequences entirely to our minds. In respect to the system, however, in which the present doctrine holds so prominent a place, we do not regard it as a harshly exclusive or denunciatory system, though very emphatic in its affirmations, and I propose, in the winding up of my discussion, to offer some remarks on the moral aspects of the subject, which may tend to correct certain unfavorable impressions on this score, that have probably arisen in the minds of some of my readers.

In the following paragraph, Swedenborg is relating the conversation of certain spirits in the other life. In the perusal I beg you will make as much or as little account as you please of his assertions, on the score of the reality of this intercourse with spirits. The grand question is rather what the Truth says on this subject, than what they are alleged to have said, yet, as I have before remarked, the evidence that they did say it, is undoubtedly enhanced in proportion to the evidence of its being intrinsically true.—The spirits were from some other earth in the universe.

"It is well to be observed, that the idea which any person entertains concerning any thing, in another world is presented to the life, and thereby every one is examined as to the nature of his thought and perception respecting the things of faith; and that the idea of the thought concerning God is the chief of all others, inasmuch as by that idea, if it be genuine, conjunction is effected with the Divine Being, and consequently with heaven. They were afterwards questioned concerning the nature of their idea respecting God. They replied, that they did not conceive God as invisble, but as visible under a human form: and that they knew him to be thus visible, not only from an interior perception, but also from this circumstance, that he has appeared to them as a man; they added, that if, according to the idea of some strangers, they should conceive God as invisible, consequently without form and quality, they should not be able in any wise to think about God, inasmuch as such an invisible principle falls not upon any idea of thought. On hearing this, it was given to tell them, that they do well, to think of God under a human form, and that many on our earth think in like manner, especially when they think of the Lord; and that the ancients also thought according to this idea. I then told them concerning Abraham, Lot, Gideon, Manoah, and his wife, and what is related of them in our Word, viz., that they saw God under a human form, and acknowledged him thus seen to be the Creator of the Universe, and called him Jehovah, and this also from an interior perception; but that at this day that interior perception was lost in the Christian world, and only remains with the simple who are principled in faith

"Previous to this discourse, they believed that our company also consisted of those, who were desirous to confuse them in their thoughts of God by an idea of three; wherefore on hearing what was said, they were affected with joy, and replied that there were also sent from God (whom they then called the Lord) those who teach them concerning Him, and that they are not willing to admit strangers, who perplex them, especially by the idea of three persons in the Divinity, inasmuch that they know that God is one, consequently that the Divine Principle is One, and not consisting of three in unanimity, unless such threefold unanimity to be conceived to exist in God as in an angel, in whom there is an inmost principle of life, which is invisible and which is the ground of his thought and wisdom, and an external principle of life which is visible under the human form, whereby he sees and acts, and a proceeding principle of life which is the sphere of love and of faith issuing from him (for from every spirit and angel there proceeds a sphere of life, whereby he is known at a distance); which proceeding principle of life, when considered as issuing from the Lord, is the essential Divine Principle which fills and constitutes the heavens, because it proceeds from the very Esse of the life of love and of faith; they said, that in this, and in no other manner, they can perceive and apprehend a threefold unity. When they had thus expressed themselves, it was given to me to inform them, that such an idea concerning a threefold unity agrees with the idea of the angels concerning the Lord, and that it is grounded in the Lord's own doctrine respecting himself; for he teaches that the Father and himself are One; that the Father is in Him and He in the Father; that whoso seeth Him seeth the Father; and whoso believeth on him believeth on the Father and knoweth the Father; also that the

Comforter, whom he calls the Spirit of Truth, and likewise the Holy Ghost, proceeds from Him, and doth not speak from himself but for Him, by which Comforter is meant the Divine Proceeding Principle. It was given me further to tell them, that their idea concerning a threefold unity agrees with the Esse and Existere of the life of the Lord when in the world : the Esse of his life was the Essential Divine Principle, for he was conceived of Jehovah, and the Esse of every one's life is that whereof he is conceived; the Existere of life derived from that Esse is the Human Principle in form; the Esse of life of every man, which he has from his father, is called soul, and the Existere of life thence derived is called body ; soul and body constitutes one man ; the likeness between each resembles that which subsists between a principle which is in effort [*conatus*], and a principle which is in act derived from effort, for act is an effort acting, and thus two are one : effort in man is called will, and effort acting is called action : the body is the instrumental part, whereby the will, which is the principal, acts, and the instrumental and principal in acting are one; such is the case in regard to soul and body, and such is the idea which the angels in heaven have respecting soul and body; hence they know, that the Lord made his 'human principle divine by virtue of the divine principle in himself, which was to him a soul from the Father. This is agreeable also to the creed received throughout the Christian world, which teaches, that '*Although Christ is God and man, yet he is not two but one Christ; yea, he is altogether one and a single Person; for as body and soul are one man, so also God and man is one Christ.*'—*E. U.* 158.

But the question which you will urge as paramount to all others is, whether the view now presented finds adequate warrant in the Scriptures fairly and legitimately interpreted. This question, of which I fully acknowledge the claims, I shall consider at length in my next.

Yours, &c.

LETTER VIII.

THE INCARNATION.

DEAR SIR,

It would not perhaps be possible to announce any proposition fraught with more momentous consequences to the interests of revealed truth, than that which I have thus far endeavored to establish, viz., that Jesus Christ is the true and only God, the Creator and Governor of the Universe, one with Jehovah, and comprising within his own Divine Person the three Essentials of the Godhead, denominated Father, Son, and Holy Spirit. How rich the discovery to the Christian, that that Being whom he had been taught to view simply as his Saviour, in some secondary character, is indeed no other than the Supreme Deity in the most absolute oneness of his nature, and not merely a proper, but the *only* proper, object of religious worship and adoration! With this view of our Lord's character firmly rooted and grounded in his mind, he knows no Father or Holy Ghost in the least degree separate from the person of Christ, and offers no prayer to any other being. The sum total of all that he knows or acknowledges of God, is concentrated in Jesus of Nazareth alone. This is "the true God and our Saviour, whom to know aright is eternal life." Such an assurance is as the blaze of a fresh revelation pouring its beams upon the dazzled eye-sight, and the soul awakes to the experience of a new-born joy in contemplating the Eternal Deity as dwelling in him who dwelt in human flesh and who accomplished his earthly sojourn in the land of Judea. The "root out of dry ground," becomes the "plant of renown," and he who was "without form and comeliness," becomes "fairer than the sons of men," his ineffable human beauties fading away into the inconceivable splendors of the Godhead. Discarded for ever from his mind is that chaos of confusion which had hitherto beset him in his attempts to put an intelligible sense upon the language of the creeds which represent God as subsisting in three persons, and Christ virtually in two.* The day-dawn of truth has at length risen upon the obscurities and mystifications of his faith, and he has ceased to be perplexed by the subtleties of the Trinitarian or the bald negations of the Unitarian dogma. He beholds the clear development of the Unity and Trinity of the Divine Nature, harmonizing all the discords of the established symbols of Christendom, and leaving intact the literal and spiritual integrity of the inspired Word. The perception of this glorious truth cannot fail to constitute an era in the experience of every soul that is visited by it, and from its inmost depths it must echo forth the response of the believing Thomas, "My LORD and my God!"

The testimony in proof of this grand position I have adduced in

---

* "The reason why the Lord is not acknowledged when his Divine principle is not acknowledged in His Human is, because in such case He is not regarded as God, but only as a man, who is not able to save : but whereas it is still believed from the Athanasian creed, that the Lord is the Son of God born from eternity, and His Divinity equal to the Divinity of the Father, and yet they separate His Human principle from His Divine, it follows, that they distinguish the Lord as it were into two persons, which they call natures, so that the Lord is one as the Son of God from eternity, and another as the Son of Mary; and whereas they thus distinguish the Lord, no one can approach Him, except he will approach him as one person, when he approaches him as God, and as another person, when he approaches Him as man. Such an idea concerning the Lord has been entertained from the first foundation of the church, as may appear from the writings of the fathers, and afterwards from those of their descendants. This division of the Lord in the church from its beginning, arose from the Word not being understood; for where the Father is mentioned by the Lord, it was believed to be the Divine principle distinct from His Human, when, nevertheless, it manifestly appears in Matthew and in Luke, that the Lord was conceived of the Essential Divine principle which is called the Father, and consequently that that Essential Divine principle is in His Human as the soul is in its body, and the soul and body are one person: and what is wonderful, the Athanasian creed, which is universally received in the Christian world, teaches this in express terms, and yet scarce any one attends to it therein; that they do not attend to it has been made evident to me from this circumstance, that many with whom I have conversed after death, both learned and unlearned, have said that they did not know it, but that they thought of the Son of God from eternity as of a divine person above His Human, sitting at the right hand of God the Father : likewise also that they had not attended to the words of the Lord which declared that the Father and He are One, likewise that the Father is in Him and He in the Father. From these considerations it may appear that the church has not acknowledged the Divine principle of the Lord in His Human, from its beginning; and that this is what is signified by the Lamb being slain from the foundation of the world."—*A. E.* 807.

copious measure in the preceding Letters. But I must have a very inadequate idea of the tenacity with which fixed opinions are held, were I to suppose that all objections would yield at once even to *any* amount of evidence that might be adduced upon the subject. So inveterate is the grasp laid upon our faith by the sermon, the catechism, and the hymn-book, which have always embodied our theology—so reluctantly is wrung from us the concession that the church of the past has failed to seize the most fundamental of all truths, and that such long lines of holy synods, erudite fathers, "angelical doctors," godly divines, learned laymen, the piously simple, and "devout women and children not a few," have disappeared from the earth with their spiritual vision filmed by an error so gross—that we must be under an equal delusion to imagine that such a result will be acquiesced in without an internal renitency of the most vigorous kind. It is a strong man armed who keeps the house that is invaded by the doctrines of the New Church. There is much more than the pride of opinion at stake. There are multitudinous *interests* involved, around which every form of partisan weaponry will rally and bristle to ward off the menacing peril. The breaking down of sects, the making bonfires of libraries, the acknowledgment of the heavenly mission of Swedenborg, are not among the pleasing objects of contemplation, and truth finds but a heartless welcome when its entrance turns so many occupants out of doors. But apart from this, I do not doubt that there are those who will be deterred from a ready assent to my previous conclusions, from a lingering but honest fear that they grow rather out of a certain vein of theosophic speculation than from the fair and unforced interpretation of the sacred text. Upon this head I am conscious of deep anxiety, for as the Divine Word is all in all with the man of the New Church, as it is with Swedenborg himself, we cannot give ear for a moment to any doctrinal proposition which will not stand the test of the Word legitimately expounded. In pursuance, therefore, of the intimation in my last, I resume the thread of my discussion at the point where it connects itself more especially with the Scriptural testimony.

That a veritable Trinity, under the threefold designation of Father, Son, and Holy Ghost, is to be recognized in the Divine nature, is a point, on which you and I can of course have no debate. The only question between us is, whether this Trinity is a Trinity of *persons* in any proper use of language. For myself, I have no idea of distinct persons which does not involve that of distinct consciousness, nor can I conceive that three distinct Divine consciousnesses should not constitute three distinct Divine Beings, however conjoined by unanimity of counsel; in other words, that they should not constitute three Gods. There is something, in fact, so palpable in this—it presses down with so much weight upon the general *consensus* of the human mind—that it is no wonder that the word *persons* has occasioned such trouble to theologians, that, like Prof. Stuart and others, they should have been anxious to get rid of it. But as this could not be decently effected, nothing has remained but to refine upon it, till it has become evacuated of its genuine import, while the ruling *idea* still underlies the doctrine, and works out its legitimate measure of mischief in the conceptions of Christendom. The consequence is, that while in controversy the Trinitarian will not allow himself to be bound to the vindication of the term, in practical operation, the tenet itself, still retains its efficiency and closes the mind against the access of all higher views. My object thus far has been to propound a higher view, and I see not why it should fail to command assent, provided it can be shown to be in accordance with the fairest construction of the oracles of truth. Let us then bring it to the test.

The doctrine is that the Father became incarnate in the person of the Son. But the Father is the Divine *esse* or Love inseparably united with the Divine *existere* or Truth. Now although all truth is a proceeding or evolution from love, yet the generating love is necessarily *in* the truth as its life and soul; consequently the Divine Love or the Father must have been *in* the Divine Truth or the Son, however it were that the Son was the object visibly manifested to the eyes of men. Accordingly Swedenborg says that although Jehovah, the Creator of the universe, descended as the Divine Truth and assumed the Human, in order to our redemption, yet that in so doing *he did not separate the Divine Good or Love.* "That God, although he descended as the Divine Truth, still did not separate the Divine Good, is evident from the conception, concerning which it is read, that 'The virtue of the Most High overshadowed Mary;' and by the virtue of the Most High is meant the Divine Good. The same is evident from the passages where he says that the Father is in Him, and He is in the Father; that all things of the Father are His; and that the Father and He are one; besides many others: by the *Father* is meant the Divine Good." Now I feel wholly at liberty to put the question, whether, if what I have previously affirmed of the constitution of the Divine nature be in itself true, it does not necessarily follow that this statement is also true, or, in other words, that the Father was essentially though invisibly present in the Son, as the *esse* is always present in the *existere?* And was he not thus most veritably *one* with Him as the true Jehovah incarnate?* Let this be a little farther explained by our author.

"There are two things which make the essence of God, the Divine Love and the Divine Wisdom; or, what is the same, the Divine Good and the Divine Truth. These two in the Word are meant also by Jehovah God; by Jehovah, the Divine Love, or the Divine Good, and by God, the Divine Wisdom or the Divine Truth; thence it is, that, in the Word, they are distinguished in various ways, and sometimes only Jehovah is named, and sometimes only God; for where it is treated of the Divine Good, there it is said Jehovah; and where of the Divine Truth, there God; and where of both, there Jehovah God. That Jehovah God descended as the Divine Truth, which is the Word, is evident in

---

* "All who belong to the Christian Church, and are under the influence of light from heaven, see and discern the Divine Nature in the Lord Jesus Christ; but such as are not under the influence of the light from heaven, see and discern in him only the Human Nature; when, nevertheless, the Divinity and the Humanity are so united in him as to make one person; for so he declares himself, 'Father, all mine are thine, and thine are mine.'"—*D. N. J.* 285.

John, where are these words: 'In the beginning was the Word, and the Word was with God, and the Word was God. All things were made by Him, and without Him was nothing made that was made. And the Word became flesh, and dwelt amongst us' (i. 1, 3, 14)."—*T. C. R.* 85.

We will now take a class of passages represented by the following,—"I *came forth* from the Father and *came* into the world." "I *proceeded forth* and *came* from God; neither came I of myself, but he *sent* me;" "The Father loveth you, because ye have believed that I *came out from God.*" How is this language to be fairly understood? It must surely have a meaning consistent with what we know to be the nature of God. If we fix our thoughts upon the simple material humanity of our Lord, he *came forth* from the womb of the virgin by a nativity similar to that of other men. Does this exhaust the meaning of the text? If understood solely in this sense, how did he proceed and come forth from the Father otherwise than do all other men? May we not all say in the words of Job, "Did not he that made me in the womb, make him? And did not one fashion us in the womb?" Is it not clear that something higher than mere natural nativity is here intended? What is it? "Who shall declare his generation?" Do you say that as he had no human father, it is an allusion to the miraculous conception? Even granting this, still the question is not answered. *What was it* that came forth from the Father? The body indeed was generated from the maternal substance, but the soul which animated the body was not from her, as the soul is evermore from the father. The soul, or inmost principle of our Lord, was from Jehovah himself, and therefore essentially divine. But as the divine essence is not divisible, it is impossible, I think, to conceive that Divinity could proceed *from* Divinity, except as Truth proceeds from Good, or the *existere* from the *esse.* Is any other kind of *proceeding* consistent with a just view of the intrinsic nature of Deity? Can we hesitate to assent to the truth of Swedenborg's remark, that "from the Divine Good, which is the Father, nothing can *proceed* or *come forth,* but what is Divine, and this which *proceeds* or *comes forth,* is the Divine Truth, which is the Son." As to any kind of idea of the *proceeding* by the Son, or *sending* by the Father, which implies a *local sojourn,* as when in this world an ambassador is sent abroad to a foreign court, you will at once unite with me in rejecting it altogether as wholly inconsistent with the nature of the subject. As God is a Spirit, and as whatever is predicated of Him must consist with spiritual attributes, so the *proceeding forth* of the Son from the Father must indicate something congruous to the properties of such a Being. I submit it then to your decision, what else can be gathered from this language than that our Lord, as the Divine Truth, *proceeded* from the Father as the Divine Good; consequently, as these principles cannot subsist apart from each other, that there is a consistent sense in which, as Swedenborg says, the Lord, by means of the assumed Human, *sent himself* into the world. If it was Jehovah who became incarnate, and if in Jehovah is the eternal Father, how can this inference be avoided? Nor in fact is the direct Scriptural testimony very remote from this.

Zech. ii. 10, 11, "Sing and rejoice, O daughter of Zion; for lo, *I come, and I will dwell in the midst of thee,* saith the Lord (Jehovah); and many nations shall be joined to the Lord (Jehovah) in that day, and shall be my people; and I *will dwell in the midst of thee,* and thou shalt know *that the Lord of Hosts hath sent me unto thee.*" Here it is clear that Jehovah, the Lord of Hosts, is both *sender* and *sent.* The same is evident from a previous portion of the same chapter, v. 8, 9, "For thus saith the Lord of hosts: After the glory hath he sent me unto the nations which spoiled you: for he that toucheth you, toucheth the apple of his eye. For behold, I will shake my hand upon them, and they shall be a spoil to their servants: and *ye shall know that the Lord of hosts hath sent me.*" The Lord of hosts is here evidently the speaker, and yet he is at the same time represented as being sent *by* the Lord of hosts.

Thus, too, when Jehovah says to Moses, "Behold, I send an angel before thee, to keep thee in the way, and to bring thee into the place which I have prepared. Beware of him, and obey his voice, provoke him not; for he will not pardon your transgressions: for my name is in him. But if thou shalt indeed obey his voice, and do all that I speak; then I will be an enemy unto thine enemies, and an adversary unto thine adversaries. For mine Angel shall go before thee, and bring thee unto the Amorites, and the Hittites, and the Perizzites, and the Canaanites, and the Hivites, and the Jebusites; and I will cut them off;" we are not to conceive of the angel as any divine person separate from Jehovah, but merely as a medium through which Jehovah's presence was manifested, as I have already had occasion to explain it. His sending an angel was, therefore, sending Himself, for that it was the supreme Jehovah, in His own person, who conducted the chosen people from Egypt, is again and again affirmed in the sacred record. Whatever, then, be the idea attached to the term *sending* in this connexion, it *must* be such as to consist entirely with the established unity and unipersonality of the Divine nature; and if this language may be properly employed in reference to the manifestation of Jehovah through an angelic medium, with the same propriety may it be employed in reference to his manifestation through the medium of the assumed Humanity. It must inevitably be a *sending of himself* in either case. So, on a smaller scale, when a man writes and publishes a book, he may be said to *send* his thoughts into the world; but he really sends himself, because his affection and thought, which are in his book, are in fact himself.

Again, the language of our Lord in Luke, xi. 13, is so peculiar, that without assuming it as an indubitable proof of the doctrine I am now advocating, I still feel at liberty to refer to it as worthy of special notice in the present connexion; "If ye then being evil know how to give good gifts to your children, how much more shall your Heavenly Father give the Holy Spirit to them that ask him?" The original exhibits the reading, πόσω μᾶλλον ὁ Πατὴρ ὁ ἐξ οὐρανοῦ, *how much more shall the Father that (is) from heaven give, &c.* This form of appellation in reference to the Father occurs nowhere else in the New Testament. There the usual phraseology is, ἐν οὐρανοῖς, *in heaven,* instead of ἐξ οὐρανοῦ, *from heaven.* Why is not the inference fair that this expression really conveys an allusion to the assumed Humanity in the person of the Saviour, who with the utmost propriety might be called the *Father* (the Divine Good) *from heaven,* and from whom also proceeds the Holy Spirit (or Divine Truth) here adverted to? The intimation need not be any less valid for being somewhat veiled. I am aware that the commentators are here also ready with their glosses and evasions by which to render pointless every form of speech that enforces the recognition of a new aspect of truth. They remark that ἐξ οὐρανοῦ, *from heaven,* is here equivalent, to οὐρανιός, *heavenly,* "as often elsewhere." But this "elsewhere" I have not been able to find; on the contrary, I am persuaded that not a single instance, apart from the present, can be adduced from Matthew to the Revelation, where the phrase ἐξ οὐρανοῦ, does not fairly imply some kind of *descent* or *proceeding* from heaven, as truly so as in Paul's expression—" The second man is the Lord *from heaven* (Κυριος ἐξ οὐρανοῦ)," which is undoubtedly tantamount to *Jehovah from heaven,* and this is in effect the same with the *Father from heaven* in the passage before us, for who is the *Father from heaven,* i. e. who descended from heaven, but Jehovah God incarnated and manifested in the person of the Son? And what other inference is forced upon us than that of the real and essential identity of the Father and the Son all the while underlying the apparent divarication and duality of the two? If it be intrinsically true that the Father descended in the person of the Son, why should it be deemed incredible that the fact is alluded to in the passage before us?

The dominant idea conveyed under the term *proceeding,* in its reference to our Lord, is so clearly set forth and illustrated in the following paragraph that I do not hesitate to insert it.

"That to *go forth* is to be of it, or its own, is evident from what goes before and from what follows, and also from the spiritual sense of that expression, for to *go forth* or *to proceed* in that sense, is to present oneself before another in a form accommodated to him, thus to present oneself the same only in another form; in this sense, *going forth* is said of the Lord in John; 'Jesus said of himself, I *proceeded forth* and *came* from God,' viii. 42. 'The Father loveth you, because ye have loved me, and have believed that I *came forth* from God: I came forth from the Father, and came into the world; again, I leave the world, and go to the Father. The disciples said, we believe that thou camest forth from God,' xvi. 27, 28, 30. 'They have known truly that I *came forth* from God,' xxvii. 8. For illustrating what is meant by *going forth* or *proceeding,* the following cases may serve. It is said of truth, that it goes forth or proceeds from good, when truth is the form of good, or when truth is good in a form which the understanding can apprehend. It may also be said of the understanding, that it goes forth or proceeds from the will, when the understanding is the will formed, or when it is the will in a form apperceivable to the internal sight. In like manner concerning the thought which is of the understanding, it may be said to go forth or proceed when it becomes speech, and concerning the will when it becomes action. Thought clothes itself in another form when it becomes speech, but still it is the thought which so goes forth or proceeds, for the words and sounds, which are put on, are nothing but adjuncts, which make the thought to be accommodately apperceived: in like manner the will becomes another form when it becomes action, but still it is the will which is presented in such a form; the gestures and motions, which are put on, are nothing but adjuncts, which make the will to appear and affect accommodately. It may also be said of the external man, that it goes forth or proceeds from the internal, yea substantially, because the external man is nothing else than the internal so formed, that it may act suitably in the world wherein it is. From these things it may be manifest, what going forth or proceeding is in the spiritual sense, namely, that when it is predicated of the Lord, it is the Divine formed as a man, thus accommodated to the perception of the believing; nevertheless each is one."—*A. C.* 5337

In like manner we infer, by parity of reasoning, that our Lord's going to the Father was in fact no local removing of himself from our globe to some distant part of the universe, called heaven, but a simple *recession,* or *returning,* into his own essential divinity, notwithstanding that it was *in appearance* an ascension in the clouds of heaven.

I could fain hope that the Scriptural testimony now adduced has not been *suborned* to the purpose of establishing a fallacious tenet of theology. As nothing can be clearer than the doctrine of the Divine Unity, and yet nothing in your view and mine more explicit than that of our Lord's divinity, I have attempted so to present the subject, as to make the Scriptures consistent with themselves.* This must be done upon some ground, or the argument yielded to the Unitarians. The mere establishment of a Trinity will go but little way towards it; for if the alleged Trinity be such as to subvert the Unity, it can never stand the ordeal to which, in this age, every doctrine of the Bible will be and ought to be subjected. That such is indeed the effect of the current doctrine of a *Trinity of persons* is, I think, beyond doubt. The mind left to the freedom of reason rejects it as a gross paralogism. The Scriptural Trinity must of necessity be such that the predicates of what are termed the *different persons* must be seen to be strictly applicable to *one person,* and to one only. The recognition of two or more persons discloses a state of mind in which the *appearances of truth* have gained an ascendancy over the *reality of truth,* no unusual result from making the simple *letter* of the Word the ultimate appeal, and building the strongest confirmations upon it. "In the sense of the letter," says Swedenborg, "it appears as if another who is superior is meant by Jehovah, but such is the sense of the letter, that it distinguishes what the internal sense unites. There are several (things or principles) in the Lord, and all are Jehovah ; thence it is that the sense of the letter distinguishes, whereas heaven never distinguishes, but acknowledges one God with a simple idea, nor any other than the Lord." Nothing therefore adverse to our view can be inferred from the use of terms so distinctive as the personal pronouns *I* and *Thou,* for as the indubitable doctrine of the Divine Unity absolutely precludes any such *real* distinction of person,

---

* On the ground of the common doctrine I believe it is impossible to assign any adequate reason why Joseph might not have been our Lord's father as well as Mary his mother. If he possessed a human soul from a human parent, why might not that soul have been propagated according to the ordinary law of generation ? That doctrine makes his Divinity to be derived solely from the *adjunction* of the Divine nature to the Human, and how could this result have been affected by his having a human father ?

The Incarnation.

so I trust it will appear from the following extract, that the solution set forth makes ample provision for the use of such language without at all weakening the ground of the main position.

"Inasmuch as all and single things in heaven, and all and single things with man, yea, in universal nature, have relation to good and truth, therefore also the Lord's Divine is distinguished into Divine Good and Divine Truth, and the Divine Good of the Lord is called Father, and the Divine Truth, Son; but the Lord's Divine is nothing else but good, yea, Good Itself, and the Divine Truth is the Lord's Divine Good so appearing in heaven, or before the angels. The case herein is like that of the sun; the sun itself in its essence is nothing else but fire, and the light which thence appears is not in the sun, but from the sun. This is the arcanum which lies hid in the circumstance, that the Lord so often speaks of His Father as if distinct, and as it were another from Himself, and yet in other places asserts that He is one with Himself. This being so, and it being so evident from the Word, it is surprising that they do not, in the Christian world, as in heaven, acknowledge and adore the Lord alone, and thus one God; for they know and teach, that the whole Trine is in the Lord. That the Holy Spirit who also is worshiped as a God distinct from the Son and the Father, is the holy of the Spirit, or the holy principle which by spirits or angels proceeds from the Lord, that is, from His Divine Good by Divine Truth, will be shown elsewhere by the Lord's Divine mercy."—*A. C.* 3704.

The last sentence of the above reminds me that in order to render the argument complete it is necessary to exhibit the evidence that the Holy Spirit is no more to be considered a Divine *person* than the Son, while yet the term as truly denotes an Essential of the Divine nature as either that of Father or Son. In this as in every other part of the discussion I shall avail myself of the light shed upon the subject by Swedenborg. And, first, I remark that the Holy Spirit is the Divine Truth *proceeding* from our Lord's Divine Human subsequent to his glorification, and that it is in effect the Lord himself. The general position is thus stated.

"That the Divine Truth is the Lord Himself, is evident from the consideration, that whatsoever proceeds from any one is himself, as, what proceeds from man, while he speaks or acts, is from his will-principle and intellectual; and the will-principle and intellectual constitutes the life of man, thus the man himself; for man is not a man from the form of the face and body, but from the understanding of truth, and the will of good. Hence it may be manifest that what proceeds from the Lord is the Lord."—*A. C.* 9407.

There is no principle of more importance than this, that what thus emanates from a being is, in fact, the being himself. We can see in this the ground on which an identity is asserted in the New Church between the Lord and the Word. Its application to the subject in hand will be seen from the paragraph that follows:—

"That the Comforter (*Paracletos*), or Holy Spirit, is Divine Truth proceeding from the Lord, manifestly appears, for it is said the Lord himself spake to them 'the truth,' and declared that, when he should go away, he would send the Comforter, 'the Spirit of Truth,' who should guide them 'into all truth,' and that he would not speak from himself, but from the Lord. And because Divine Truth proceeds from the human principle of the Lord glorified, and not immediately from his Divine itself, inasmuch as this was glorified in itself from eternity, it is therefore here said, 'The Holy Spirit was not yet, because that Jesus was not yet glorified.' It is greatly wondered at in heaven that they who compose the church do not know that the Holy Spirit, which is Divine Truth, proceeds from the human principle of the Lord, and not immediately from his Divine, when notwithstanding the doctrine received in the whole Christian world teaches that,—'As is the Father, so also is the Son, uncreate, infinite, eternal, omnipotent, God, Lord, neither of them is first or last, nor greatest or least. Christ is God and man: God from the nature of the Father, and man from the nature of the mother; but although he is God and man, yet nevertheless they are not two, but one Christ; he is one, not by changing the divinity into the humanity, but by the divinity receiving to itself the humanity. He is altogether one, not by a commixture of two natures, but one person alone, because as the body and soul are one man, so God and man is one Christ.' This is from the Creed of Athanasius. Now forasmuch as the divinity and humanity of the Lord are not two, but one person alone, and are united as the soul and body, it may be known that the Divine Proceeding, which is called the Holy Spirit, goes forth and proceeds from his Divine principle by the Human, thus from the Divine Human, for nothing whatsoever can proceed from the body, unless as from the soul by the body, inasmuch as all the life of the body is from its soul. And because, as is the Father so is the Son, uncreate, infinite, eternal, omnipotent, God and Lord, and neither of them is first or last, nor greatest or least, it follows that the Divine Proceeding, which is called the Holy Spirit, proceeds from the Divinity itself of the Lord by his Humanity, and not from another Divinity, which is called the Father, for the Lord teaches that he and the Father are one, and that the Father is in him, and he in the Father. But the reason why most in the Christian world think otherwise in their hearts, and hence believe otherwise, the angels have said is grounded in this circumstance, that they think of the Human principle of the Lord as separate from his Divine, which nevertheless is contrary to the doctrine which teaches that the Divinity and Humanity of the Lord are not two persons, but one person alone, and united as soul and body. Inasmuch as the Divine Proceeding, which is Divine Truth, flows into man, both immediately and mediately, by angels and spirits, it is therefore believed that the Holy Spirit is a third person, distinct from the two who are called Father and Son; but I can assert that no one in heaven knows any other Holy Divine Spirit, than the Divine Truth proceeding from the Lord."—*A. E.* 183.

At the risk of trespassing a little on your patience, I give another extract which has come before me since penning the foregoing.

"In the Doctrine of the New Jerusalem concerning the Lord, it has been shown that God is one in person and in essence, that there is a trinity in Him, and that that God is the Lord; also, that His trinity is called Father, Son, and Holy Spirit, and that the Divine from whom all things are, is called the Father, the Divine Human, the Son, and the Divine proceeding, the Holy Spirit. Although the latter is called the Divine proceeding, yet no one knows why it is called proceeding: this is unknown, because it is also unknown that the Lord appears before the angels as a sun, and that heat, which in its essence is divine love, and light, which in its essence is divine wisdom, proceeds from that sun. These truths being unknown, it was impossible to know that the Divine proceeding was not divine by itself, and thus the Athanasian doctrine of the trinity declares that there is one person of the Father, another of the Son, and another of the Holy Spirit: but when it is known that the Lord appears as a sun, a just idea may be had of the Divine proceeding, or the Holy Spirit, as being one with the Lord, yet proceeding from Him, as heat and light from the sun; which is the reason why the angels are in divine heat and divine light in the same proportion as they are in love and wisdom. No one who is ignorant that the Lord appears in the spiritual world as a sun, and that His Divine

Spirit proceeds from Him in this manner, could ever know what is meant by proceeding, whether it only means communicating those things which are of the Father and the Son, or illuminating and teaching. Still, even in this case, there is no ground for enlightened reason to acknowledge the Divine proceeding as separately divine, and to call it God, and make a distinction, when it is known that God is one, and that He is omnipresent."—*D. L. & W.* 146.

This will doubtless suffice on this head, as it is less necessary to dwell upon the identity of the Holy Spirit with Jehovah, inasmuch as there will be comparatively little difficulty in admitting it, when once the identity of the Son with the Father is conceded. That the prevailing idea, in the Church, of the Holy Spirit is that of a *person* in some way proceeding from the Father, or from both, is beyond question. This is conclusively met in one of Swedenborg's Memorable Relations where he was auditor to a discussion on this subject. One of the speakers says, "'What then is the Holy Ghost, mentioned in the writings of the evangelists and Paul, by whom so many learned men of the clergy, and particularly of our church, profess themselves to be guided? Who at this day in the Christian world denies the Holy Ghost and his operation?' Upon this, one who sat on the second row of seats, turned himself, and said, 'The Holy Spirit is the divinity proceeding from Jehovah the Lord; you insist that the Holy Spirit is a person by himself and a God by himself, but what is a person going forth and proceeding from a person except it be operation going forth and proceeding? One person cannot go forth and proceed from another through a third, but operation can. Or what is a God going forth and proceeding from a God, but divinity going forth and proceeding? One God cannot go forth and proceed from another, and by another, but divinity can go forth and proceed from one God. Is not the Divine Essence one and indivisible, and since the Divine Essence or the Divine Esse is God, is not God one and indivisible?' After hearing these things, they that sat on the seats came to this unanimous conclusion, that the Holy Ghost is not a person by itself, nor a God by itself, but that it is the holy divine going forth and proceeding from the one only omnipresent God who is the Lord. To this the angel who stood at the golden table, on which was the Word, said, 'It is well; we do not read in any part of the Old Testament that the prophets spake the Word from the Holy Spirit, but from Jehovah the Lord; and wherever the Holy Spirit is mentioned in the New Testament, it signifies the proceeding divinity, which is the divine, that illustrates, teaches, vivifies, reforms, and regenerates.'"—*A. R.* 962.

On the whole I see not but that I am entitled to propose the question, whether the view above presented of the *Divine Trinity in Unity*, is not one that fairly meets the demands of the most rigid exegesis of the Scriptures, and at the same time, of the most enlightened reason? Does it not adequately harmonize all the discordant theories which have been offered on the subject, and propose a common ground on which all can meet who receive the Old and New Testament as embodying the inspired counsels of heaven, and constituting the infallible rule of faith? While it dissolves in rational light the alledged *mystery* hanging over the *manner* in which the Trinity exists, it still leaves, without the attempt to penetrate it, the mystery of the Divine Essence, of which we can only say that it *is*, while it must for ever be incompetent to created beings to comprehend *what* it is. That the expose which I have attempted, rests in great measure upon the asserted illumination of Swedenborg, cannot vacate the intrinsic evidence of truth accruing to it from its obvious agreement with the genuine import of Scripture. You can never show that the claim which he prefers is a mere nullity. There is nothing in the laws of the human mind—nothing in the known order of the Divine Providential government of the world—which absolutely forbids the expectancy of such a mission as that with which he declares himself to have been invested. Nor can you say with any justice, that his advocates are following a mere *ignis fatuus* in embracing the doctrines he has announced. It is impossible for a fair mind to charge with absurdity a single extract that I have given, or to say that the credence yielded to their truth implies a mental weakness in their recipients. "These are not the words of him that hath a devil or is mad." Our calmest reason assents to his propositions from their self-evidencing power, nor have we the least fear that their soundness can be soundly impugned; and it is upon internal testimony equally strong, that we receive all parts of his amazing disclosures. In regard to no feature of the system do we find the evidence less luminous or convincing. That it often contravenes established dogmas—that it brings against them the most emphatic charges of fallacy and falsity—is with us no argument of error, but rather the reverse. We should believe him less if he respected them more. We perceive that in all cases his principles and premises necessitate his conclusions, and we find too that his *principles*, as they are unassailable, never are assailed by opponents, but always the conclusions. In the present case the fundamental principle laid down is that of a necessary and eternal distinction between the *Esse* and *Existere* of the Divine nature. Is not this true? What is the import of the sublime declaration, "I AM THAT I AM?" Is not this a synonim of JEHOVAH, and does it not imply the absolute and underived *Esseity* of the Most High? What can be more pertinent to this point than the striking elucidations of Prof. Lewis in his chapter on the "Philosophy of the verb *To Be?*" where he contends that εἰμί, *I am*, "expresses *essential, eternal, necessary, self-existent, independent, uncaused essence or being;*" and where too he says that it denotes "a general and most important proposition, namely, that the idea of *goodness* is not merely relative or accidental, or the result of the mind's generalization from outward facts, but an absolute and eternal verity; that it has an absolute existence in the Divine Mind, and that there is a fixed foundation for the absolute, and not merely relative, nature of moral distinctions."—(*Plat. Theol.*, p. 171, 173). This is by no means remote from Swedenborg's incessant inculcation, that the Divine *esse* is the Divine Good, of which the Divine Truth is the *existere* in form. And what is the distinction in effect between the two, but that between εἰμί, *to be*, and γίνομαι, *to become*, which Prof.

The Incarnation.

Lewis has so clearly developed, and to which he justly attaches so much importance?

But having already transcended the proper limits of a single letter I forbear to enlarge upon the various aspects of the subject which invite discussion. Several points of interest to which I have hitherto barely alluded, will come before us hereafter for fuller consideration, especially the grounds on which the idea of *disjunction* between the Father and the Son has established itself in the minds of most Christians. For the present, I conclude by presenting from Swedenborg, a kind of *resumé* of the whole subject.

"That by the Father, when he is mentioned by the Lord, is understood the Dvine Good which is in the Lord and from the Lord, is, because the Lord called the Divine principle which was in him from conception, his Father, and which was the *esse* of his life, to which Divine principle He united His Human, when he was in the world. That the Lord called this principle his Father, appears manifest from this circumstance, that he thought that he himself was one with the Father; as in John: 'I and my Father are one.' Again: 'Believe that the Father is in me, and I am in Him.' Again: 'He that seeth me seeth him that sent me.' Again: 'If ye had known me, ye should have known my Father also; and from henceforth ye knew him, and have seen him. Philip saith unto him, Lord, show us the Father. Jesus saith unto him, Have I been so long time with you, and yet hast thou not known me, Philip? he that hath seen me hath seen the Father; and how sayest thou then, show us the Father? Believest thou not that I am in the Father, and the Father in me? The Father that dwelleth in me he doeth the works. Believe me, that I am in the Father, and the Father in me.' Again: 'If ye had known me ye should have known my Father also.' Again: 'I am not alone, because the Father is with me.' Inasmuch as the Lord is one with the Father, therefore he also declares, that all things of the Father are his, and his are the Father's: that all things that the Father hath are his; that the Father hath given all things into the hand of the Son; and that all things are delivered to him by the Father; that no one knoweth the Son but the Father, nor any the Father except the Son; also, that no one hath seen the Father except the Son, who is in the bosom of the Father, that the Word was with God, that the Word was God, and that the Word was made flesh. From this latter passage it is also manifest that they are one, for it is said that 'the Word was with God, and the Word was God.' It is plain, too, that the Human principle of the Lord was God, for it is said, 'and the Word was made flesh.' Inasmuch then as all things of the Father are also the Lord's, and inasmuch as he and the Father are one, therefore the Lord, when he ascended into heaven, said to his disciples, 'All power is given to me, in heaven and in earth;' by which he taught his disciples that they should approach him alone, because he alone can do all things, as he also said to them before, 'Without me ye can do nothing.' Hence it appears how these words are to be understood: 'I am the way, the truth, and the life; no man cometh unto the Father but by me;' namely, that the Father is approached when the Lord is approached. Amongst many other reasons why the Lord so often named the Father as another, was this, that by Father, in the internal or spiritual sense, is understood the Divine Good, and by Son, the Divine Truth, each in the Lord and from the Lord; for the Word is written by correspondences, and is thus adapted both for men and angels. The Father, therefore, is mentioned, that the Divine Good of the Lord may be perceived by the angels, who are principled in the spiritual sense of the Word; and the Son of God and the Son of Man are mentioned, that the Divine Truth in like manner may be perceived.

"To what has been said above, it is here to be added, as an appendix, that if it be assumed as doctrine, and acknowledged, that the Lord is one with the

Father, and that his Human principle is Divine from the Divinity in himself, light will be seen in every particular of the Word; for what is assumed as doctrine, and acknowledged from doctrine, appears in light when the Word is read. The Lord also, from whom all light proceeds, and who has all power, enlightens those who are in this acknowledgment. But, on the other hand, if it be assumed and acknowledged as doctrine, that the Divine principle of the Father is another principle separate from that of the Lord, nothing will be seen in light in the Word; inasmuch as the man who is in that doctrine turns himself from one Divine being to another, and from the Divinity of the Lord, which he may see, which is effected by thought and faith, to a Divinity which he cannot see, for the Lord says: 'Ye have never heard his (the Father's) voice at any time, nor seen his form;' and to believe in and love a Divine being, which cannot be thought of under any form, is impossible."—*A. E.* 200.

Yours, &c.

LETTER IX.

THE GLORIFICATION.

DEAR SIR,

THE course of the present discussion up to this point has been mainly devoted to the attempt to unfold the true constitution of our Lord's person, both before and after the advent, and to develop the grounds on which the New Church holds to a Trinity in the Divine nature, while at the same time most strenuously rejecting the Tripersonality which that doctrine has been supposed to involve. I have endeavored to show that a Divine Humanity pertains essentially to Jehovah, and that in the Incarnation this Divine Humanity "passed from first principles to last." On no other grounds do we hold such an incarnation to be possible, and contend, consequently, that the prevalent doctrine of Christendom, by ignoring the fact of such a Divine Humanity, does in effect deny the fundamental verity of the incarnation, and substitute for it the fallacy of the simple *adjunction* of the Divine to the Human nature. This is the inevitable issue of ascribing to our Lord a human soul as well as a human body derived from the virgin mother. Let it be understood, on the other hand, that the inmost element of our Lord's being was, by conception, from the Father, and therefore as the Divine essence is indivisible, was the Father Himself, and we have a clear and consistent enunciation of the doctrine of Christ's Divinity, without the least invasion of the great truth of the absolute Unity of the Godhead. We behold God and man united in Him in one person, and the key afforded us, on this view, for a rational explication of the various and sometimes apparently conflicting texts of Scripture bearing upon the subject.

With such a presentation of the grand theme before us, it is at least sufficiently curious to contemplate in juxtaposition with it the following extract from Professor Norton's "Statement of Reasons," in which he unequivocally denies the possibility of the truth of such a doctrine as Swedenborg has proposed.

"With the doctrine of the Trinity, is connected that of the HYPOSTATIC UNION, as it is called, or *the doctrine of the union of the divine and human natures in Christ, in such a manner that these two natures constitute but one person.* But this doctrine may be almost said to have pre-eminence in incredibility above that of the Trinity itself. The latter can be no object of belief when regarded in connexion with that of the Divine Unity; for these two doctrines directly contradict each other. But the former, without reference to any other doctrine, does in itself involve propositions as clearly self-contradictory, as any which it is in the power of language to express. It teaches that Christ is both God and man. The proposition is very plain and intelligible. The words *God* and *man*, are among those which are in most common use, and the meaning of which is best defined and understood. There cannot (as with regard to the terms employed in stating the doctrine of the Trinity) be any controversy about the sense in which they are used in this proposition, or, in other words, about the ideas which they are intended to express. And we perceive that these ideas are wholly incompatible with each other. Our idea of God is of an infinite being; our idea of man is of a finite being; and we perceive that the same being cannot be both infinite and finite. There is nothing clear in language, no proposition of any sort can be affirmed to be true, if we cannot affirm this to be true,—that it is impossible that the same being should be finite and infinite; or, in other words, that it is impossible that the same being should be man and God. If the doctrine were not familiar to us, we should revolt from it, as shocking every feeling of reverence toward God;—and it would appear to us, at the same time, as mere an absurdity as can be presented to the understanding. No words can be more destitute of meaning, *so far as they are intended to convey a proposition which the mind is capable of admitting*, than such language as we sometimes find used, in which Christ is declared to be at once the Creator of the universe, and a man of sorrows; God omniscient and omnipotent, and a feeble man of imperfect knowledge.

"The doctrine of the Trinity, then, and that of the union of two natures in Christ, are doctrines, which, when fairly understood, it is impossible, from the nature of the human mind, should be believed. They involve manifest contradictions, and no man can believe what he perceives to be a contradiction. In what has been already said, I have not been bringing arguments to disprove these doctrines; I have merely been showing that they are intrinsically incapable of any proof whatever; for a contradiction cannot be proved;—that they are of such a character, that it is impossible to bring arguments in their support, and unnecessary to adduce arguments against them."—*Norton's Statement of Reasons*, p. 17-19, 22.

You will see from this that it is not possible to array two distinct exhibitions of Christian doctrine in more direct antagonism with each other than is done by the citation of this passage in connexion with the scope of my previous reasonings. To what extent the author will be admitted as an accredited expounder of Unitarian sentiments, I know not; but yourself and my other readers must judge on which side the truth lies, if the inspired oracles are to be the standard of faith; and also where there is any intermediate ground on which the Lord's essential Divinity can be safely made to rest. For myself, I see none. If the doctrine of Swedenborg on that head is not the true doctrine, I despair of finding it either in the Bible or out of it, and I should despair too of successfully refuting the above argument on the basis of the common Trinitarian theory. If you feel competent to the task, I hope you will undertake it. For myself, my only resource is to array against it the tenor of the foregoing course of argument.

According to the plan proposed, having treated at some length the *mode* of the incarnation, I am now brought to the consideration of the *ends* to be accomplished by it. This would, perhaps, most naturally enforce upon me the direct and formal discussion of the doctrine of the Atonement, which is commonly regarded as embodying or concentrating within itself the ends of the Divine Benevolence in ordaining the assumption of human nature on the part of the Son of God. That doctrine I shall submit to examination as I proceed, but my purpose is to anticipate what would perhaps appear to be the regular course of the argument, and to devote the present letter to the subject of our Lord's Glorification. I do this because in the views of the New Church, the process of glorification stands in most intimate connexion with the incarnation, as it commenced with the assumption of the natural humanity and reached its acme simultaneously with the laying it aside. As the design, in fact, of his becoming incarnate was that he might be glorified, and by being glorified might become the Saviour of men, this fact prescribes the more orderly mode of discussion, and the subject thus treated will virtually cover the ground of the Atonement, as it will evince that nothing of a *vicarious* character is involved in the economy of redemption. By showing what the Atonement *is*, we show at the same time what it *is not*, and if there be any basis of truth to what I shall now advance, it will at least be made clear that the essence of our Lord's atonement was *not* concentrated in his death on the cross, or in what is termed the *sacrifice* there offered up to Divine justice. But of this you will be able to judge better hereafter.

That the Lord was appointed to pass through a process termed *glorification* is abundantly evident from the following among other passages:—"After Judas had gone out, Jesus said, Now is the Son of man *glorified* and God is *glorified* in Him. If God be *glorified* in Him, God shall also *glorify* Him in Himself, and shall straightway *glorify* Him." "Father, the hour is come, *glorify* thy Son that thy Son also may *glorify* Thee." "Now is my soul troubled; and He said, Father *glorify* thy name ; and there came a voice from heaven, saying, I have both *glorified* it and will *glorify* it again." "Ought not Christ to have suffered these things, and to enter into his *glory ?*" The question occurs, what is to be understood by this language? What is the precise idea to be attached to the word *glorify* in these connexions? It can hardly, I think, be doubted that the common conception awakened by the term is that of exaltation, dignity, majesty, dominion. The *glory* of an earthly sovereign consists in the power, wealth, splendor, and pre-eminence with which he is invested, and this idea we naturally transfer to Christ after his resurrection from the dead, when we regard him as seated at the right hand of the Father, and surrounded with all the insignia of celestial royalty. The dominant impression, therefore, produced by the term is that of a certain Divine *splendor* which the mind connects with the prerogatives that He enjoys in his risen and ruling state.

But it is evident that all such conceptions amount to nothing except so far as they agree with the intrinsic and elemental nature of the Divine Being. The *glory* predicated of him must be very different from any kind of *outward display* of dignity or majesty. It must have direct reference to the Love and Wisdom which are the all in all of his essence and perfection. Imagine for a moment the application of the term to a human being. So long as he abides in the flesh, in the present world, it will inevitably refer itself to some kind of imposing *external manifestation*, to something in his *circumstances*, his *achievements*, or his *possessions*—but still to the external and bodily man. But suppose the man to be divested of the material body; contemplate him as a pure spirit in the spiritual world, and if aught of *glory* be predicated of him it must pertain to his spirit solely; it must be some property, phase, or attribute of his love or intellect or both; in a word, it must be something which is appropriate to the interior and essential nature of a being composed of the fundamental principles of will and understanding. So also in reference to the Lord Himself. He is essentially Love and Wisdom, and his *glory* must be the glory of these principles in some form or other of their manifestation; for we are continually remanded, in the theology of Swedenborg, to the very *first principles* of all things. Consequently he says again and again that God *is* heaven, because when heaven is analysed it resolves itself into the very being of God. So he says also that a spirit *is* his own love, because his love is his essence. It is on this ground, moreover, that he informs us that every thing in the Word has an ultimate reference to the Lord. The natural, the spiritual, the celestial senses are, as it were, unrolled, as so many swathings, and then the Divine appears. Hence, Abraham, Isaac, and Jacob interiorly represent the Lord, each in some one of the aspects in which he is to be viewed. And who can doubt this when it is said of the people of Israel as representing the church, "My servant David shall rule over them." Is not the Lord ultimately indicated under the title David? And was not Abraham, for instance, as fit a representative of the Lord as David?

You will perceive from this that the idea conveyed by the term *glorification* as applied to our Lord, is far different from that of a mere *splendid* or *glorious state* resulting from the exercise of kingly dominion or from the bare *display* of the most exalted prerogatives whether in the midst of angels or men. It is a term applicable to an internal or subjective condition which in the case of our Lord, viewed in his Humanity, brought him into the capacity of saving the human race. On the common theory of Redemption the glorification of Christ was a mere resulting effect, in the Divine economy, from the previous state of humiliation and suffering to which he condescended to stoop, and could not be said even to have commenced so long as that state continued. Indeed it is for the most part spoken of as a *reward* for the voluntary endurance of the pains and afflictions which he underwent on our behalf, and our ideas of it are governed by the letter of such texts as the following:—" Who for the joy that was set before him endured the cross, despising the shame, and is now set down on the right hand of God." But on the higher and truer view, as I conceive it to be, of the New Church, the glorification commenced from the outset of the earthly humanity of Jesus and ran parallel with it to the termination of his career in the flesh, when it reached its culminating and consummating point in the complete deposition of everything that bore the taint of the maternal infirmity. So far from being a mere result and sequence of the atoning work of the Saviour it was the very essence of the atonement itself, apart from which the term loses entirely its genuine force. Instead of indicating a state into which a transition was first made upon his emergence from the depth of his humiliation into the height of his exaltation, it denotes an interior process which was going on through the whole course of his earthly pilgrimage, and which resulted in the complete unition of the Human with the Divine, somewhat as the process of regeneration in a man results in " his body of vileness being fashioned like unto the glorious body of Christ.* That there is a difficulty in bringing this sublime doctrine down to the comprehension of the natural man we are forced to admit, because it involves the recognition of the process of regeneration which can never be adequately grasped except by one who has in some degree experienced it.† Still the fact that a doctrine of revelation may require, in order to its full apprehension, the higher intelligence of the spiritual mind, cannot fairly be urged as an argument of its falsity, so long as the apostolic declaration holds good, that "the natural man receiveth not the things of God; for they are foolishness unto him; neither can he know them, because they are spiritually discerned." Nevertheless, I have assumed the task of endeavoring to enunciate the truth on this head, and those that are spiritual, who "judge all things," will find in themselves a criterion of judgment as to the claims of the doctrine.‡

---

* " The regeneration of man is an image of the Lord's glorification; that is, in regeneration as in a kind of image it appears how the Lord glorified his human, or what is the same, made it divine; for as the Lord altogether changed his human state into divine, so also the Lord with man when he regenerates man, altogether changes his state, for he makes his old man new."—*A. C.* 3296.

† " That the Lord as to the human was made new, that is, glorified, or what is the same, was made divine, no one can ever conceive, thus neither believe, who is in worldly and corporeal loves; he is altogether ignorant what the spiritual and celestial is, nor indeed is he willing to know; but he who is not in worldly and corporeal loves, is capable of perceiving this, for he believes that the Lord is one with the Father, and that from him proceeds all that is holy; consequently that he is divine even as to the human, and whoever believes in his manner (or measure) perceives."—*A. C.* 3212

‡ " Inasmuch as it now follows concerning the separation of the former human, which the Lord had from the mother, and at length concerning its full rejection, it is to be known that the Lord successively and continually, even to the last of his life, when he was glorified, separated from himself, and put off that which was merely human, viz., what he derived from the mother, till at length he was no longer her son, but the son of God, as well with respect to nativity as to conception, and thus one with the Father, and himself Jehovah. Moreover, as to what concerns the separation and putting off of the maternal human, they do not comprehend this, who have merely corporeal ideas concerning the

The Glorification. 91

If I have at all succeeded in my object hitherto I have made it somewhat obvious not only that Jesus Christ is the true and only Jehovah, but also that a Divine Humanity, in "first principles" is to be predicated of his very nature. In his incarnation this Divine Humanity passed into "last principles," and He became God in Human flesh. The human nature, however, received from the mother was a *fallen* nature, as she could impart no other.* It was consequently *liable* to temptation, to suffering, and to sin, though "he knew no sin," nor was "iniquity found in his lips." But it was in the economy of redemption that this fallen, infirm, and peccable humanity, hereditarily received from the mother, should be gradually put off, and a perfectly Divine humanity, received from the Father, gradually put on. "He put off the human," says Swedenborg, "taken from the mother, which in itself was like the human of another man, and thus natural, and put on a Human from the Father, which was in itself like his Divine, and thus substantial, from which the Human also was made Divine." The process by which this was effected was our Lord's *glorification*. This is thus explained.

"The Lord, by the most grievous temptation-combats, reduced all things in himself into divine order, insomuch that there remained nothing at all of the human which he had derived from the mother; so that he was not made new as another man, but altogether divine; for man, who is made new by regeneration, still retains in himself an inclination to evil, yea evil itself, but is withheld from evil by an influx of the life of the Lord's love, and this by exceedingly strong power; whereas the Lord entirely cast out every evil which was hereditary to him from the mother, and made himself divine, even as to the vessels, that is, as to truths; this is what in the Word is called glorification."—*A. C.* 3318

But in order to a clearer discovery of this great truth, it is important to advert to certain principles in the constitution of our nature which rendered such a process necessary. Among the remarkable developments made by Swedenborg is that of a clear distinction between the *external* and the *internal* man. This is not a distinction simply between the body and the spirit. It is rather a distinction between the *animal* or *sensitive*, and the *spiritual* and *heavenly* nature, though pertaining to each. Still it is one which recognizes the animal or *psychical* affections and appetencies as bearing a very close relation to the body, and as manifesting their power

---

Lord's human, and think concerning it as concerning the human of another man, whereby they are offended at it; such persons are not aware that as the life is, such is the man, and that the Lord had by conception, a Divine Esse of life, or Jehovah, and that a like esse of life had existed in his human by union."—*A. C.* 2649.

* "The Lord's divine good natural, is what was Divine to Him from nativity, for He was conceived from Jehovah; hence He had a Divine esse from nativity, which was to Him for a soul, and consequently the inmost of his life. This was exteriorly clothed by those things which He assumed from the mother, and because this from the mother was not good, but in itself evil, therefore He expelled it of his own proper power, chiefly by temptation-combats, and afterwards conjoined this human, which he made new in Himself, with the divine good which He had from nativity."—*A. C.* 4641.

and predominance chiefly through it. The following extracts develop the distinction more in detail:—

" What the internal man is, and what the external, is known to few, if any, in the present day. It is generally supposed that they are one and the same; and the reason of this supposition is, because the generality of persons believe that they do what is good, and think what is true of themselves, or from proprium, this being a necessary consequence of submission to its influence. . . . The internal man is as distinct from the external as heaven from earth. Both the learned and the unlearned, when reflecting on the subject, entertain no other conception respecting the internal man but as consisting of thought, because it is within; and believe that the external man is the body, with its sensual and voluptuous principle, because they are without. Thought, however, which is thus ascribed to the internal man, does not, in fact, belong thereto; for in the internal man there are nothing but goods and truths derived from the Lord, conscience being implanted in the interior man by the Lord. Thus the wicked, yea, the very worst of men, and even those who are destitute of conscience, have a principle of thought; hence it is evident that the faculty of thought does not belong to the internal, but to the external man. That the material body, with its sensual and voluptuous principle, does not constitute the external man, is manifest from this consideration, that spirits, who have no material bodies, have an external man as well as men on earth. . . . . The internal man is formed of what is celestial and spiritual; and the external man of sensual things, not belonging to the body, but derived from bodily things; and this is the case not only with man, but also with spirits."—*A. C.* 978

" They who have only a general idea concerning the internal and external man, believe that it is the internal man which thinks and which wills, and the external which speaks and acts, since to think and to will is somewhat internal, and thence to speak and to act is external. But it is to be noticed that not only the internal man thinks and wills, but also the external."—*A. C.* 9702, 9703

" It is scarcely known at this day what the external man is; for it is supposed that the things appertaining to the body alone constitute the external man, as his sensuals, namely, the touch, the taste, the smell, the hearing, and the sight; as also the appetites and pleasures. But these only constitute the outermost man, which is merely corporeal. The external man properly is constituted by scientifics appertaining to the memory, and affections appertaining to the love with which man is imbued; also by the sensuals which are proper to spirits, with the pleasures which likewise appertain to spirits. That these properly constitute the external or exterior man, may appear from men in another life, or from spirits who, in like manner have an external man, and an interior, and consequently an internal man. This body is only as an integument or shell, which is dissolved, in order that man may truly live, and that all things appertaining to him may become more excellent."—*A. C.* 1713.

If this be sound we are shut up to the conclusion that the external man is by no means identical with the bodily fabric. It stands, indeed, in close relation to the body and is the seat of sensation, and as there is always some degree of thought where there is sensation, so the power of thought belongs to the external man. Hence it follows that the Lord received not merely a body from the virgin mother, but also an external or *psychical* man, and for this reason we cannot say, without qualification, that He had no human soul; for in strict propriety of speech the word *soul* ($\psi\nu\chi\eta$, *psyche*) denotes this very element of our nature which we have above described as constituting the external man. Such an element our Lord did undoubtedly derive from his maternal origin, and in virtue of this it could be said that he grew in wisdom and knowledge. But this psychical or natural principle was neither in him, nor is it in us, the inmost *esse* of being, although it is true that in the prevailing usages of speech the term *soul* is applied to denote such an inmost principle of life and being. In the case of our Lord his internal essence was Jehovah or the essential Divine itself, and when we say that he had no human soul we always *mean* this, although aware that it is not a rigidly exact mode of speech, according to which he *had* a human soul, that is to say, an external man, as above described.

These two principles, the external and the internal, are opposed to each other, the internal man inclining to heaven and heavenly things, and the external to earth and earthly things, and the end of regeneration is to bring them into harmony. The external is thus to be made not only a fit instrument, but a living image, of the internal, and to incline, like it, to heavenly things, and only to earthly in subordination to heavenly. Now in order that our Lord might be truly a man it was necessary that he should be possessed of both these principles, and in order that he might be a Saviour, competently endowed, that they should both be brought to act in unison. But in His case that which answers to *our* internal man was Jehovah, or the Essential Divinity itself, whereas his external, being derived from a human parent, was subject to human infirmity, and therefore before He could enter into perfect oneness with the Father his external man was to be formed anew, so as to become the exact image of his internal; in other words, his Human was to become Divine. In this process consisted his glorification, and this process was gradual. It is thus more fully explained by one of the ablest expounders of Swedenborg.

" The Lord Jesus Christ, while in the world, *so far* as he had anything appertaining to him from the mother, or *so far* as He was the Son of Mary, was not strictly One with the Father: but in proportion as what He received from her was *put off*, and a Divine Human Nature, received or brought forth from the Father, *put* on in its place, He advanced towards perfect union, till at length, all the life of the maternal nature being extinguished at the passion of the cross, and the Divine life from the Father being brought down into the lowest natural principle in lieu of it at the resurrection, He thenceforward, and for ever, was, and is, One with the Father,—One God in One Divine person; his Divine Soul being the very Father or what is called God in his inmost essence, and his Divine Body being the Son of God, or a clothing of the Divine Essence, brought forth solely from that Essence itself, to be the medium of its manifestation to mankind."—*Noble's Lectures*, p. 118, 119.

* * * * *

" Even the natural body, it is to be remembered, was conceived of Jehovah, and was, as to its inmost principles, divine from conception, having for its inmost soul the whole Divine Essence. The Divine Essence, while the Lord Jesus Christ was living as a man in the world, was in the continual effort to assimilate the assumed Humanity to itself. In the interior forms of that human nature a glorifying process was going on, from the first to the last moment of his life. The Divine Principle within kept descending lower and lower, imparting its own divine nature to the interior forms of the human essence in succession; extirpating everything that partook of infirmity,—everything, in fact, that was derived from the mother; but yet retaining every human principle entire, though rendered infinitely perfect and truly divine. When all that belongs to man beyond or above the mere shell of clay had been submitted to this wonderful process, the crucifixion took place: and then, the merely human life being altogether extinct, the divine life descending to the extremes of the bodily frame, renewing the whole by its descent. This fully accomplished, He arose again with his human form complete, nothing being lost or left behind,—a truly Divine Man, having in his Glorious Person every thing, and every principle, which is found in the constitution of man, but all perfectly assimilated in nature to the pure Divinity Itself. In this Divine Humanity, therefore, He is truly the Alpha and the Omega, the First and the Last, —the very immediate *Esse* or Source of being to everything that exists, the immediate Upholder and Supporter of all things, both in heaven and earth. Thus the child once born, the son once given, is of a truth the Mighty God, the Everlasting Father upon whose shoulders, of right, the government rests, and to whom belong glory and dominion for ever."—*Ibid.* 140, 141.

I could fain hope that the main position has been so stated as to be exempt from the charge of disparaging in any degree the pure and perfect character of the Saviour, but in order to guard still further against any misapprehension, I insert the following paragraph, unfolding the sense in which alone evil is predicable of his nature.

"It may be a matter of surprise to many, to hear it said that hereditary evil from the mother was with the Lord; but . . . it cannot be doubted that it was so. It is altogether impossible for any man to be born of a human parent, but he must thence derive evil. But there is a difference between hereditary evil which is derived from the father, and that which is derived from the mother. Hereditary evil from the father is more interior, and remains to eternity, for it can never be eradicated: the Lord had no such evil, since he was born of Jehovah as his Father, and thus, as to internals, was Divine, or Jehovah. But hereditary evil from the mother appertains to the external man: this was attached to the Lord. Thus the Lord was born as another man, and had infirmities as another man. That he derived hereditary evil from the mother, appears evidently from the circumstance of his enduring temptations; for it is impossible that any one should be tempted who has no evil, evil being that in man which tempts, and by which he is tempted. That the Lord was tempted, and that he endured temptations a thousand times more grievous than any man can possibly sustain, and that he endured them alone, and by his own proper power overcame evil, or the devil and all hell, is also manifest. It is not possible for any angel to be tempted by the devil, because, being in the Lord, the evil spirits cannot approach him even distantly, as they would be instantly seized with horror and fright; much less could hell approach to the Lord, if he had been born Divine, that is, without an adherence of evil from the mother. That the Lord also bore the iniquities and evils of mankind, is a form of speaking common with preachers; but for him to take upon himself iniquities and evils, except in an hereditary way, was impossible. The Divine Nature is not susceptible of evil: wherefore, that he might overcome evil by his own proper strength, which no man ever could, or can do, and might thus alone become righteousness, he was willing to be born as another man. There otherwise would have been no need that he should be born; for he might have assumed the Human Essence without nativity, as he had formerly done occasionally, when he appeared to those of the Most Ancient Church, and likewise to the prophets. But in order that he might also put on evil, to fight against and conquer it, and might thus at the same time join together in himself the Divine Essence and the Human Essence, he came into the world. The Lord, however, had no actual evil, or

The Glorification. 95

evil that was his own; as he himself declares in John: 'Which of you convicteth me of sin?' viii. 46."—*A. C.* 1573..

Our Lord's external man, then, was to be brought into a state of complete and harmonious union with the internal, which is otherwise expressed by saying that his Human was to be, as it were, merged in his Divine, and when this was fully effected he was fully glorified, of which the passion of the cross was the last and consummating step. The rationale of the process is thus strikingly unfolded in the Arcana.

"It is known that the Lord was born as another man, and that when an infant He learnt to speak as another infant, and that He next grew in science, also in intelligence and wisdom; hence it is evident, that his human was not Divine from nativity, but that He made it Divine by his own proper ability. That it was done by his own proper ability was because He was conceived by Jehovah, and hence the inmost of his life was Jehovah Himself; for the inmost of the life of every man, which is called soul, is from the father, but what that inmost puts on, which is called body, is from the mother. That the inmost of life, which is from the father, is continually flowing in and operating upon the external, which is from the mother, and endeavoring to make this like to itself, even in the womb, may be manifest from sons, in that they are born to the natural inclination of the father, and in some cases grandsons and great-grandsons to the natural inclinations of the grandfather and great-grandfather: the ground and reason of this is, because the soul, which is from the father, continually wills to make the external, which is from the mother, like to itself. Since this is the case with man, it may be manifest that it was especially the case with the Lord. His inmost was the Divine Itself, because Jehovah Himself, for He was his only-begotten Son; and inasmuch as the inmost was the Divine Itself, could not this, more than in the case of any man, make the external, which was from the mother, an image of itself, that is, like to itself, thus make the human, which was external, and from the mother, Divine? and this by his own proper ability, because the Divine, which was inmost, from which He operated into the human, was his, as the soul of man, which is the inmost, is his. And whereas the Lord advanced according to divine order, He made his human when He was in the world, to be divine truth; but afterwards, when He was fully glorified, He made it to be divine good, thus one with Jehovah."—*A. C.* 6716.

The drift of these remarks affords us a clew to the solution of the apparent paradox of our Lord's praying to the Father as to another person, when in fact, as I have endeavored to show, He was one with the Father, as the Divine Truth is ever really one with the Divine Good. It is doubtless this circumstance more than any other which has tended to beget and confirm that idea of *disjunction* and *duality*, in relation to the Father and the Son, which has become so deeply inwrought in the mind of Christendom, and which is at the same time so utterly at war with all consistent views of the Divine Unity. The general impression on this score derived from the literal import of the Scriptures, in a multitude of passages, is in fact so strong as to have produced a virtual denial of one only God manifested in the person of Jesus of Nazareth, and the virtual assertion of three Gods in three persons. I do not say that this belief is formally avowed, but I say that the prevalent doctrine constructively amounts to this, and that every attempted explanation which would render the alleged Trinity consistent with the admitted Uni'y avoids a logical contradiction only by running on the fog-banks of mystery— a mystery inscrutable, unapproachable, defiant alike of angelic and human inquisition. To the view of the New Church all mystery *on this score* is completely banished. We see an entire consistency between these apparently repugnant aspects of our Lord's character. The solution given in the ensuing paragraphs of the seeming inconsistency is to us perfectly satisfactory.

" So long as the Lord was in a state of temptation, he spake with Jehovah as with another; but so far as his Human Essence was united to his Divine, he spake with Jehovah as with himself. This is evident from many passages in the evangelists, and also from many in the prophets, and in David. The reason is plain from what has been said above concerning the hereditary from the mother; in proportion as anything of this remained, he was as it were absent from Jehovah, but in proportion as this was extirpated, he was present and was Jehovah himself."—*A. C.* 1745

" So far as the Lord was in the human not yet made Divine, so far He was in humiliation; but so far as He was in the human made Divine, so far He could not be in humiliation, for so far He was God and Jehovah. That He was in humiliation when in the human not yet made Divine, was because the human which He derived from the mother was hereditary evil, and this could not approximate to the Divine without humiliation: for man in genuine humiliation divests himself of all ability to think and do anything from himself, and leaves himself altogether to the Divine, and thus accedes to the Divine. The Divine was indeed in the Lord, because he was conceived of Jehovah, but this appeared remote, so far as his human was in the maternal hereditary; for in spiritual and celestial things, dissimilitude of state is what causes removal and absence, and similitude of state is what causes approach and presence; and it is love which makes similitude and dissimilitude. From these things now it may be manifest, whence was the state of humiliation with the Lord when he was in the world; but afterwards when he put off the human which he derived from the mother, insomuch that he was no longer her son, and put on the Divine, then the state of humiliation ceased, for then he was one with Jehovah."—*A. C.* 6866.

"Whereas the Lord had from the beginning a humanity from the mother, and successively put off the same; therefore, during his abode in the world, he passed through two states, one a state of humiliation, or emptying himself, and the other a state of glorification, or union with the divinity which is called the Father: the state of humiliation was at the time and in the degree that he was in the humanity from the mother; and the state of glorification, at the time and in the degree that he was in the humanity from the Father. In the state of humiliation he prayed unto the Father, as to one different from himself; but in the state of glorification he spake with the Father as with himself: in this latter state he said, that the Father was in him, and he in the Father, and that the Father and he were one; but in the state of humiliation, he underwent temptations, and suffered the cross, and prayed unto the Father not to forsake him: for the divinity could not be tempted, much less could it suffer the cross. Hence then it appears, that by temptations, and continual victories therein, and by the passion of the cross, which was the last of those temptations, he entirely conquered the hells, and fully glorified the humanity, as was shown above. That the Lord put off the humanity from the mother, and put on the humanity from the divinity himself, which is called the Father, appears also from this consideration, that so often as the Lord spake by his own mouth unto the mother, he did not call her mother, but woman."—*Doct. of the Lord*, 35.

The Glorification. 97

Is there anything in this calculated to stumble one who appreciates what may be termed the twofold personality of the old and new man in the regenerating Christian? Is anything more palpable than the conflict which is continually going on in the bosom of such an individual, and which is so graphically described by Paul in the record of his own experience? "For that which I do I allow not: for what I would, that do I not; but what I hate, that do I. If then I do that which I would not, I consent unto the law that it is good. Now then it is no more I that do it, but sin that dwelleth in me. For I know that in me (that is, in my flesh,) dwelleth no good thing: for to will is present with me; but how to perform that which is good I find not. For the good that I would I do not: but the evil which I would not, that I do. Now if I do that I would not, it is no more I that do it, but sin that dwelleth in me. I find then a law, that, when I would do good, evil is present with me. For I delight in the law of God after the inward man: but I see another law in my members, warring against the law of my mind, and bringing me into captivity to the law of sin which is in my members. O wretched man that I am! who shall deliver me from the body of this death? I thank God through Jesus Christ our Lord. So then with the mind I myself serve the law of God; but with the flesh the law of sin."—*Rom.* vii. 15-25.

Here is the "law of the mind" and the "law of the flesh" in direct antagonism with each other, each striving for the mastery, and each alternately claiming to be the real *ipseity* or self-hood of the man. Now is it not evident that so long as this contest continues, the man is internally divided in himself, and that just in proportion as the opposition is strong the external man is remote from the internal, and as it grows weaker, that they come into conjunction? The end of regeneration is that they may both be brought *at one*, and this, in respect to our Lord, was the very essence of *atonement* (*at-one-ment*), as will perhaps be made more obvious in the sequel. But at present I would exhibit, in a still clearer manner, the analogy between regeneration and glorification, which I do in the words of our author.

"The state of the Lord's glorification may in some manner be conceived from the state of the regeneration of man, for the regeneration of man is an image of the Lord's glorification; when man is regenerated, he then becomes altogether another, and is made new, therefore also when he is regenerated, he is called born again, and created anew; then, although he has a similar face, and a similar speech, yet his mind is not similar; his mind, when he is regenerated is open towards heaven, and there dwells therein love to the Lord, and charity towards his neighbor with faith ; it is the mind which makes another and a new man; change of state cannot be perceived in the body of man, but in his spirit, the body being only the covering of his spirit, and when it is put off, then his spirit appears, and this in altogether another form when he is regenerated, for it has then the form of love and charity in beauty inexpressible instead of its pristine form, which was that of hatred and cruelty with a deformity also inexpressible; hence it may appear what a regenerate person is, or one that is born again, or created anew, viz., that he is altogether another and a new man. From this image it may in some measure be conceived what the glorification of the Lord is ; he was not regenerated as a man, but was made divine, and this from the veriest divine love, for he was made divine love itself;

7

what his form then was, was made apparent to Peter, James, and John, when it was given them to see him, not with the eyes of the body, but with the eyes of the spirit, viz., that his countenance shone like the sun, Matt. xxvii. 2; and that this was his divine human, appears from the voice which then came out of the cloud, saying, 'This is my beloved son,' verse 5."—*A. C.* 3212.

In all this it is carefully to be noted, that, although Swedenborg occasionally applies the term "regenerated" to the Lord, he would yet be understood to mean that the process, unlike what takes place with man, is not effected by any influence or agency foreign to Himself, but it is due solely to his "own proper ability"—it is all in Himself and from Himself. It is thus but another term for "glorified." This is very clearly announced in the following passage. "That the Lord might make the human divine, by an ordinary way, he came into the world, that is, was willing to be born as another man, and to be instructed as another, and as another to be re-born, but with the difference, that man is re-born of the Lord, but that the Lord not only regenerated himself, but also glorified himself, that is, made himself divine; further, that man is made new by an influx of charity and faith, but the Lord by love divine, which was in him, and which was his; hence it may be seen, that the regeneration of man is an image of the glorification of the Lord; or, what is the same, that in the process of the regeneration of man, as in an image, may be seen, although remotely, the process of the Lord's glorification."—*A. C.* 3138.

I have thus endeavored to exhibit somewhat of a correct view of the doctrine of our Lord's glorification as taught in the illuminated theology of the New Church. It is the doctrine of the gradual deposition of the natural Humanity received from the mother, and of the gradual assumption of a Divine Humanity received from the Father. That our Lord, viewed as to his essential nature, had a Divine Human from eternity, is undoubtedly true, but in coming into the world he *superinduced*, says Swedenborg, a natural Humanity upon the Divine, and this natural Humanity he successively glorified by victories over temptation, which continually tended to *bring down* the Divine influx into its forms, and thus eventually fill them with its own plenitude.*—But upon this and several other phases of the subject I shall dwell at greater length in another letter.

Yours, &c.

---

* "He who is in the combats of temptation, and conquers, acquires to himself more and more power over evil spirits, till at length they dare not assault him; but in every victory obtained, the Lord reduces to order the goods and truths from which the combat was supported; when, consequently, these are purified; and, in proportion as they are purified, the celestial things of love are insinuated into the exterior man, and a correspondence is effected. Whosoever supposes that the external man can be reduced to correspondence without the combats of temptations, is deceived."—*A. C.* 1717. If *harmony* be here substituted instead of *correspondence*, the idea will be perhaps more obvious to the common reader.

LETTER X.

THE GLORIFICATION.

DEAR SIR,

I MAY perhaps presume that the tenor of my two last letters has conveyed to you somewhat of a correct general idea of the doctrine of the Lord's Glorification as held by the New Church. You will have seen that it is something altogether different from that state of post-resurrection glory and grandeur which is usually understood by the term. It is the designation of an internal process which was continually going on in the Lord's human nature, as the result of that series of temptation-combats by which alone the hereditary evils of the maternal principle could be expelled, and a Divine humanity be substituted in its stead.* It is in this view of the subject that we see the ground of the analogy between the glorification of our Lord and the regeneration of his people, to which I have already adverted. Swedenborg has in fact given to the world what may be termed a *philosophy of temptation* which constitutes one of the most remarkable features of his system, and, as it lies at the very foundation of the doctrine of regenerate and glorified life, I shall dwell at some length upon it as essential to a right apprehension of the grand scope of my argument. And first, as to the *fact* of a continued series of temptations endured by the Lord throughout the whole period of his earthly sojourn.

"That the life of the Lord, from his earliest childhood even to the last hour of his life in the world, was a continual temptation and continual victory, appears from several passages in the Word of the Old Testament; and that it did not cease with the temptation in the wilderness, is evident from these words in Luke: 'After that the devil had finished all the temptation, he departed from him for a season,' iv. 13; also from this, that he was tempted even to the death of the cross, thus to the last hour of his life in the world. Hence it appears that the Lord's whole life in the world, from his earliest childhood, was a continual temptation and continual victory; the last was, when he prayed on the cross for his enemies; thus for all on the face of the whole earth. In the Word of the life of the Lord with the Evangelists no mention is made, except the last, of any other than his temptation in the wilderness; others were not disclosed to the disciples; those which were disclosed, appear, according to the literal sense, so light, as scarcely to be anything; for so to speak and so to answer is not any temptation: when yet, it was more grievous than any human mind can conceive or believe. No one

---

* "With respect to the Lord's essential life, it was a continual progression from the human to the Divine, even to absolute union; for that he might fight with the hells and overcome them, it was needful that he should fight from the human, inasmuch as there can be no combat with the hells from the Divine; therefore he was pleased to put on the human as another man, to be an infant as another, and to grow up into sciences and knowledges. That the Lord's progression from the human to the Divine was such can be doubted by no one, who only considers that he was an infant, and learned to speak as an infant, and so forth; but there was this difference, that the essential Divine was in him, as being conceived of Jehovah."—*A. C.* 2523.

can know what temptation is unless he has been in it. The temptation which is related in Matt. iv. 1–11 ; Mark i. 12, 13 ; Luke iv. 1–13, contains in a summary the Lord's temptations, namely, that, out of love towards the whole human race, he fought against the loves of self and of the world, with which the hells were replete. All temptation is made against the love in which man is, and the degree of the temptation is according to the degree of the love. If it is not against the love, there is no temptation. To destroy any one's love, is to destroy his very life ; for love is life. The life of the Lord was love towards the whole human race, which was so great, and of such a nature, as to be nothing but pure love. Against this his life were admitted continual temptations, as already stated, from his earliest childhood to his last hour in the world. During all this time the Lord was assaulted by all the hells, which were continually overcome, subjugated, and conquered by him; and this solely out of love towards the human race. And because this love was not human but divine, and all temptation is great in proportion as the love is great ; it may be seen how grievous were his combats, and how great the ferocity with which the hells assailed him. That these things were so I know of a certainty."—*A. C.* 1690.

"That the Lord, more than all in the universe, underwent and sustained most grievous temptations, is not so fully known from the Word, where it is only mentioned that he was in the wilderness forty days, and was tempted of the devil. The temptations themselves which he then had, are not described except in a few words ; nevertheless these few involve all; as what is mentioned in Mark, chap. i. 12, 13, that he was with the beasts, by which are signified the worst of the infernal crew ; and what is elsewhere related, that he was lead by the devil upon a pinnacle of the temple, and upon a high mountain, which are nothing else but representatives of the most grievous temptations which he suffered in the wilderness."—*A. C.* 1663.

The end to be attained by this indispensable process of temptation-combats, accompanied always by victory, was the gradual reduction of the external man to conformity or correspondence with the internal, and the final union of the Human Essence with the Divine in the Lord, which is but another name for his glorification.* The general principle is thus stated by our author.

"Temptations have for their end the subjugation of what is external in man, that they may thereby be rendered obedient to what is internal; as may appear to any one who reflects, that so soon as man's loves are assaulted and broken, as during misfortunes, sickness, and grief of mind, his lusts begin to subside, and he at the same time begins to talk piously ; but as soon as he returns to his former state, the external man gets the dominion, and he scarcely thinks at all on such subjects. The like happens at the hour of death, when corporeal things begin to be extinguished ; and hence every one may

---

* " Temptation is the means of the conjunction of the internal man with the external, inasmuch as they are at disagreement with each other, but are reduced to agreement and correspondence by temptations."—*A. C.* 3928.
" The external things that are discordant, which were spoken of above, are the only things that hinder the external man, when it acts upon the external, from making it one with itself. The external man is nothing else but an instrumental or organical something, having no life in itself, but receiving life from the internal man, and then it appears as if the external man had life from itself. With the Lord, however, after he had expelled hereditary evil, and thus had purified the organicals of the Human Essence, these also received life ; so that the Lord, as he was life with respect to the internal man, became life also with respect to the external man. This is what is signified by glorification."—*A. C.* 1603.

see what the internal man is, and what the external; and the mode in which lusts and pleasures, which are of the external man, hinder the Lord's operation by the internal."—*A. C.* 857.

In the following extract the same view is expanded from a deeper ground and a strong light shed upon the rationale of the whole subject. The theology of the schools sounds no such depths as those that are reached by Swedenborg's plummet. The intimation of organic and recipient *vessels* in the soul of man into which the influx of life from the Lord is received, may, at first blush, outrage your psychology, but I have no hesitation to adduce it, as it is a very natural sequence from the admission which even you yourself would probably make, that the *soul is a substance,* and a substance, too, receptive of life from a Divine source, which it must be unless it have life in itself independent of the uncreated and self-subsisting life that pertains to the Lord alone. But if the soul be a substance adapted to the reception of influent life, we see no reason to doubt what Swedenborg has affirmed, that this substance is *organized* for that purpose, as we find throughout the whole domain of vegetable and animal existence that *organized forms* are the fixed receptacles of vital influx. And if this holds in the lower departments of the universe, why not in the higher? What is the difficulty of conceiving that there may be spiritual substances duly organized as well as material? Assuming then as a postulate, what every intelligent receiver of Swedenborg is prepared argumentatively to maintain, that the human mind is as truly distinguished by recipient vessels as the body is by a cellular tissue, I transfer the paragraph in question.

"Good cannot be conjoined with truth in the natural man without combats, or, what is the same, without temptations; that it may be known how the case is, in respect to man, it may be briefly told; man is nothing else but an organ, or vessel which receives life from the Lord, for man does not live from himself; the life, which flows in with man from the Lord, is from His divine love; this love, or the life thence, flows in and applies itself to the vessels, which are in man's rational, and which are in his natural; these vessels with man are in a contrary situation in respect to the influent life in consequence of the hereditary evil into which man is born, and of the actual evil which he procures to himself; but as far as the influent life can dispose the vessels to receive it, so far it does dispose them. . . . . Good itself, which has life from the Lord, or which is life, is what flows in and disposes; when therefore these vessels, which are variable as to forms, are in a contrary position and direction in respect to the life, as was said, it may be evident that they must be reduced to a position according to the life, or in compliance with the life; this can in nowise be effected, so long as man is in that state into which he is born, and into which he has reduced himself, for the vessels are not obedient, being obstinately repugnant, and opposing with all their might the heavenly order, according to which the life acts; for the good which moves them, and with which they comply, is of the love of self and the world, which good, from the crass heat which is in it, causes them to be of such quality; wherefore, before they can be rendered compliant, and be made fit to receive anything of the life of the Lord's love, they must be softened; this softening is effected by no other means than by temptations; for temptations remove those things which pertain to self-love, and to contempt of others in comparison with self, consequently things which pertain to self-glory, and also to hatred and revenge thence arising; when therefore the vessels are somewhat tempered and subdued by temptations, then they begin to become yielding to, and compliant with the life of the Lord's love, which continually flows in with man; hence then it is, that good begins to be conjoined to truths, first in the rational man, and afterwards in the natural. . . . . . Hence is the reason why man is regenerated, that is, is made new, by temptations, or, what is the same, by spiritual combats, and that he is afterwards gifted with another temper or disposition, being made mild, humble, simple, and contrite in heart: from these considerations it may now appear what use temptations promote, viz., this, that good from the Lord may not only flow in, but may also dispose the vessels to obedience, and thus conjoin itself with them. . . . . . But as to what respects the Lord, he, by the most grievous temptation-combats, reduced all things in himself into divine order, insomuch that there remained nothing at all of the human which he had derived from the mother, so that he was not made new as another man, but altogether divine; for man, who is made new by regeneration, still retains in himself an inclination to evil, yea is evil itself, but is withheld from evil by an influx of the life of the Lord's love, and this by exceedingly strong power; whereas the Lord entirely cast out every evil which was hereditary to him from the mother, and made himself divine even as to the vessels, that is, as to truths; that is what in the Word is called glorification."—*A. C.* 3318.

The bearing of this upon the case of the Lord will not be of difficult apprehension. Receiving, as he did, a humanity from the mother tainted from the necessity of its nature with hereditary evil, this element of evil was to be gradually put away, and a Divine humanity assumed, in consequence of which, he, in fact, ceased from that time to be the son of Mary, his infirm human being entirely lost and swallowed up in the Divine. The former state was that of the Lord's humiliation, but the latter that of his glorification. "In the former state, viz., that of humiliation, when he had yet with himself an infirm human, he adored Jehovah as one distinct from himself, and indeed as a servant, for the human is respectively nothing else."—*A. C.* 2159.

That the prevailing theology of Christendom involves no such view of a progressive glorification in the Lord is beyond debate. That theology maintains that, whatever may have been the change in circumstances and state, still the *nature* of Jesus Christ was the same before and after the event termed his glorification. Accordingly, all those passages in which the letter represents the Lord as distinct from the Father, and in which he prays to Him in the hour of his agony, appear to the mass of Christians as equally applicable to the Lord sojourning on earth and to the Lord reigning in heaven. They do not recognize the fact of his having undergone an inward change of nature still more marked than anything that occurred in the vicissitudes of his outward lot. Thus, the dogma of Catholicism has established that Mary is still the mother of our Lord, and the result has been a glorification of her little short of that ascribed to her Son. Protestantism, though rejecting the Mariolatry of the Romanist, is still equally explicit in recognizing the complete separation between Jehovah and Jesus. The Son offers himself a sacrifice to propitiate the Father; as, otherwise they must hold that God died to propitiate himself, which is of course absurd. It holds, moreover, that the Son, in virtue of his atoning sacrifice, perpetually intercedes in behalf of his elect. He is, therefore, practically regarded as distinct from the Being with or before whom he intercedes. How exceedingly diverse from all this is the view presented by Swedenborg may be seen from his statement of the true Scriptural doctrine of Intercession.*

"The Lord's intercession for the human race was during his abode in the world, and indeed during his state of humiliation, for in that state he spake with Jehovah as with another; but in the state of glorification, when the human essence became united to the Divine, and was also made Jehovah, he does not then intercede, but shows mercy, and from his Divine (principle) administers help and saves; it is mercy itself which is intercession, for such is its essence."—*A. C.* 2250.

This view of intercession we hold to result necessarily from the doctrine of the Divine unity. As there is but one God, and Jesus Christ is himself that God, we find it as impossible to conceive of his interceding *with* himself as of his making an atonement *to* himself; and we can admit no requisition upon our faith to acknowledge any doctrine as divine which clearly conflicts with the fundamental tenet of the supreme Deity and absolute Unipersonality of Jehovah-Jesus.

Still objections suggest themselves. If the inmost soul of Jesus was Jehovah, then the Lord in praying to the Father prayed to his own soul. Unquestionably he did, on the principle before alluded to, and which is clearly developed in the two following paragraphs, which I give at length from the very great importance of the subject-matter as throwing light upon one of the profoundest arcana of revelation, to wit, the manner in which the duality of the letter is to be reconciled with the unity of the sense, in what is related of our Lord's intercourse with the Father.

"The internal of the Lord, that is, whatever the Lord received from the Father, was Jehovah in him, because he was conceived of Jehovah. There is a difference between what man receives from his father, and what he receives from his mother. Man receives from his father all that is internal, that is, his very soul or life; but he receives from his mother all that is external: in a word, the interior man, or the spirit, is from the father, but the exterior man, or the body, is from the mother. This every one may comprehend merely from this; that the soul itself is implanted from the father, which begins to clothe itself with a bodily form in the ovary, and whatsoever is afterwards added, whether in the ovary or in the womb, is of the mother, for it receives no addition from elsewhere. Hence it may appear, that the Lord, as to his internals, was Jehovah; but as the external, which he received from the mother, was to be united to the Divine or Jehovah, and this by temptations and victories, as was said, it must needs appear to him in those states, when he spake with Jehovah, as if he was speaking with another, when, nevertheless, he was speaking with himself; so far, that is, as conjunction was effected."—*A. C.* 1815.

"That the Lord adored and prayed to Jehovah his Father, is known from the Word in the Evangelists, and this as if to a Being different from himself,

---

* See the subject of our Lord's Intercession treated with consummate ability by Mr. Noble, in his "Lectures on the Important Doctrines of the True Christian Religion."— *Lectures* XVII and XVIII.

although Jehovah was in him. But the state in which the Lord then was, was his state of humiliation, the quality of which was described in the First Part, namely, that he was then in the infirm human derived from the mother. But so far as he put off that human, and put on the Divine, he was in a different state, which is called his state of glorification. In the former state he adored Jehovah as a Person different from himself, although he was in himself; for, as stated above, his internal was Jehovah: but in the latter, namely, the state of glorification, he spake with Jehovah as with himself, for he was Jehovah himself. But how these things are cannot be conceived, unless it be known what the internal is, and how the internal acts upon the external: and, further, how the internal and external are distinct from each other, and yet joined together. This, however, may be illustrated by its like, namely, by the internal in man, and its influx into, and operation upon, his external. The internal of man is that by which man is man, and by which he is distinguished from brute animals. By this internal he lives after death, and to eternity; and by this he is capable of being elevated by the Lord amongst angels: it is the very first form by virtue of which he becomes, and is, a man. By this internal the Lord is united to man. The heaven nearest to the Lord consists of these human internals; this, however, is above the inmost angelic heaven; wherefore these internals are of the Lord himself. Those internals of men have not life in themselves, but are forms recipient of the life of the Lord. In proportion, then, as man is in evil, whether actual or hereditary, he is as it were separated from this internal, which is of the Lord and with the Lord, consequently, is separated from the Lord: for although this internal be adjoined to man, and inseparable from him, still, as far as man recedes from the Lord, so far he, as it were, separates himself from it. This separation, however, is not an evulsion from it, for man would then be no longer capable of living after death; but it is a dissent and disagreement of those faculties of man which are beneath it, that is, of the rational and external man. In proportion to this dissent and disagreement, there is a disjunction; but in proportion as there is no dissent and disagreement, man is conjoined by the internal to the Lord; and this is affected in proportion as he is in love and charity, for love and charity conjoin. Thus it is in respect to man. But the internal of the Lord was Jehovah Himself, inasmuch as he was conceived of Jehovah, who cannot be divided and become another's, as the internal of a son who is conceived of a human father; for the divine is not capable of division, like the human, but is one and the same, and is permanent. With this internal the Lord united the Human Essence; and because the internal of the Lord was Jehovah, it was not a form recipient of life, as the internal of man is, but was life itself. His Human Essence also, by union, was in like manner made life; wherefore the Lord so often says that he is life; as in John: 'As the Father hath life in himself, so hath he given to the Son to have life in himself,' chap. v. 26; besides other passages in the same Evangelist, as chap. i. 4; v. 21; vi. 33, 35, 48; xi. 25. In proportion, therefore, as the Lord was in the human which he received hereditarily from the mother, he appeared distinct from Jehovah, and adored Jehovah as one different from himself; but in proportion as he put off this human, the Lord was not distinct from Jehovah, but one with him. The former state, as remarked above, was the Lord's state of humiliation, but the latter was his state of glorification."—*A. C.* 1999.

The same mystery, then, if we may so term it, is to be recognized in its degree in every man who becomes a subject of regeneration. This work is carried on by a process of temptation, or, in other words, of conflict between the flesh and the spirit, equivalent to the external and internal man. Just in proportion to the disagreement between these two principles, the man feels himself possessed, as it were, of a double personality, the one yielding, the other resisting.

In this state of inward self-divulsion it is not difficult to conceive of one department of the man's being addressing the other, as we find in the case of David;—" Why art thou cast down, O my soul, and why art thou disquieted within me? Hope thou in God, for I shall yet praise Him." The case of Paul, as exhibited in the epistle to the Romans (Ch. vii.) I have already cited as strikingly illustrative of the grand position. This conscious antagonism of the two natures becomes less and less as the victories are multiplied over temptation, for the effect of this is evermore to bring the soul into harmony and unity with itself, and this is in truth an image in miniature of the sublime conjunction of the Human and the Divine, which constituted the glorification of the Lord. As this, however, was a result accomplished by degrees, as it was the issue of a process extending through the whole term of the Lord's terrestrial life, and was brought to a consummation by the passion of the cross, which was the last stage of his temptations—at once his sorest trial and his crowning triumph—so the conclusion presses upon us, that the regeneration of man, which is conformed to this exemplar, is not an instantaneous act but a gradual process.

That the plenary glorification of the Lord was accomplished by the death on the cross, he himself teaches in John xiii. 31, 32; "Therefore when he was gone out Jesus said, Now is the Son of man glorified, and God is glorified in him. If God be glorified in him (ἐν αὐτῷ), God shall also glorify him in himself, (ἐν ἑαυτῷ), and shall straightway glorify him." Here the glorification is predicated both of God the Father and of God the Son, since God is glorified *in him*, and if so, he will glorify him *in himself*, clearly evincing that the glorification was an act of union and identification between the Father and the Son, in consequence of which the Son was henceforth to be so merged in the Father that they could no longer be viewed as in a state of even apparent separation. This was effected at the crisis of the crucifixion when the mysterious process reached its acme; "Father, the hour is come; glorify thy Son that thy Son also may glorify thee." The son of Mary is nailed to the cross and suffers the agony of dissolution, and in the article of death the union of the Divine and Human becomes completed: the man Christ Jesus is fully identified with the one only God, Jehovah, and hence is he now known in the New Church by the distinguishing and appropriate title of THE LORD. At this eventful moment the bonds of his terrestial relationships were severed, the Lord rejected whatever he held in common with the *fallen* race of men, and Mary ceased to be his mother; "*Woman*, behold thy son," and to the disciple whom he loved, "Behold thy mother." These words, in conjunction with what follows, denote the completed work of glorification: "After this, Jesus, knowing that all things were now accomplished, that the scripture might be fulfilled, saith, I thirst—and when he had received the vinegar he said, IT IS FINISHED: and he bowed his head and gave up the ghost."*

---

* "When the Lord said, '*It is finished*,' all was accomplished that can properly be called Glorification, as answering to man's regeneration, for the Resurrection, properly speaking, was no part of the Glorification (any more than man's resurrection is a part of his regeneration), but only a result from it, or manifestation of it, as previously accomplished."—(*Mason's Answer to Eight Questions, p.* 54.)

The Lord, however, was not to be holden of the bonds of the grave; he therefore arose and appeared to his disciples in such a measure of his glory as they were able to bear, while his body in outward semblance bore the aspect of the body of the son of Mary which hung upon the cross and rested in the tomb of Joseph. "Behold," said he to his disciples, "behold my hands and my feet, that it is I myself: handle me and see; for a spirit hath not flesh and bones as ye see me have." As if for confirmation, Thomas was allowed to put his fingers into the prints of the nails, and subsequently the Lord sat down with his disciples to a meal of broiled fish and honeycomb.

These are the passages on which the christian church relies, in teaching that our Lord was entirely the same before his death and after his resurrection. But it is obvious that the body with which he rose was divested of material properties, as it enabled him to enter a room with closed doors and to appear and disappear at pleasure to the view of his disciples. He was, therefore, at this time in a glorified body because in a glorified state; but *in what precise manner* this body was divested of sensible material properties, and emancipated from its liability to the laws of the natural world, is doubtless beyond the ken of mortal apprehension. I am as much at liberty to call upon you for explanation on this score as you upon me. We must both admit that an immense change took place in the properties of the body, and yet that the *personal likeness*, as witnessed by the disciples, remained unchanged. *We*, however, are taught—what you would be also if you could receive it—that the post-resurrection appearances of the Lord were not perceived by the natural but by the spiritual senses of the spectators, just as we suppose that the body of the transfiguration, which shone as the sun, was seen by interior and not by exterior vision.

The mystery of our Lord's glorification is dimly shadowed out in the process which takes place in ourselves. The soul during its sojourn in the body makes use of it as a vestment and an instrument. Every day and every hour it is laying aside the old and assuming new substances. The life on earth is an incessant death and an incessant resurrection. The body of the child is not, as to substance, identically one with that of the adult man, nor that of the adult man with that of the old man. How then can we maintain that precisely the same material body will arise, when the same flesh is not, for a single day, subject to the same soul? By this analogy we may comprehend the sublime process of our Lord's glorification, as far as it is given to the finite of man to grasp the infinite of God.*

---

* The following extract from the Lectures of Rev. B. F. Barrett presents a pertinent but still inadequate view of the subject, by means of a striking illustration. As our argumentative scope is substantially the same, it serves both our purposes equally well.

"Our conception of this divine operation may perhaps be somewhat aided if we reflect upon how the case is in that natural phenomenon which is called petrifaction—a process by which wood or any other organic substance is changed to stone. As often as a particle of the organized substance which undergoes this operation is removed, a particle of mineral or silicious matter comes in and takes its place. And thus, when the process is completed, the substance of the wood has all been removed, and replaced by

The Lord, however, successively laid aside the substances received from the virgin mother, not to borrow and substitute for them new *material* substances, but to put on in their stead the spiritual substances of his Divine Humanity, such as it appeared, by anticipation, to Peter, James, and John, on the hallowed mount of transfiguration. The completion of this process was the consummated union or unition of the Human with the Divine Essence, in virtue of which the Lord is now able to put forth a redeeming and saving power towards our lost race which would otherwise have been for ever impossible consistently with those laws of order from which the Most High cannot depart without denying his own nature. But upon this point I propose to dwell more at length in another letter.

Yours, &c.

LETTER XI.

THE ATONEMENT.

DEAR SIR,

Pursuant to previous intimations, I propose to devote the present letter to the subject of the Atonement. Its intimate connection with the general theme thus far treated is obvious at a glance. It is the exigency in which Atonement is supposed to originate that brings so prominently into view, and renders so indispensable, the threefold distinction of persons which is held to constitute the true doctrine of the Trinity. The essential element in the prevailing theory of the Atonement is that of vicarious sacrifice or substituted suffering, and this doctrine of satisfaction obviously rests upon the assumed tenet of the tripersonality of Jehovah, inasmuch as it is held to be offered by one of these persons to the other and the essential divinity of the offerer is what gives its redeeming efficacy to the offering. On the basis of the prevailing scheme of Atonement, the Trinity of persons in the Godhead is an equally indispensable element with the Divinity itself. The law which had been violated by sin was so infinitely pure and so sternly inexorable, and the ability of the sinner to fulfil its demands had become so completely prostrated and extinct, that nothing short of the intervention of the second person of the triune Godhead could avail to propitiate the clemency of the Fa-

---

mineral matter; yet so gradual has this process been, that the form and organic structure of the wood has been completely preserved. And so perfectly is this the case, that it appears as if the wood had been *changed* to stone. Something similar to this is also taking place continually in our bodies. Particles are constantly passing off, and their place is supplied by new ones; yet the form and organic structure of our bodies is still preserved. —(*Barrett's Lectures, p.* 307).

In the eighth of Noble's Lectures the reader will find the subject here alluded to treated with distinguished ability.

ther, vindicate his injured justice, and open the way for the bestowment of pardon, peace, and eternal life upon the guilty. In the execution of this merciful purpose he came fully into our place as a fulfiller of the violated law, and by his perfect obedience and unparalleled sufferings wrought out and brought in an everlasting righteousness, the merit of which is made over by imputation to the believer who receives the Divine testimony, and with a strong confidence appropriates to himself the proffered grace. As the grand virtue of the Redeemer's work is concentrated in his passion on the cross, or in the blood shed on that occasion, so it is an act of faith put forth in a special manner upon the efficacy of this blood that constitutes the genuine ground of the believer's justification in the sight of God. In this way he receives the full benefit of a gratuitous salvation, while the law, that brooks no infraction, is magnified and made honorable in the eyes of its Author and of the whole universe.

There are various other items comprised in this peculiar scheme of theology, to which I have not adverted, although they enter essentially into the integrity of the system considered as a whole; such, for instance as the doctrine of election, of perseverance, and of instantaneous regeneration, to which we may add the dogma respecting the *Divine Anger*. It is all along assumed as a postulate that indignation and wrath, in the most genuine sense of the terms, pertain to the Most High, and that without the placating or propitiating of the Divine wrath, the exercise of his saving love towards sinful men is effectually estopped and can only find vent for itself in the channel opened by the shedding of the blood of Christ upon the cross. The effect of this sacrifice of the Son of God, it is contended, is to quench the burning flames of the Father's anger, and to remove that moral disability under which he was laid by the law of his perfections on the score of the bestowment of pardon and eternal life upon fallen creatures. This atoning blood, however, has been shed, its efficacy acknowledged by Him to whom it was offered, and now its priceless benefits are to be appropriated by an act of faith in virtue of which the believer may repose peacefully in the confidence of salvation. There is indeed no real righteousness or merit in such a faith, yet it is *imputed* to him for righteousness, and on the ground of it he may safely count upon being able to stand with acceptance before the Lord in the day of final audit.

It would, doubtless, be doing injustice to the system under consideration, to say, that it makes no account of a good life, or that it does not, in some sense, provide for it and insist upon it. Bad as human nature is, and liable to be warped into the grossest falsities of persuasion, there is still a deep-seated and ineradicable conviction abiding in its bosom, that the essence of religion is in the *life*—that a man who lives well is a religious man, and that a man who lives ill is an irreligious man. This is confirmed by the express declaration of holy writ, that the sum and substance of all religion—the conclusion of the whole matter—is to fear God and keep his commandments. It is hardly possible for any form of creed or confession to plant itself in the belief of Christendom, in which *life* does not enter as an avowed element, and as holding a prominent place, and yet I think it obvious that the basis for this doctrine in the present scheme is a very slender one, and that it involves a complete inversion of the true order by which *life* is made to result from principles. Upon this point I shall dwell more at length by and by. At present, I would simply advert to the fact, which cannot but be admitted as a marked feature of the scheme, that no previous change of character is requisite in order to the appropriation of all the promises of the Gospel, provided there is the exercise of a fiducial trust in the divine assurances, so that if the sinner, at the last hour of life, puts forth a vigorous act of faith, his former iniquities are all canceled, and he comes at once into the full privileges and prerogatives of a state of grace. As the vital act of faith is put forth at once, and this act is the essence of regeneration, it follows that regeneration is instantaneous; and as regeneration is the grand requisite to salvation, while to the former nothing is requisite but faith, it is obvious that the demands of a holy life are practically all but annulled in the vicarious scheme of atonement. The legitimate results of the system are thus propounded by Swedenborg:—

"The modern faith is, that it is to be believed, that God the Father sent His Son, who suffered upon the cross for our sins, and took away the curse of the law by the fulfilment thereof, and that this faith without good works will save every one, even in the last hour of death : by this faith impressed from childhood, and afterwards confirmed by preachings, it has come to pass, that no one flees from evils from a. principle of religion, but only from a civil and moral law, thus not because they are sins, but because they are hurtful : consider now, whilst man thinks that the Lord suffered for our sins, that He took away the curse of the law, and that to believe those things, or that the faith of those things alone, without good works, saves, whether all the precepts of the decalogue are not lightly esteemed, and all the life of the religion prescribed in the Word, and moreover all the truths which teach charity ; separate therefore these, and remove them from man, and say whether there appertains to him any religion ; for religion does not consist in only thinking this or that, but in willing and doing that which is thought, and there is no religion when willing and doing are separated from thinking : hence it follows, that by the modern faith, spiritual life, which is the life of the angels of heaven, and the essential Christian life, is destroyed."—*A. E.* 902.

I am not conscious of having, in the above sketch, exaggerated or misrepresented the leading features of the theory of atonement upon which I am commenting. It surely is not necessary to invest it with any factitious enormities in order to intensify its repulsiveness to every right mind. Such an effect, however, will be more likely to follow from arraying it somewhat directly in contrast with what we believe to be the genuine doctrine of the Word on this subject. This doctrine we find embodied in the theology of the New Church, and the sequel will show the strong points of contrariety between the two.

And, first of all, this divine theology teaches that there is no real anger or wrath in the Deity. All those forms of speech which, viewed in the letter, would seem to imply this, are the language of *appearances*, and not of *genuine truth* as it is apprehended in heaven. The Lord is essential *love*, and *love* is inconsistent with *wrath*. The virtual assertion of anger as a quality of the divine mind is founded upon the sensible *effect* produced by the contrariety between the state of the man in evil and the Divine affection, which conveys to him the impression of the Lord's being moved by wrathful emotions towards him. So to an inflamed condition of the eyes, the sun's light is painful, and a vague impression is produced of some kind of antagonism between the grand luminary of day and the organ of vision, whereas it is wholly to a diseased state of the organ that this impression is owing, as the light of the sun is always genial and pleasant to the healthy eye. The language of the Scripture in all those passages which ascribe irascible passions to the Deity is but giving a name to the *appearance* instead of the *reality;* just as when it is said, in reference to the apparent motion of contiguous objects beheld from a railroad car in rapid transit, that they *fly past* one with winged speed.

"That Jehovah has not any anger, is evident from this, that He is love itself, good itself, and mercy itself, and anger is the opposite, and also is an infirm principle, which cannot be imputed to God: wherefore when anger in the Word is predicated of Jehovah or the Lord, the angels do not perceive anger, but either mercy, or the removal of evil from heaven. . . . . That anger in the Word is attributed to Jehovah or the Lord, is because it is a most general truth, that all things come from God, thus both evils and goods; but this most general truth, which infants, young people, and the simple, must receive, ought afterwards to be illustrated, namely, by teaching that evils are from man, but that they appear as from God, and that it is so said, to the intent they may learn to fear God, lest they should perish by the evils which themselves do; and afterwards may love Him, for fear must precede love, that in love there may be holy fear; for when fear is insinuated into love, it becomes holy from the holy of love, and then it is not fear lest the Lord should be angry and punish, but lest they should act against good itself, because this will torment the conscience. . . . . The reason why by anger is meant clemency and mercy, is because all the punishments of the evil exist from the Lord's mercy towards the good, lest these latter should be hurt by the evil; but the Lord does not inflict punishments upon them, but they upon themselves, for evils and punishments in the other life are conjoined. The evil inflict punishments on themselves principally, when the Lord does mercy to the good, for then their evils increase, and thence punishments; it is from this ground that instead of the anger of Jehovah, by which are signified the punishments of the evil, mercy is understood by the angels. From these considerations it may be manifest, what the quality of the Word is in the sense of the letter, also what the quality of the truth divine is in its most general sense or meaning, namely, that it is according to appearances, by reason that man is of such a quality, that when he sees and apprehends from his sensual, he believes, and what he does not see, neither apprehend from his sensual, he does not believe, thus does not receive. Hence it is, that the Word in the sense of the letter is according to those things which appear; nevertheless in its interior bosom it contains a store of genuine truths, and in its inmost bosom truth divine itself, which proceeds immediately from the Lord, thus also divine good, that is the Lord Himself."—*A. C.* 6997.

" I have conversed with good spirits, that many things in the Word, and more than any one could believe, are spoken according to appearances, and according to the fallacies of the senses; as that Jehovah is in wrath, anger, and fury, against the wicked, that he rejoices to destroy them and blot them out, yea, that he slays them. But these modes of speaking were used, that persuasions and lusts might not be broken, but might be bent: for to speak otherwise than man conceives, which is from appearances, fallacies, and persuasions, would have been to sow seed in the water, and to speak what would instantly be rejected. Nevertheless, those things may serve as common vessels for the containing of things spiritual and celestial, since it may be insinuated into them, that all things are from the Lord; afterwards, that the Lord permits, but that all evil is from diabolical spirits; next, that the Lord provides and disposes, that evils may be turned into goods; lastly, that nothing but good is from the Lord. Thus the sense of the letter perishes as it ascends, and becomes spiritual, afterwards celestial, and lastly divine."—*A. C.* 1874.

The prevailing tenet is, of course, opposed to Swedenborg's statement on this head. It acknowledges no such distinction between *real* and *apparent* truth. The Divine mind would have been eternally the seat of inexorable wrath towards the race of men had not Christ Jesus interposed in their behalf, and by his voluntary oblation of himself, "changed the wrath to grace." But we find, in this view of the subject, a difficulty insuperable. While it is denied that the Divine love could be exercised towards fallen man without an atoning sacrifice, yet this very love provided the sacrifice in the first instance. Jesus Christ is the free gift of God. He provided the ransom. "God so loved the world that he gave his only begotten Son, that whosoever believeth in him should not perish, but have everlasting life." We are then constrained to ask how it is, that if God the Father was relentlessly angry with the human race, he did not previously require to be pacified before he thought of thus providing the requisite satisfaction? This is a question which we believe to be unanswerable on the accredited theory of atonement. To say that Christ satisfied the justice of God, at the same time that the satisfaction was of God's own procuring, is the same as to say, that one who is indebted, to a large amount, to another, discharges the debt by money given him out of the creditor's own pocket. Or, to vary the illustration, suppose a poor man—one so utterly impoverished as to be unable to refund a penny—deeply in debt to a rich man who insists upon the liquidation of his claim. Aware, however, of the circumstances of his debtor, and disposed to aid him in an emergency, while keeping up the form of exact dealing, he brings forward his own son as surety for the poor man, and yet himself supplies that son with all the pecuniary resources that enable him to stand good for the demand. Is it not clear that the creditor becomes, after all, his own surety? And what real satisfaction is there in all this? Is it not palpably a feint, a simulation, a mockery? Is the debtor any more a real object of favor after such a *quasi* or *ideal* satisfaction than he was before? So much, then, for a theory of atonement built upon the assumption of positive wrath existing in the bosom of Deity.

But is it to be inferred from this that the salvation of men could have been as easily compassed without the mediation of Christ as with it? Was the incarnation, life, works, sufferings, and death of the Son of God an empty and useless expenditure of the Divine mercy? Far from it. It was a procedure of absolute and indispensable necessity; not however as a vicarious or propitiatory sacrifice— not as a vindication of the honor of a law which sinful man had broken—but as the only possible medium of effecting renewedly that conjunction with the Divine nature in which stands the happiness of every created soul and which had been violently disrupted and sundered by sin. This we are taught to regard as the very essential element of atonement, as it is the genuine signification of the original word (καταλλαγη, *katallage*,) thus rendered, which you are aware has in its genuine sense the import of *reconciliation*. I am well aware, however, that this view of the subject, which represents the essence of all true religion to lie in *conjunction* with the Divine, is one which the advocates of the popular theology invariably disrelish and shun. They do not like the term because they do not like the thing. It militates directly with their dominant and favorite notions of the *legal* and *governmental* character of the transaction. Their views of atonement involve so much of a *forensic* element—they are built upon such inveterate preconceptions respecting the dignity and sanctity of an outward or objective law—a law which *must* be fulfilled, although man has lost his power to fulfil it—that they seem utterly incapable of entertaining the idea of union or conjunction with the Divine Being as the very essence of heaven, and consequently of salvation. The term, therefore, is a suspected and discarded term, as it is intuitively seen to be completely at war with their chosen hypothesis of an atonement effected by the Saviour's plenary satisfaction of the demands of a violated law.

Now the man of the New Church goes deeper than all this. He recognizes an inward law more primary, organic, and fundamental than any outward law or code could be, though written on tables of stone by the Divine finger itself. He looks down into the law of his own nature. He sees that the evil consequent upon his apostacy is an evil that has seized upon the inmost vitalities of his being, which must of necessity work out the most deplorable miseries unless they are reached in their fountain-head by the appropriate remedy. He sees no process by which a putative transfer of righteousness can avail to eradicate the deep sin-stain which has struck into the very core of his moral life. He perceives also a fundamental fallacy in the very first conception of the fulfilling of law on the part of man—the conception, to wit, that man, in his integrity, had an inward power of perfect obedience, which he has lost by the fall, and that consequently a necessity has arisen for the obedience of a substitute, who should perfectly fulfil its utmost requirements, while the fruits of this obedience are made to redound to the benefit of the delinquent. Instructed in the deeper theology of the New Church, such an one perceives, that, from the very nature of dependent life, neither man in innocence, nor the highest angel in glory, has one particle of self-potency from which to obey law or to do good. From the fact that his being—his *esse*—is derived, his power of doing anything good is derived also, and Adam in Eden was no more competent, in himself considered, or *by his own ability*, to keep the law of the Decalogue than the lowest devil of the pit.* Consequently, every assumption which in-

---

* "It is of divine order that man should act from freedom, since to act from freedom according to reason is to act of himself. Nevertheless, these two faculties, FREEDOM and REASON, are not man's own, but are the Lord's within him; and so far as he is man, they

volves the opposite view is founded upon a central fallacy which will vitiate the whole system throughout. The idea that Christ's mediation was founded on the demands of an outward law which man had lost the power to fulfil, is inevitably false, because he never did and never could possess such a power.

How then was man's redemption from the power of evil, i. e. from the power of hell, to be effected, and what was the precise nature and end of that intervention of God incarnate which is everywhere held forth in the Scriptures as so indispensable to the compassing of the objects of the Divine beneficence? The answer to this question will obviously be determined, on my part, by the tenor of the whole foregoing series of letters. If I have at all succeeded in establishing my main position in regard to the Divine unity, or, in other words, in regard to the absolute identity of Jehovah and Jesus, that peculiar aspect of the doctrine which represents the atonement as a satisfaction or expiation offered by the second person of the Godhead to the first, the virtue of which was especially concentrated in the death of the cross, cannot possibly be just. The fact that the whole Trinity is to be recognized in the one person of the Lord the Saviour, for ever bars the supposition that an atoning sacrifice should be any more required to be offered to the Father than to the Son. As their nature and personality are one and the same, the moral demands made by the perfections of each are also the same. On this ground, therefore, I feel abundantly authorized to say what the end of the Saviour's mission was *not*—that it was *not* to make a vicarious atonement for sin—and the statement of a negative often helps us directly to the establishment of an affirmative. In the present case there surely cannot be many alternatives. If the work of Christ was not expiatory, what remains to conclude respecting it but that it was simply salvatory? The fact that in Christ was not merely one person of the Trinity, but the whole Trinity, or, in other words, that he was the one, supreme, and absolute Jehovah, clothed with humanity, cannot but enforce upon us the conclusion, that the end of the incarnation was in some way to restore us back to that saving conjunction with Himself from which we had so rashly torn ourselves away. The more fully we can divest ourselves of the idea of Christ as a third person or party

---

are not taken away from him, inasmuch as without them he could not be reformed; for he could not do the work of repentance; he could not fight against evils, and afterwards bring forth fruits worthy of repentance. Now since freedom and reason are with man from the Lord, and man acts from them, it follows that he does not act of himself, but *as* of himself."—*Doct. of Life of N. J.* 101.

"Man cannot think any thing, or will any thing from himself. Every thing which he thinks and wills, flows into him from the spiritual world; good and truth from the Lord through heaven, thus through the angels who are attendant on man, and thus into man's thought and will. There is not any man, spirit, or angel, who in any case hath life from himself, thus neither can he think and will from himself; for man's life consists in thinking and willing, while speaking and acting is the life thence derived. For there is only one life, namely, the Lord's, which flows in into all, but is variously received, according to the quality which man has by his life induced upon his soul."—*A. C.* 5846, 5847.

"The case with man as to his affections and as to his thoughts, is this, no person whatsoever, whether man, or spirit, or angel, can will and think from himself, but only from others; nor can these others will and think from themselves, but all again from others, and so forth; and thus each from the first source or principle of life which is the Lord; that which is unconnected doth not exist."—*A. C* 2886.

mediating between God and us, and distinct from both, so much the more nearly shall we approximate to the true view of his entire redemption or salvation work. He acts, or acted as Mediator, indeed, but then the mediatorial function pertained solely and exclusively to the Human which was assumed, and not the Divine which assumed it. This Divine we are evermore to regard as being the essential Jehovah himself. When we realize, therefore, that there is no other God in the universe than He who is to be recognized in Christ—no Divine Father *beyond* or *out of* the Son—the inference would seem to be irresistible that the action of the infinite love in our recovery from sin and death puts itself forth irrespective of any propitiatory measure designed to remove obstacles in the way of its exercise. It will not suffice to reply to this, that the whole drift of the apostolic representations, confirmed by the peculiar genius of the typical ritual of the Jews, speak continually the language of vicarious oblation; for the question first of all to be determined is, whether Jesus Christ be intrinsically Jehovah God—the point which I have been laboring throughout. If he be, then I take the ground without hesitation that the sustaining of such an office by our Lord is a downright impossibility, and, consequently, that some other interpretation *must* be put upon the scriptural language in which it is spoken of.

But you will still remind me that I have not yet distinctly propounded the precise grounds on which the incarnation of Jehovah became necessary or the exact mode in which it becomes available to our salvation. The true response flows legitimately from what I have hitherto advanced on the general subject. Man had broken the bond of connection which allied him to the beatific source of his being. He had done this in the perverted exercise of his freedom as man, and in so doing had thrown himself within the disastrous sphere of infernal influences from which, unless he were liberated, he must inevitably perish. But in this liberating process, the freedom of man and the freedom of evil spirits must be sacredly preserved, for this is that *peculium* of the rational nature which Jehovah guards as the apple of his eye. Neither in time nor in eternity—neither in heaven nor in hell—does he ever suffer this gem of the soul to be touched with the finger of violence or constraint, as such a thing would be to extinguish the very principle of humanity in man. The first step, then, in the recovering work of Heaven's mercy was the breaking of the bondage of evil into which man had fallen—the disanulling of that covenant with death and that agreement with hell into which he had so rashly entered. This could only be effected by subjugating the powers of hell, and the agency by which this was to be brought about must necessarily be such as to be consistent with the essential freedom of the enemies to be subdued, for the All-Wise never deals with his creatures as a potter would with vessels that so displeased him in the making as to prompt him to dash them in pieces. He never treats men as machines. He pays respect to the high moral nature he has given them, even when that nature is grievously abused. The end, therefore, at which his boundless benevolence aimed could not be attained if they were to be dealt with by the direct putting forth of the Divine power towards them. Before the naked arm of Omnipotence they could not stand for a moment. It was not, therefore, in the way of Omnipotence that infinite Wisdom deemed it meet to engage with the infernal hosts, since this could not be done but in total disregard of their moral nature. They were to be met upon their own plane. Jehovah must in some way come down to their level, and yet it would be impossible that he should do this without instantaneously consuming them, unless he approached them through a medium, and that medium, we learn, was the assumed Humanity. Veiling the consuming ardor of his infinite love under this investment, he could come in contact with man's spiritual foes. Devoid of the Humanity thus put on, it would have been impossible for him to have admitted into himself the temptations, the fierce and direful assaults, of the infernal legions, as the pure Divine is infinitely removed beyond the reach of their infestations. Yet, unless he had been assailed in every possible way by the utmost malignity of the hells, he could not have subdued them, and thus could not have glorified his Humanity, or have "atoned, or reconciled the world to himself," that is, could not have accomplished the work of redemption. This, however, he *has* accomplished, and it is in virtue of his glorious victories in this behalf that he has removed the grand obstacles that stood in the way of *man's recovering himself* by repentance and a new life of love and faith. There now perpetually flows forth from the glorified and Divine Humanity of the Lord, a sphere of quickening spiritual life which is capable of resuscitating those who were previously dead in trespasses and sins. Operating through his Divine Word, which is but another name for his Divine Truth, he draws the souls of men to himself, as the central sun might be supposed to draw back to itself, by an augmented power of attraction, a planet that had wandered out of its orbit. This is *atonement* in its true interior sense, which is that of *reconciliation* or *renewed conjunction;* in a word, it is *at-one-ment.* And it is ever to be borne in mind that all this is the work of the one, absolute Jehovah, existing, loving, and acting in one person made Immanuel, *God with us,* by the wondrous fact of incarnation. The whole theme is totally misconceived the moment we fix our thoughts upon what is termed the second person of the Trinity going through this process in obedience to the will, in vindication of the justice, and in the display of the glory, of the first.

Unquestionably to human view a great mystery must, on any solution, hang round an event so stupendous as the incarnation of a God. It is a mystery ineffably profound how the Divine could pass "from first principles to last," embodying his pure essence in the ultimates of our gross and fallen humanity. But however mysterious, the fact has to be admitted. No one can fairly reject it who believes, as you undoubtedly do, that "the Word which was with God and was God, became flesh and dwelt among us." This transcendant fact stands revealed on the very threshold, as it were, of the Christian oracles, and in this fact, in its interior import, we read the genuine doctrine both of Atonement and Redemption, the former the issue of the latter. It is here that we find an adequate clew to that wonder of wonders, the Glorification—an internal process constituting the very heart and core of the Saviour's mediatorial life, and which is yet as completely ignored in the prevailing schemes of atonement, as though it had never taken place. These theories take no note of any such hidden process or progress in our Lord's interior state during his sojourn on earth. The evangelic record that he was born an infant, that he advanced to childhood, that he increased in stature and wisdom, that he became a man of sorrows and acquainted with grief, and that he finally died a painful and humiliating death on the cross, is of course admitted, and this is substantially the history of his mere external man. But prior to the revelations of the New Church, who of the advocates of the modern theories of atonement had ever obtained a glimpse of that inner world of mysterious experience, in which lay the germ of earth's redemption? It is evermore this view of our Lord which is most prominent in the mind of a New Churchman. He looks incomparably more at what he *was* in his inner life than at what he *did* in his outer works. He knows of no other atonement than that which consists in the actual *reconciliation* of the human of man to the Divine of Jehovah, for it was in this that the glorification of Jesus consisted, and in this he sees the prototype of his own regeneration.

Such then is the view which we are taught by Swedenborg to entertain of the subject before us. The end of the incarnation was not to satisfy law or glorify justice, in the outward or forensic relations of either. Divine law can never fail to satisfy itself, either in the cordial obedience rendered it, or by the punishment inseparably annexed to violation. The end for which the Lord assumed the Human, was to provide a medium through which the saving Divine influx might reach us. This influx may be compared to that of the light. If a dense cloud intervene, the luminous ether cannot reach and penetrate the dark places that need illumination. Let the cloud be removed and the light finds its way to the regions and recesses which it could not visit before. Thus the mediatorial agency of the Son of God, which is the Divine Human, is to remove the obstructing cloud, and give access to the rays of light, while at the same time it affords a medium by which the rays of the Divine heat shall be so tempered as not to consume its objects. The great error in theology we conceive to have been in losing sight of the atonement as an actual re-uniting, or *putting at one*, opposing parties, and interpreting the term as expressive solely of the *propitiatory* or *pacificating* work on which the actual union or reconciliation is supposed to rest. This propitiation, moreover, is supposed, by a large portion of the Christian world, to involve a designation of the particular objects to whom it shall be applied, and who are determined by a so-called decree of election. From this designation it is usually understood that the heathen are excluded, being shut up under the ban of reprobation. Every one feels indeed the pressure of the problem on this score, but as it is the inevitable logical result of the theory advocated, its upholders sit down silent, if not quiet, under the oppressive burden of doubt which it imposes. While they shudder at the thought of such tremendously preponderating masses of the race sinking into the yawning abyss of an eternal hell, the authority of the dogma still schools the impulses of their hearts into acquiescence with the dread result. On the principles of the New Church this difficulty disappears. We are taught by them that as the divine influence is not confined to the understanding, but flows into the affections, so those among the heathen who live a good life according to the dictates of their religion, are saved to the measure of their capacity, and in the other life receive such instructions from the angels as shall bring them to the acknowledgment of the truths that are in accordance with their good. The nature of the influx now descending from the Lord in his glorified state, is such as to dispense with the absolute necessity of the written Word as the medium of salvation. The Word is indeed of pre-eminent value to those who possess it, as being the grand vehicle of the Divine Truth, and the instrumental means of conjunction with heaven; but the virtue of the Lord's incarnation and redemption reaches the wills of men where the light of revelation does not reach their understandings, and spiritual life has its seat in the will rather than in the intellect. This position, however, no more enforces the inference that *all* the heathen are saved, than we are to infer that such influences in Christian lands are available to the salvation of *all* who enjoy them. Man is universally left to the freedom of his own will. Heaven is not *forced* upon any one, whether Christian or Pagan, Jew or Gentile, Barbarian or Scythian, bond or free.

But the bearing of this and of every Christian doctrine upon *life* is after all the grand test. Tried by this standard we do not see how the inference can be avoided, that the system which we have above set forth, as held by the mass of the Protestant Church, is to be pronounced wanting. It is clear beyond dispute that its requisitions are made mainly on faith and not on love or life; but faith pertains primarily to the understanding, while love is referable to the heart or will. Now the life is invariably the expression of the love, and not of the intellect. Whatever a man loves supremely, that he will act out and ultimate in his life. But what is the scope of love on the scheme presented? It is at best but the love of gratitude. Its language is :—" The Lord has been so unspeakably kind and merciful as to touch my hard heart with the finger of his love, and to write me, against all my deserts, an heir of heaven; and shall I not, therefore, henceforth direct towards him the full ardor of my renovated affections?" I would not, be it observed, speak disparagingly of love on this score, in itself considered, but who would not say that there is a higher form of love than gratitude? A man who has generously risked his life to save another from drowning or from the hands of pirates, may be held in grateful and affectionate remembrance for so noble and benevolent an act; but *he* surely would not prize this form of love as he would that which fixed itself upon him for his own sake—for the various moral qualities calculated to engage affection. So in regard to the Divine Being. He is in himself, without relation to us, infinitely lovely, and it is upon this character mainly that all genuine love fixes.

Now this we affirm to be the distinguishing principle of the New Church. Its very essence is love to the Lord, and love to the neighbor, and it is the restoration of this love that was the object and aim of the incarnation and atonement. And as love is the fulfilling of the law, we take the precepts of the Decalogue as the great rule of life, and without, in some good degree, keeping these commandments we know there is no such thing as entering into life. We repudiate altogether a species of faith which is a *supersedeas* to good works, and the legitimate operation of which is described in the following extract.

"Let every one therefore beware of this heresy, that man is justified by faith without the works of the law, for he who is in it, and does not fully recede from it before his life's end, after death associates with infernal genii; for they are the goats, of whom the Lord says, 'Depart from Me, ye cursed, into everlasting fire, prepared for the devil and his angels' (Matt. xxv. 41); for of the goats the Lord does not say that they did evil, but that they did not do good; the reason why they did not do good is, because they say to themselves, 'I cannot do good from myself, the law does not condemn me, the blood of Christ cleanses me and delivers me, the passion of the cross has taken away the sentence of sin, the merit of Christ is imputed to me through faith, I am reconciled to the Father, am under grace, am regarded as a son, and our sins He reputes as infirmities, which He instantly forgives for the sake of His Son, thus does He justify by faith alone, and unless this was the sole medium of salvation, no mortal could be saved; for what other end did the Son of God suffer on the cross, and fulfil the law, but to remove the sentence of condemnation for our transgressions?' Thus do they reason with themselves, and in consequence thereof do not do any good which is good in itself, for out of their faith alone, which is nothing but a faith of knowledges, in itself historical faith, consequently nothing but science, no good works proceed; for it is a dead faith, into which no life and soul enters, unless a man immediately approaches the Lord, and shuns evils as sins as of himself, in which case the good which he does as of himself, is from the Lord, and consequently is good in itself; on which subject it is thus written, in Isaiah: 'Wo unto the sinful nation, laden with iniquity, a seed of evil doers, children that are corrupted; when ye spread forth your hands, I hide mine eyes from you, even though ye multiply prayers I hear not: wash you, make you clean, remove the evil of your works from before mine eyes, cease to do evil, learn to do good: then, though your sins be as scarlet, they shall be as white as snow; though they be red like purple, they shall be as wool' (i. 4, 15, 16, 17, 18)"—*A. E.* 1250.

But how, on the other hand, must the Decalogue be regarded by those who rely solely on faith as the ground of their salvation? In the nature of the case they must look upon it as a very ancient and venerable document, given, as to the letter and form, some three or four thousand years ago, in very solemn circumstances, though it had existed in fact from the beginning, and which was as really broken in its spirit by our father Adam, as it was in its tables of stone by Moses, and which we can no more keep than we can now journey to Mount Sinai and gather up the sacred fragments into which it was shivered by the pious zeal of the leader of Israel. Consequently the works of obedience to that law have virtually no more demand upon us as believers in Christ. We have come out from under it, and as we are not to be judged by it, its demands are essentially vacated and abrogated in regard to us. It will be seen accordingly that by the advocates of the solifidian theory, all those passages which are found in the Gospels insisting upon works, are strangely overlooked. They do not see them. However palpable to others, they do not come within the field of their vision. As Cowper says;—

> "The text that suits not to his darling whim,
> Though clear to others, is obscure to him."

Why is it, otherwise, that such perpetual reference is made to texts that speak of believing in Christ? We are indeed to believe in him, not however, as a ground of exemption from the fulfilment of the law, but as a medium of ability for fulfilling the law. If we have recourse to his own words in cases where he answered inquiries as to the terms of salvation, we shall by no means find that his answer was uniformly to believe in him as the very first and paramount duty. In some instances he commands the selling of one's goods, of parting with all to the poor, and coming and following him. In others he directs immediately to the keeping of the commandments. In others to the doing good to the neighbor, like the good Samaritan. In others, the first duty is love to the brethren. And in the epistles we learn that "pure religion and undefiled before God and the Father is to visit the fatherless and widows in their affliction and to keep himself unspotted from the world." What then can be more evident than that life is the grand requisition, the crowning command, of the Gospel? And yet is any thing more palpable than that a view of Atonement which suspends salvation upon a naked act of faith is most adverse to the claims of a life of charity and use?

I have thus endeavored, according to my ability, to disclose the essential distinguishing characteristics of two very diverse systems of religious doctrines—the one a doctrine of faith, the other a doctrine of life. You will not fail to perceive that if the one is true, the other must inevitably be false. If the one be light, the other is darkness, and if darkness, how great is that darkness! In looking abroad upon the actual state of the Christian world, is there not too much reason for resting in the justice of Swedenborg's declaration, that the Church that has been has actually come to an end—that it is morally defunct before God. Not but that there may be good men and good women existing in the membership of such churches; but they are the exception and not the rule. There is, doubtless, both goodness and truth in the creeds and in the conduct of those churches; but this goodness and truth is so vitiated, adulterated, and falsified by pernicious mixtures of evil and error, that a new Church, founded upon charity and life, is indispensable to the moral welfare of the world. That such a church has been founded and entered upon its incipiency we are happy to believe. It is a Church which fully retains every cardinal and essential truth involved in the prevailing systems, and, at the same time, repudiates all their errors. It utterly disclaims all merit on the part of the creature, and makes the most sincere and unreserved ascription of all power and ability for good to the Lord himself, and thus meets the demand of the most self-renouncing and man-abasing Calvinist. On the other hand, it insists, in the most strenuous terms, upon the highest active agency in working out our salvation and bringing forth the fruits of righteousness, and thus satisfies the most rigid Arminian. Again, it holds for the Trinitarian a real and threefold distinction in the Divine nature, answering to Father, Son, and Holy Ghost, and, at the same time, meets the Unitarian by denying that these three distinctions are three *persons*, and thus maintains with him the most absolute unity of the Godhead. It does, indeed, hold that this unity is concentrated in the Lord Jesus Christ, than whom we know no other God in the universe, and this the Unitarian must receive *if he can*. But whether he does or not, it does not affect the stability of our assurance, that if there is such a book as the Bible, and it teaches a single truth to be believed by the human mind, it teaches as plainly as "words can wield the matter," the supreme, sole, and exclusive Deity of Jesus Christ. For that Jesus is Jehovah is taught in so many words, and no one can maintain that there are two Jehovahs.

We ask ourselves, then,—we ask our fellow-men—whether the view now presented has not all the evidence that can be rationally desired of being in very deed the truth of God. Can that be the true interpretation of Christianity which exalts faith above charity and life, or which indicates any other mode of salvation than keeping the Commandments?

Yours, &c.

LETTER XII.

PRACTICAL RESULTS.

"Upon a just idea of God, the universal heaven, and the church universal on earth, are founded, and in general the whole of religion; for by that idea there is conjunction, and by conjunction, light, wisdom, and eternal happiness."—*Swedenborg—Preface to A. R.*

DEAR SIR,

The earnest advocate who attempts to plead the cause of Scriptural truth has not unfrequently a double task to perform; first, to vindicate the apprehended or alleged truth from error; secondly, to show that it is a truth worth vindicating,—the latter not seldom the most difficult task of the two. It is, however, a requisition that will hardly hold in the present case. You cannot fail to agree with me in assigning the highest possible estimate to the importance of the doctrine of our Lord's essential Divinity, however you may refuse to concede the soundness and the *scripturalness* of the view which I have thus far aimed to present. With one who maintains so strenuously as you do the supremacy of the claims of inspiration to govern our views of religious doctrine, it cannot be necessary to construct a formal argument to prove, that if the conclusions already announced do in fact accord with the genuine teachings of scripture, they are of transcendent moment to every Christian man. The only question which you and I can debate is, whether the *doctrine of the Lord*, as taught by Swedenborg, is really the doctrine of the Lord as taught by Himself and his Apostles. This question I, on my part, have largely discussed in the foregoing series of Letters. The ground already traversed it will be needless again to go over. I would simply reaffirm my previous positions, and close this branch of the argument by adverting to some results which seem to grow naturally out of it.

You will of course have seen that, throughout the discussion, I have claimed to present the true, and the *only* true, view of the scriptural doctrine of our Lord's nature as conjointly divine and human, and becoming known to us as Jehovah-Jesus, God-man in one person, in which person subsists the Trinity of Father, Son, and Holy Spirit. For the correctness of this view, I have adduced a long array of evidences, which may or may not have carried weight to your mind. The light however in which you regard them does not affect their intrinsic character. They are as valid after rejection as before. In my own estimate, the ground assumed is impregnable, but you are of course at liberty to demonstrate the contrary if you feel competent to do it, and deem it expedient to be done. Assuming, meantime, the validity of my conclusions, I proceed to exhibit, from the sources from which I have hitherto drawn, certain practical issues that will be seen to be important just in proportion to the soundness of the data on which they rest. These issues bear equally upon the prevalent Trinitarian and the prevalent Unitarian tenet on this head. Viewed in the light of Swedenborg's exposé of the doctrine, they both involve an essential denial of the cardinal truth of the Incarnation of Jehovah, the true basis of the divine work of Redemption. They therefore necessarily lay themselves open to the consequences which it is my present purpose to unfold—consequences, as you will see, far, very far, from being of slight concern to those who are chargeable with them, while at the same time they leave the system inaccessible to the stigma of uncharitableness, intolerance, or bigotry, to which at first blush it might seem to render itself liable.

Nothing, you are well aware, is more frequent in our Lord's discourses, than the solemn affirmation of the absolute necessity of a true knowledge of, and a true faith in, Him, in order to eternal life. The grounds of this necessity is the point to which you will allow me to call your attention, and if I draw freely upon Swedenborg in support of my remarks, it will be simply because I regard him as having drawn largely and directly upon the fountain of eternal truth. However it might appear to a superficial view that the demand of a cordial belief in the divine testimony was an arbitrary demand, and to be obeyed simply from a religious respect and reverence for the Divine will, yet, upon deeper reflection, it will be seen to result from the very nature and necessity of things. It is evident that all saving truth, communicated by God to man, must not only be intellectually apprehended, but cordially acknowledged. It must be received not merely with *cognition*, but also with *agnition*, as otherwise it barely floats through the understanding, and lodges itself in the memory, the outer court of the mind, where it is as far from being practically received and incorporated into the life, as is a sparrow from becoming a worshiper, merely because she builds her nest near the altar of the Lord's house. But even acknowledgment, unless prompted by the affection of the heart, comes short of being the proper entertainment of divine truth, as it comes short of genuine faith. "It is one thing," says Swedenborg, "to know truths, another to acknowledge them, and yet another to have faith in them. Merely to know what relates to faith, is an act of the memory, without the consent of the rational principle; to acknowledge what is of faith is the assent of the rational principle, influenced by certain causes, and with a view to certain ends; but to have faith is an act of the conscience, or of the Lord operating by means of conscience."—(*A. C.* 896.)

We may safely affirm, then, that in order to the adequate reception of all Divine truth, and especially of that which is of the highest import, there must be in the recipient a certain subjective state of adaptation, congruity, or accordance with the truth which is to be believed. As I endeavored to show in a previous letter, truth divine comes into the mind by influx from its Author, somewhat as light comes to the eye from the sun, and unless it finds the fitting vessels in the spiritual organization of the soul, an adapted or orderly reception is impossible.

We can scarcely gain an adequate conception on this head without mentally divesting man of his body and resolving him into his last analysis, which is that of understanding and will, or intellect and affection. Suppose him in this condition of elementary being to be brought into contact with the Deity as the source of his happiness, is it not obvious that there must of necessity be a reciprocal congruity or inter-adaptation between the great truth of the Divine nature and character, and the intellectual and moral state of the recipient spirit? This mutual relation may be illustrated by that which subsists between the atmosphere and the human lungs in the matter of respiration. Unless the lungs were so formed as to be receptive of the aerial influx, the respiratory function could never be performed. In like manner, unless the intrinsic *status* of the human mind be in accordant relation with those attributes and aspects of the Divine nature in which it is presented, it is plainly impossible that a saving *conjunction* between the soul and God can ever take place.

The use which I have now made of the word *conjunction* defines, in fact, what I conceive, and what you will perhaps grant to be the true and fundamental idea of salvation. For a created, intelligent being like man, there is no such thing as salvation but in interior vital union with the Lord as the self-subsisting and infinite fountain of life and bliss. But as the very ground-elements of the Divine nature are Goodness and Truth, or Love and Wisdom, so it is requisite that there should be a deep-laid conformity to that nature in the spiritual state of the creature, and such a spiritual state is in fact *a spiritual organism.* It is only in such a state that Divine truth can be cordially *acknowledged,* for as truth is the *actuality* or *verity of things,* the state of the soul must be in unison with the state of the things with which it is to be united, in order that the heartfelt acknowledgement of the truth may ensue. Let the soul be once in that moral posture which quadrates with the reality of things, and the profoundest and sincerest acknowledgement will be the result, an acknowledgment not so much of the lips as of the heart.

Abiding then in the soundness of the principle thus far maintained, the great question of questions which is at the foundation of the whole debate is, What is the precise idea of the Lord which corresponds with the truth?—for it is by that idea, with its appropriate affection, that the soul is conjoined to the Lord and in that conjunction, and in that only, is salvation. To this question there is, I conceive, but one answer. The only correct idea of the Lord, as revealed in the Word, is that which answers to the following formula: " That Jehovah God, the Creator and Preserver of heaven and earth, is Love Itself and Wisdom Itself, or Good Itself and Truth Itself. That He is one, both in essence and in person, in whom, nevertheless, is the Divine Trinity of Father, Son, and Holy Spirit, which are the Essential Divinity, the Divine Humanity, and the Divine Proceeding, answering to the soul, the body, and the operative energy in man : and that the Lord and Saviour Jesus Christ is that God."

This, then, is the paramount asserted and constitutive truth of the New Jerusalem—the essential Divinity and the assumed but now glorified Humanity, co-existing in the one person of the Lord the Saviour, in whom also is the divine trinity of Father, Son, and Holy Spirit, equivalent to the three distinct principles of Love, Wisdom, and Operation in the Divine nature, and shadowed out in soul, body, and act, as pertaining to man and angel. The true conception, therefore, will be that of One and not of Three, except as three combined in one, in the sense just enunciated, so that the idea of unity shall still be predominant. This august verity, as we are informed by Swedenborg, is expressly revealed " for the comfort and instruction of those who shall be admitted into the New Jerusalem." It is the very badge of discipleship and fellowship in that divine dispensation. No one who receives this grand truth in heart and life is really *without* the New Church; no one who rejects it *ex animo* is *within* it. The declarations on this head are very explicit, as will appear from the following extracts, which I give without reserve, because I am not at liberty to disguise from myself or others any important shade of a doctrine upon which such momentous consequences depend.

" They who live within the pale of the Church, and do not acknowledge the Lord Jesus Christ and his Divinity, can have no union with God ; and of consequence can have no place with the angels in heaven; for no one can be united with God but by the Lord and in the Lord."*—*H. D.* 283.

---

* " By the Lord the Redeemer we mean Jehovah in the Human ; for that Jehovah himself descended and assumed the human, for the purpose of accomplishing redemp-

"All who belong to the church, and are under the influence of light from heaven, see and discern the Divine nature in the Lord Jesus Christ; but such as are not under the influence of light from heaven see and discern in Him only the human nature ; when nevertheless the Divinity and the Humanity are so united together in Him as to make one person : for so he Himself declares ; 'Father, all mine are thine and thine are mine.'"—*Ib.* 285.

"They who entertain an idea of three persons in their conceptions of the Godhead, cannot possibly have an idea of one God ; for though they say with their lips there is but one God, yet in their minds they conceive three. But they who in their conceptions of the Godhead entertain an idea of a Trinity in one person may have an idea of one God, and both with their lips and with their hearts confess that there is but one."—*Ib.* 289.

"The first and grand fundamental of the Church is to know and acknowledge its God ; for without such acknowledgment there can be no conjunction with Him."—*Ib.* 236.

"All who come into heaven have their place allotted them there, and thence everlasting joy, according to their idea of God, because this idea reigns universally in every particular of worship ; the idea of an invisible God is not determined to any God, nor does it terminate in any, therefore it ceases and perishes; the idea of God as a spirit, when a spirit is thought of as ether or air, is an empty idea ; but the idea of God as a man, is a just idea, for God is divine love and divine wisdom, with every quality belonging thereto, and the subject of these is man, and not ether or wind. The idea of God in heaven is the idea of the Lord, he being the God of heaven and earth, as he himself taught. Of how great importance it is to have a just idea of God may appear from this consideration, that the idea of God constitutes the inmost thought of all those who have any religion, for all things of religion and divine worship have respect unto God ; and inasmuch as God is universally and particularly in all things of religion and worship, therefore unless it be a just idea of God, no communication can be given with the heavens. Hence it is that in the spiritual world every nation has its place according to its idea of God as a man, for in this and in no other is the idea of the Lord."—*Ib.* 163.

As the view of the subject I am now endeavoring to present is obviously one of the most urgent and imperative claims upon the church, if true, you will pardon the insertion of a somewhat extended paragraph from Swedenborg. He is speaking of interior rejection of the Lord.

"The Lord is said to be rejected, when he is not approached and worshiped, and also when he is approached and worshiped only as to his human

---

tion, will be demonstrated in what follows. The reason why it is said the *Lord*, and not *Jehovah*, is because *Jehovah*, in the Old Testament, is called the *Lord* in the New, as is evident from these passages: it is said in Moses, 'Hear, O Israel, *Jehovah* your God is one *Jehovah* ; and thou shalt love *Jehovah* thy God with all thy heart and with all thy soul' (Deut vi. 4, 5) ; but in Mark, 'The *Lord* your God is one *Lord*, and thou shalt love the *Lord* thy God with all thy heart and with all thy soul' (xii. 29, 30). Also in Isaiah, 'Prepare a way for *Jehovah* ; make smooth in the desert a path for our God' (lx 3); but in Luke, 'Thou shalt go before the face of the *Lord*, to prepare a way for him' (i. 76) ; besid s in other passages. And also the *Lord* commanded his disciples to call H m *Lord*, and therefore He was so called by the apostles, in their Epistles, and afterwards by the apostolic church, as appears from their creed, which is called the 'Apostle's Creed.' The reason was, because the Jews durst not use the name *Jehovah*, on account of its sanctity ; and also, by *Jehovah* is meant the Divine Esse, which was from eternity, and the Human, which he assumed in time, was not that Esse. For this reason, here, and in what follows, by the *Lord*, we mean *Jehovah in his Human*."—*T. C. R.* 1.

principle, and not at the same time as to his divine; wherefore at this day he is rejected by those within the church who do not approach and worship him, but pray to the Father to have compassion on them for the sake of the Son, when notwithstanding no man, or angel, can even approach the Father, and immediately worship him, for the divinity is invisible, with which no one can be conjoined in faith and love; for that which is invisible does not fall into the idea of thought, nor, consequently, into the affection of the will; and what does not fall into the idea of thought, does not fall into the faith, for what pertains to the faith must be an object of thought. So likewise what does not enter into the affection of the will, does not enter into the love, for the things which pertain to the love, must affect the will of man, as all the love which man has resides in the will. But the Divine Human Principle of the Lord falls into the idea of thought, and thus into faith, and thence into the affection of the will, or into the love; hence it is evident, that there is no conjunction with the Father unless from the Lord, and in the Lord. This the Lord himself teaches very clearly in the Evangelists; as in John: 'No one hath seen God at any time; the only begotten Son, who is in the bosom of the Father, he hath declared him' (i. 18). Again, 'Ye have neither heard his voice at any time, nor seen his shape' (v. 37). And in Matthew, 'Neither knoweth any man the Father save the Son, and he to whomsoever the Son will reveal him' (xi. 27). And in John: 'I am the Way, and the Truth, and the Life, no man cometh unto the Father but by me' (xiv. 6). Again, 'If ye had known me, ye should have known my Father also; he that hath seen me hath seen the Father; believest thou not that I am in the Father, and the Father in me? believe me, that I am in the Father, and the Father in me' (xiv. 7-11). 'I and my Father are one' (x. 30, 38). Again, 'I am the vine, ye are the branches; without me ye can do nothing' (xv. 5). Hence it is plain, that the Lord is rejected by those within the church, who immediately approach the Father, and pray to him to have compassion for the sake of the Son; for these cannot do otherwise than think of the humanity of the Lord as of the humanity of another man, not at the same time of his Divinity in the humanity, and still less of his Divinity conjoined with his humanity, as the soul is conjoined with the body, according to the doctrine universally received in the Christian world. Who, in the Christian world, that acknowledges the Divinity of the Lord, is willing that this acknowledgment should be such as to place his divine principle out of his human; when nevertheless to think of the human principle alone, and not at the same time of the divine in the human, is to view them separate, which is not to view the Lord, nor both as one person, when yet the doctrine received in the Christian world is, that the Divinity and Humanity of the Lord make not two persons, but one person? They who constitute the church at this day do, indeed, think concerning the divine principle of the Lord in his human, when they speak from the doctrine of the church, but altogether otherwise when they think and speak with themselves without that doctrine; but let it be known, that man is in one state when he thinks and speaks from doctrine, and in another when he thinks and speaks without it. Whilst man thinks and speaks from doctrine, his thought and speech are from the memory of his natural man; but when he thinks and speaks out of doctrine, his thought and speech are then from his spirit; for to think and speak from the spirit, is to think and speak from the interiors of his mind, wherefore what he thence speaks is his real faith. From these considerations it also appears how it is to be understood, that the Lord is rejected at this day by those who are within the church, namely, that from doctrine indeed it is allowed that the Divinity of the Lord is to be acknowledged and believed in the same degree as the Divinity of the Father, for the doctrine of the church teaches, 'that as is the Father, so also is the Son, uncreate, infinite, eternal, omnipotent, God, Lord, neither of them greater or less, before or after the other.' Notwithstanding this, however, they do not worship the Lord as divine, but worship the Divinity of the Father, as is the case when they pray to the Father, that he may have compassion on them for the sake of his Son, and when they use these words, they do not at all think of the divine principle of the Lord, but of his human separate from the divine, thus of his humanity, as similar to that of another man. On such occasions they think not of one God, but of two, or three. To think thus concerning the Lord, is to reject him; for not to think of his divine principle in conjunction with his human, is by separation to exclude the divine, which nevertheless are not two persons but one person, and make a one as soul and body."—*A. E.* 114.

From all this, the inference is very clear that a conception of the Lord, according to the absolute truth of his being and attributes, is all important in order to salvation; and the ground of this is, that in no other way can that conjunction take place which is the very essence of eternal life. It is here pre-eminently that the distinctive character of the New Church appears conspicuous. It worships a visible God with whom there may be conjunction.

"The reason why this New Church is the crown of all churches that have heretofore existed on this earthly globe is, because it will worship one visible God, in whom is the invisible God, as the soul is in the body; and the true ground and reason why the conjunction of God with man is thus, and in no other way, possible, is, because man is natural, and consequently thinks naturally, and conjunction is effected in thought, and thereby in the affection of love, and such conjunction takes place when man thinks of God as a man. Conjunction with an invisible God is like the conjunction of ocular vision with the expanse of the universe, of which it sees no end; it is also like vision in the midst of the ocean, which falls on air and water, and is lost in their immensity; but conjunction with a visible God is like the sight of a man in the air or the sea, stretching forth his hands and inviting to his embraces; for all conjunction of God with man must be likewise reciprocal on the part of man with God, and this is not possible but with a visible God."—*T. C. R.* 787.

I am well aware, however, that in speaking of *conjunction with the Lord* as salvation, I am using a term that is for the most part extremely unwelcome and unpalatable to those whose theological system is run in the moulds of Wittemberg, Geneva, or Westminster. Having formed to themselves the idea of a salvation founded on vicarious atonement and made available by means of forensic imputation, they inevitably cherish a latent aversion to a term which involves, by implication, a virtual denial of the whole scheme, and resolves the very element of religious principle into harmonious and vital union with the Lord. They cannot well refrain from charging it as *mystical*, to say nothing of the disparagement that some may throw upon it by representing it as really subversive of the work of Christ viewed as a satisfaction for sin, and as confounding justification with sanctification. But all this passes with the man of the New Church unheeded as objection, though awakening sad sentiments as evidence of moral state in the objector. With such a ground work for our position as we find laid in the following extracts, we should be strangely wanting to ourselves to abate an iota of the strength of our confidence in its impregnability.

"Inasmuch as the church at this day does not know that conjunction with the Lord constitutes heaven, and that conjunction is effected by the acknowledgment that he is the God of heaven and earth, and at the same time by a life according to his commandments, therefore it may be expedient to say something on this subject. A person altogether ignorant of these matters may possibly say, What signifies conjunction? how can acknowledgment and life occasion conjunction? what need is there of these things? may not every one be saved from mercy alone? what need is there then for any other medium of salvation but faith alone? is not God merciful and omnipotent? But let him know, that in the spiritual world all presence is effected by knowledge and acknowledgment, and that all conjunction is effected by affection which is of love. . . . . Faith and the consequent presence of the Lord is given by the knowledges of the truths of the Word, especially by those concerning the Lord himself there, but love and consequent conjunction is given by a life according to his commandments, for the Lord saith, 'He that hath my *commandments and keepeth them*, he it is that loveth me, and I will love him, and will manifest myself to him' (John xiv. 21)."—*A. R.* 913.

"The very essential principle of the Church is the acknowledgment of the union of the Divine itself in the Human of the Lord, and this must be in all and singular the things of worship. The reason why this is an essential of the Church, and hence an essential of worship is, because the salvation of the human race depends solely on that union."—*A. C.* 10,370.

If then the idea of God in heaven be the idea of the Lord Jesus Christ in his Divine Humanity, and saving conjunction with him can ensue only from this view of his nature, surely the idea of a tri-personal Deity is not only false in itself, but, if confirmed, absolutely destructive of genuine truth and fatal to the possibility of that conjunction in which salvation is enwrapped.* Equally disastrous to the interests of the soul is the Unitarian tenet when fully inwrought into the deepest convictions of the holder, because it is equally at war with that essential truth with which the spirit of man must be in what we may term *organical accordance* in order to be saved. It is one of the prominent positions of Swedenborg that "every man *is* his own will and his own understanding; because the will is the receptacle of love and thus of all the goods which are of that love, and the understanding is the receptacle of wisdom, and thus of all the things of truth which are of that wisdom, it follows, that every man is his own love and his own wisdom; or, what is the same, his own good and his own truth. Man is not man from any thing else, and not any thing else with him is man. He who thinks, and speaks nothing but truth, becomes that truth; and he who wills and does nothing but good, becomes that good." If this be so—and I see not how it can be denied—the same principle must hold good as to what one holds and believes to be truth, though in reality it be falsity; consequently, as a man's apprehension of truth becomes the very form of his being, as its goods does its essence, how can this being be to him a source of happiness unless the belief within him corresponds to the truth without him?

That the positions above assumed should be at one time of a more urgent and imperative character than at another might seem at first blush incredible, but the following passage implies that causes are

---

* "They who are in falsities, and yet in the good of life, according to their religion, cannot be saved until their falsities are removed, so that truths may be implanted in their place."—*A. E.* 478.

operating at the present day to give additional solemnity and sanction to the conclusions already announced.

"To confirm this further, I will relate what I know, because I have seen, and therefore I can testify what follows ; that the Lord, at this day, is forming a new angelic heaven, and that it is formed of those who believe in the Lord God the Saviour, and go immediately to Him ; and that the rest are rejected. Wherefore, if any one hereafter comes from Christendom into the spiritual world, into which every man does come after death, and does not believe in the Lord, and go to Him alone, and then is not able to receive this, because he lived wickedly, or has confirmed himself in falses, he is repelled at his first approach towards heaven. Every man also in Christian countries, who does not believe in the Lord, is not hereafter heard with acceptance ; his prayers, in heaven, are like ill-scented odors, and like eructations from ulcerated lungs ; and if he thinks that his prayer is like the perfume of incense, still it does not ascend to the angelic heaven, otherwise than as the smoke of a fire, which is driven back by a violent tempest, into his eyes, or as the perfume from a censer under a monk's cloak; thus, after this time, it is with all piety which is determined to a divided trinity, and not to one conjoined."—*T. C. R.* 108.

This will no doubt be set down by many as the mere overflowing of the gall of bitterness with which the spirit of the writer is supposed to be surcharged whenever he comes to speak of those who hold the views generally entertained in the Christian world. It will be regarded as of a piece with his emphatic declaration (*D. N. J.* 289), that "they who entertain an idea of three persons in their conceptions of the Godhead, cannot possibly have an idea of one God; for though they say with their lips that there is but one God; yet in their minds they conceive three. But they who, in their conceptions of the Godhead, entertain an idea of a Trinity in one person may have an idea of one God, and both with their lips and with their hearts confess that there is but one." This of course must be left to the judgment of each individual reader. However much it may savor of intolerance, it is still to be pronounced upon according to the weight of the *reasons* on which the sentence is founded. It may go somewhat, I trust, to soften the apparent asperity of the statement for the reader of it to be informed, that Swedenborg teaches no other exclusion from the happiness of heaven than that which is *necessary*, resulting from the dominant moral state of the person. He knows nothing of any immediate and arbitrary act of the Divine will ordaining such a lot of rejection. No one is shut out of the blissful mansions but he who shuts himself out.

But I am here reminded of the frequent protestations made on the score of the views actually entertained by Trinitarians in regard to the subjects which I have thus far discussed. The tritheistic tendency, which is all along virtually alleged of the current doctrines of the Divine nature, is stoutly denied, and the assertions of New Church writers charged as little short of a downright slander upon a large body of religionists. To this again I reply in the first instance by exhibiting Swedenborg's testimony on this head, and submitting the question of its truth to the candid decision of yourself and others into whose hands the present discussion may chance to fall.

"At the end of the Church the Lord is indeed preached, and also from doctrine Divinity is attributed to Him like to the Divinity of the Father; but notwithstanding scarce any one thinks of his Divinity, by reason of their placing it above or without His Humanity, wherefore when they look to His Divinity they do not look to the Lord, but to the Father as to another; when notwithstanding the Divinity, which is called the Father, is in the Lord, as He Himself teaches in John, chap. x. 30, 38; chap. xiv. 7: hence it is that man does not think of the Lord otherwise than as of a common man, and from that thought flows his faith, howsoever he may say with his lips that he believes His Divinity : let any one explore, if he can, the idea of his thought concerning the Lord, whether it be not such as is here described, and when it is such, he cannot be conjoined to Him in faith and love, nor by conjunction receive any good of love and truth of faith: hence then it is, that in the end of the Church, there is not any acknowledgment of the Lord, that is, of the Divine [principle] in the Lord and from the Lord : it appears, indeed, as if the Divine [principle] of the Lord was acknowledged, because it is affirmed in the doctrine of the Church; but whilst the Divine [principle] is separated from His Human, His Divine [principle] is not yet acknowledged inwardly, but only outwardly, and to acknowledge it outwardly is to acknowledge it only with the mouth, and not in the heart, or with speech only, and not in faith. That this is the case, may appear from Christians in the other life, where the thoughts of the heart are manifested : when it is granted them to speak from doctrine, and from what they have heard from preaching, then they attribute Divinity to the Lord, and call it their faith; but when their interior thought and faith is explored, it is found that they have a different idea concerning the Lord, which is as of a common man, to whom nothing divine can be attributed : the interior thought of man is the real ground of his faith, wherefore, such being the thought and thence the faith of his spirit, it is evident, that there is not any acknowledgment of the Divine [principle] in the Lord and from the Lord, in the Christian world, at the end of the Church. In a word, there is indeed an external acknowledgment of the Divine [principle] of the Lord, but no internal, and external acknowledgment is of the natural man alone, but internal acknowledgment is of his spirit itself; and the external is laid deep after death, but the internal, being of his spirit, remains."—*A. E.* 649.

The present, according to Swedenborg, is the period of the "end of the Church," that is, of the Christian church, both Protestant and Roman, because this, as we learn, is the period of the Second Advent, when the former church is consummated by the extinction of charity and consequently of true faith, and a new one, the church of the New Jerusalem, is established. In this state of things, while the Divinity of Christ is ostensibly maintained, our author affirms that it is really denied, inasmuch as the Divinity and Humanity are in effect so completely sundered from each other in the popular conception, that the one stands as the representative of the sole Jehovah or the Father, while the latter sinks to the level of the common manhood of the race, so that the genuine doctrine of a Trinity is in effect dissipated into thin air. The truth is, the idea of a threefold principle or character in one person is the only true idea of the Scriptural Trinity, and this idea can never be entertained but when it is perceived that the Divinity itself or the Father, the Divine Humanity or the Son, and the Divine Proceeding or Holy Ghost, are all concentrated in the single person of our Lord, Jesus of Nazareth, the Saviour of the world. Let any one who thinks he can entertain an idea of one God existing in three separate Divine persons, honestly and ingenuously examine his own mind, and see whether he can *really* think of God *out of* Christ and yet consider Christ as God; or whether he can really think of Christ as God at all, when he thinks of the Father as distinct from him. We imagine that this test alone faithfully applied would be sufficient to determine the question of the truth of Swedenborg's averments as so frequently cited above.*

The consideration of the charges of intolerance and bigotry I reserve to another letter.

Yours, &c.

LETTER XIII.

PRACTICAL RESULTS.

DEAR SIR,

As intimated in my last, I am prepared to encounter the objection which will scarcely fail to be urged, if not by yourself, at least by others ;—to wit, that of uncharitableness, intolerance, and bigotry in the system. As the New Church claims to be pre-eminently, a dispensation of love—as its doctrines are frequently termed *heavenly* doctrines—as its genius is often avowed to be angelic, which at the least implies mild, gentle, benignant—how can such a severe and exclusive spirit consist with such professions? Are there not multitudes of good men who sincerely embrace, some the Trinitarian and some the Unitarian dogma? And if they are good will they not be saved? I have hinted a doubt whether you yourself would urge this objection, for my impression is, that with you the great question is the intrinsic truth of the doctrine advanced, and that when once satisfied on that head you are prepared for the most stern and stringent issues that may legitimately ensue. Your profound reverence for the divine oracles, in all the length and breadth of their genuine purport, would rather lead you to exclaim—" Purity before peace—let God be true, but every man a liar—let the truth stand though the heavens fall." But this is not the mood of multitudes. There is a certain sentiment of *soi-disant* liberality and charity which frowns upon and denounces every thing in the shape of an asserted fundamen-

---

* " If this divine truth is not received, that the Lord's Human is Divine, it necessarily hence follows that there is a trine which is to be adored, but not a one, and also that half of the Lord is to be adored, namely his Divine, but not his Human; for who adores what is not divine? And is the Church anything where a trine is adored, one separately from the other, or what is the same, where three are equally worshiped? For, although three are called one, still the thought distinguishes and makes three, and only the discourse of the mouth says one. Let every one weigh this with himself, when he says that he acknowledges and believes one God, whether he does not think of three; and when he says that the Father is God, the Son is God, and the Holy Spirit is God, and they also distinguished into persons, and distinguished as to offices, whether he can think that there is one God, except so that three distinct among themselves make one by concordance, and also by condescension so far as one proceeds from another; when, therefore, three Gods are adored, where is then the Church? But if the Lord alone be adored, in whom there is a perfect trine, and who is in the Father and the Father in Him, as He himself says; then there is a Christian church."—*A. C.* 4766.

tal doctrine of faith. In the system of the New Church we have such a doctrine, and that is the *doctrine of the Lord,* upon which I have thus far descanted. We are taught to regard this doctrine as vital to salvation, and yet I shall hope to show that notwithstanding the rigor of demand on this score, nothing of undue severity or revolting exclusiveness is, on that account, really chargeable upon the system. It will be the height of injustice to impute an intolerant or anathematizing spirit to Swedenborg if he gives an adequate reason for his sentence, founded in the very nature of things. Let the question first be settled whether the principles above stated, respecting acknowledgement and conjunction, be *true,* and then let it be determined whether he is justly open to the reproach of a bigoted intolerance. The fact is, the decision of this point is suspended upon that of another, viz., whether Swedenborg speaks on this subject in his private personal capacity, or as a divinely commissioned messenger of heaven to men. If the latter, then his enunciations are to be referred to a higher source than his own spirit, and are merged in the dictates of eternal truth. Since, however, we have no hope that this question will be entertained by the mass of the Christian world, we are happy to be able to rest his vindication on another basis, and one of a character so truly philosophical that it can hardly fail, when rightly understood, to win back the confidence and esteem which may have been chillingly repulsed by the literal assertions above adduced.

A fundamental principle of the New Church theology, as expounded by Swedenborg, is that the closest and most indissoluble relation exists between Goodness and Truth, as there does also between Evil and Falsity. Truth in the understanding is the normal and legitimate product of goodness in the will (*voluntas*), which with Swedenborg is but another name for *love* or *affection,* as a man wills what he loves. The *voluntary* principle is accordingly thus distinguished from the *intellectual.* In saying that truth is the legitimate outbirth of good, I do not of course mean to imply that no degree of the false is found in conjunction with good, and no degree of truth in conjunction with evil. I only mean that when such conjunctions do exist they are abnormal and illicit. The true relation is that which I have stated above, and we learn, that, in virtue of this relation, truth and falsity virtually change their nature accordingly as they are severally in alliance with good or with evil. Genuine truth is not truth to him who is in evil, and absolute is only apparent falsity to him who is in the good of life. The teachings of Swedenborg on this subject are so immeasurably in advance of any thing before given to the world, and are so instinct with a wisdom that savors of the superhuman, that I shall presume upon your indulgence in offering somewhat copious extracts. You will see from these that it is *confirmation* which determines the effect of a man's intellectual errors upon his destiny.

"From the contrariety existing between good and evil, the true and the false, it is plain that truth cannot be joined with evil, nor good with the false that originates in evil; for if truth be joined with evil, it is no longer truth, but becomes false, inasmuch as it is falsified: and if good be joined with the false of evil, it is no longer good, but becomes evil, inasmuch as it is adulterated. Nevertheless the false, which has not its ground in evil, is capable of being joined with goodness."—*T. C. R.* 398

"From evil exist all falses; but the falses which are not from evil, in the external form indeed are falses, but not in the internal; for there are falses given with those who are in the good of life, but interiorly in those falses there is good, which causes the evil of the false to be removed; hence that false before the angels does not appear as the false, but as a species of truth; for the angels look at the interior things of faith and not at its exterior: hence it is that every one, of whatsoever religion he be, may be saved, even the Gentiles who have no truths from the Word, if so be they have respected the good of life as an end."—*A. C.* 10,648.

"All are saved who are in the good of life according to the dogmas of their religion which they believed to be truths, although they were not truths, for what is false is not imputed to any who lives well according to the dogmas of his religion, for the good of life according to religion contains within itself the affection of knowing truths, which such persons also learn and receive, when they come into another life, for every affection remains with man after death, and especially the affection of knowing truths, because this is a spiritual affection, and every man when he becomes a spirit is his own affection; of consequence the truths which they desire they imbibe, and so receive them deeply in their hearts."—*A. E.* 455.

"From the fact, that appearances of truth may be taken for naked truths, and confirmed, have sprung all the heresies which have been and still are in the Christian world. Heresies themselves do not condemn men; but confirmations of the falsities, which are in a heresy, from the Word, and by reasonings from the natural man and an evil life, do condemn. For every one is born into the religion of his country, or of his parents, is initiated into it from infancy, and afterwards retains it; nor can he extricate himself from its falses, both on account of business in the world, and on account of the weakness of the understanding in perceiving truths of that sort; but to live wickedly and confirm falses, even to the destruction of genuine truth, this does condemn. For he who continues in his religion, and believes in God, and in Christendom, believes in the Lord, and esteems the Word holy, and from religion lives according to the commandments of the decalogue, he does not swear to falses; wherefore, when he hears truths, and in his own way perceives them, he can embrace them, and thus be led out of falses; but not he who had confirmed the falses of his religion, for the false, when confirmed, remains, and cannot be extirpated; for a false, after confirmation, is as if one had sworn to it, particularly if it coheres with the love of himself, or with the pride of his own intelligence.

"I have spoken with some n the spiritual world, who lived many ages ago, and confirmed themselves in the falses of their own religion, and I have found that they still remained firmly in the same; and I have also spoken with some there, who were in the same religion, and thought like those, but had not confirmed its falses in themselves, and I have found, that, when instructed by the angels, they have rejected falses and received truths; and that these were saved, but not those. Every man is instructed by the angels after death, and those are received who see truths, and from truth, falses; but those only see truths who have not confirmed themselves in falses; but those who have confirmed themselves are not willing to see truths: and if they do see, they turn themselves back, and then either laugh at them or falsify them; the genuine cause is, that confirmation enters the will, and the will is the man himself, and it disposes the understanding according to its pleasure; but bare knowledge only enters the understanding, and this has not any authority over the will, and so is not in man, otherwise than as one who stands in the entry, or at the door, and not as yet in the house."—*T. C. R.* 254, 255.

As this subject is treated at great length in various parts of Swedenborg's works, I will content myself with transcribing the following references to the *Arcana*, which contain an argument in themselves.

" That there are falses of religion which agree with good, and falses which disagree, n. 9259; that falses of religion, if they do not disagree with good, do not produce evil except with those who are in evil, n. 8318; that falses of religion are not imputed to those who are in good, but to those who are in evil, n. 8051, 8149; that truths not genuine, and also falses, may be consociated with genuine truths with those who are in good, but not with those who are in evil, n. 3470, 3471, 4551, 4552, 7344, 8149, 9298; that falses and truths are consociated by appearances from the literal sense of the Word, n. 7344; that falses are verified and softened by good, because they are applied and made conducive to good, and to the removal of evil, n. 8148; that the falses of religion with those who are in good, are received by the Lord as truths, n. 4736, 8149; that the good whose quality is from a false principle of religion, is accepted by the Lord if there be ignorance, and if there be in it innocence and a good end, n. 7887; that the truths which are with man are appearances of truth and good, tinctured with fallacies, but the Lord nevertheless adapts them to genuine truths with the man who liveth in good, n. 2053; that falses in which there is good exist with those who are out of the church, and thence in ignorance of the truth, also with those within the church where there are falses of doctrine, n. 2589-2604, 2861, 2863, 3263, 3778, 4189, 4190, 4197, 6700, 9256."—*A. E.* 452.

If all this may be said of the heathen, who have never enjoyed a written revelation, how much more may we suppose it to hold good of thousands who have lived and died in Christian lands? You will hardly fail to draw from it, at any rate, the inference, that one may be internally in such a state of good, as it concerns the affections, as to counterbalance and neutralize the errors of the intellect. Consequently, as this good has a powerful elective affinity for truth, the presumption is, that in the other life, if not in this, the good will come into conjunction with its appropriate truth, and when this result takes place, salvation cannot but ensue; for it is in this that salvation consists. The imputation of narrowness and denunciation grows legitimately out of the current views of human destiny in the other life. It is taught in all the popular theologies, that man goes at death either to heaven or to hell, and that anything like *instruction* is superseded by the full blaze of truth flashing at once upon the translated spirit, and revealing to it an eternal inheritance of bliss or woe, according to its moral state. From Swedenborg we learn an entirely different doctrine of the future, and by his own revelations are his decisions as to character and state to be judged. He teaches from alleged direct illumination, that there is an intermediate state into which man enters upon leaving the present world, and that in that state a process takes place by which his interior loves and thoughts shall be developed in freedom, and his lot finally determined according as goodness and truth shall predominate over evil and falsity, or the reverse. It is a state in which every spirit is instructed by angels, and if he be found to have been interiorly principled in good, the truths which he may, from various causes, have refused to receive in this life are then seen to be truths, and as such cordially embraced. When this result is fully accomplished, the spirit is prepared for heaven, for the conjunction of good and truth is heaven. "It is not permitted," says Swedenborg, " to any one in heaven nor in hell to have a divided mind, that is, to understand one thing and to will another; but what he wills he must also understand, and what he understands he must also will. Wherefore, in heaven, he who wills good must understand truth, and in hell he who wills evil must understand what is false; therefore, with the good falses are then removed and truths are given agreeable and conformable to their good, and with the evil truths are removed, and falses are given agreeable and conformable to their evil."—*H. & H.* 425.

With these fundamental principles before us, we can see how it is that two such apparently conflicting classes of declarations, as are represented in the following extracts, may still be perfectly consistent with each other.

"The reason why there is no appropriation of good with those who do not acknowledge the Lord is, because for man to acknowledge his God is the first principle of religion, and with Christians to acknowledge the Lord is the first principle of the Church, for without acknowledgment there is no communication given, consequently no faith, thus no love; hence the primary tenet of doctrine in the Christian Church is, that without the Lord there is no salvation; for whatsoever he calls true and believes, and whatsoever he calls good and loves, cannot be called true and good, unless it be from the Divine, thus unless it be from the Lord, for that man from himself cannot believe and do good, that all truth and all good comes from above, is also a known thing; hence it is manifestly evident that they within the Church who do not acknowledge the Lord, cannot have faith, thus neither can they have love to God, consequently neither can they be saved. Hence it may be manifest what is the lot of those in the other life, who have been born within the Church, and yet in heart deny the Lord, whatsoever may be their quality as to moral life; by abundant experience also it hath been given to know, that they cannot be saved; which the Lord teaches openly in John, 'He that believes in the Son, hath eternal life, and he who doth not believe the Son, shall not see life, but the anger of God abideth in him,' iii. 36."—*A. C.* 10,112.

"With respect to Christians and Gentiles in another life, the case is this; Christians, who have acknowledged the truths of faith, and at the same time have led a life of good, are accepted before Gentiles, but such Christians at this day are few in number; whereas, Gentiles, who have lived in obedience and mutual charity, are accepted before Christians who have not led a good life. For all persons throughout the universe are, of the mercy of the Lord, accepted and saved, who have lived in good, good itself being that which receives truth, and the good of life being the very ground of the seed, that is, of truth ; evil of live never receives it; although they who are in evil should be instructed a thousand ways, yea, the instruction should be most perfect, still the truths of faith with them would enter no further than into the memory, and would not penetrate into the affection, which is of the heart; wherefore, also, the truths of their memory are dissipated, and become no truths in another life."—*A. C.* 2590.

On the whole, may I not venture to regard the vindication of Swedenborg, on the score of uncharitableness and bigotry as complete? Is not this seeming sternness of requisition on the score of faith in the Lord as God-man that of truth itself? As an expositor of the profoundest laws of man's moral nature, could he lower the standard of requirement on this head? At the same time, is it not perfectly obvious that the very soul of Christian charity breathes through his teachings, which so explicitly lay the foundation of eternal life in the love instead of the understanding, and declare, that nothing but a falsity confirmed by an evil love will put the soul beyond the pale of salvation? What more could you desire of a teacher professing to derive his doctrines from heaven? Could you accord to him your credence, if he addressed his fellow-men in any other strain?

Permit me, in this connexion, to adduce the following pertinent paragraph from my "Reply to Dr. Woods," in which I am endeavoring to meet this very objection of uncharitableness.

"But we are pressed by the consequences. If the doctrines held and taught by such men as Leighton, Baxter, Scott, Edwards, Brainerd, Payson, and others of similar stamp, really involved grand and essential errors, do we not, by the very force of the allegation, pronounce sentence upon the men, and cut them off from all hope of heaven? Do we not consign them over to a fatal fellowship with 'the dragon and his crew?' No other inference could well be drawn from the above presentation of the subject, and yet no inference could be more unjust or injurious to our author and to the true character of his system. Not the least striking among its wonderful features is that of the enlarged and catholic charity which it breathes towards every degree of real *good*, with whatever error of understanding it is found in conjunction. The fundamental distinction upon which it every where insists between the *love* or *life principle*, and the mere intellectual conviction of *truth*, upon the former of which, and not upon the latter, salvation is suspended, enables him to recognize the heirs of eternal life in multitudes of those whose doctrinal belief is widely at variance with that which he inculcates. Indeed, I have often been deeply and admiringly impressed by the *tender solicitude* he evinces so to discriminate between the falsities of the head and the heart as to embrace as many as possible within the range of the Lord's saving goodness. Nothing approaching to a spirit of stern and gloomy denunciation is to be found in his writings. It is only when falsities are intelligently *confirmed* and thence wrought into the texture of the *life*, that he despairs of a happy result. And it would certainly be strange if one who assures us that even the well-disposed heathen, who live up to the light of their convictions, are saved as far as their goodness and truth will admit, should still exclude from the prospect of heaven such men as the pious worthies whose names you have recited. That their *faith* was at fault so far as it coincided with the leading popular dogmas upon which I have dwelt, is undoubtedly true, but you will see from the extracts which follow, that their errors might still consist with a salvable state, though they must necessarily detract from that completeness and symmetry of character, which results from the fair and full conjunction of Goodness and Truth."— (P. 165.)

As then our venerated author has so abundantly disclosed the *grounds* of his averments on this head, and referred his decisions, not to arbitrary enactment, but to the intrinsic necessity of things, founded upon the laws of being, it is to be hoped that he may stand acquitted of the charge of undue severity, or harshness of judgment, in respect to the moral state of those who fail to receive the truth as by him announced. In fact, the real question is not whether he is severe or mild, but whether he is true or false. If his grand positions relative to the genuine doctrine of the Lord, and to the interior constitution of man's nature, be sound—if he has clearly evinced that there is an absolute truth in respect to the former which must be really responded to by the dominant state of the latter—then I do not perceive that any solid basis exists for the disparaging imputations which many may be prompted to cast upon him on this account. He does indeed insist upon a cordial *acknowledgment* of what he clearly teaches to be the paramount truth of heaven and the universe, in order to receiving the benefit of that truth in our own soul. And is he not warranted in thus teaching? If our Lord himself declares that eternal life is suspended on the condition of BELIEVING IN HIM, must not that belief be a belief of the truth respecting his nature and character? As this salvation consists essentially in conjunction with the Divine Being, and this conjunction demands acknowledgment, can any other acknowledgment avail than the acknowledgment of that which is true in itself? Will the acknowledgment of a false or unreal God be attended with the same effect? In a word, is there not the most ample evidence of the soundness of Swedenborg's positions on this head? And have we any sufficient reasons for repudiating his statement, that "hereafter no one can come from Christians into Heaven, unless he believes in the Lord God, the Saviour, and goes to him alone?" If this sounds a note abhorrent to Unitarian ears, let them set over against it all the force of the argument hitherto adduced in its support, and let them also give its due weight to the following paragraph which protests with equal emphasis against the leading error of the Trinitarians, while it lays at the same time a foundation of hope for both Trinitarian and Unitarian who come within the scope of its provisions.

"It is necessary to know, first, who is the God of heaven, since all other things depend on this. In the universal heaven, no other is acknowledged as the God of heaven but the Lord (i. e. the Lord Jesus Christ). It is three said, as he Himself taught, that "He is one with the Father;" that "the Father is in Him, and He in the Father;" and that "whosoever seeth Him seeth the Father;" and that "every thing which is holy proceedeth from Him." I have frequently conversed with the angels on this subject, and they constantly said, that they cannot in heaven distinguish the Divine into three, because they know and perceive that the Divine is One, and that it is One in the Lord. They said also that they of the Church who come from the world, and have entertained an idea of three Divine persons, cannot be admitted into heaven, because their thought wanders from one to another, and it is not allowable there to think of three, and to confess One, because every one in heaven speaks from thought. Speech there is cogitative speech, or thought speaking; wherefore they in the world who have distinguished the Divine into three, and have conceived a separate idea of each, and have not made and concentrated it into one in the Lord, cannot be received; for in heaven there is a communication of the thoughts of all, wherefore if any one should come thither thinking of three and confessing one, he would be immediately discovered and rejected. It is however to be noted, that all those who have not separated truth from good, or faith from love, when instructed in the other life, receive the heavenly idea concerning the Lord, namely, that He is the God of the universe ; but it is otherwise with those who have separated faith from life, that is, who have not lived according to the precepts of a true faith."*—*H. & H.* 2.

But I forbear further enlargement. The grand purpose which I had in view in entering upon the present series of Letters, is now accomplished. Under the most positive and abiding conviction that the prevalent views of Christendom on the sublime and central doctrine of the TRINITY IN UNITY are radically erroneous, and therefore morally pernicious, I have aimed to set forth, with all the distinctness in my power, that form of the doctrine which we find so luminously developed in the theology of the New Church. It is this doctrine mainly which gives character to that Church, and in which we find, in fact, the chief testimony to its heavenly origin. We can appeal to no higher proof of the Divine genius of this dispensation than the fact, that it bears in its bosom a doctrine so immeasurably in advance of anything ever delivered in the schools of theology—so conformed to Scripture, so consonant with reason—and, in a word, so lucent with the light which beams from the celestial sphere. I am, indeed, aware that it is very easy to turn aside the point of the whole preceding train of reasoning, by assuming to one's self, that it is a system resting solely upon the authority or the bare *ipse dixit* of a man who had given himself up to the enthusiastic conceit of possessing a divine illumination, by virtue of which all sacred mysteries were laid open to him. But I do not perceive how such a verdict can proceed from any candid mind after perusing the long chain of extracts embodied in the preceding pages. I should be at a loss upon which one of the whole series of paragraphs to fix as most likely to come under the imputation of incoherence, irrationality, or phantasy. Is there any one of them which *might* not have come from the most sedate and sober mind that ever pronounced itself upon theological themes? To take, for instance, the following, with which I close the list:—

"They who come at this day into the other life from the Christian church

---

* "They who are truly men of the Church, that is, who are in love to the Lord, and in charity towards their neighbor, know and acknowledge a Trine, but still they humble themselves before the Lord, and adore him alone, inasmuch as they know, that there is no access to the essential Divine, which is called the Father, but by the Son, and that all the holy, which is of the Holy Ghost, proceeds from Him ; and when they are in this idea, they adore no other than Him, by whom and from whom are all things; consequently they adore One, nor do they divide their ideas upon three, as is the case with many within the Church, and as may appear from many in another life, even from the learned, who in the life of the body have imagined themselves to possess more than others the arcana of faith. These being explored in respect to the idea they have had of one God, whether there be three uncreate, three infinite, three eternal, three omnipotent, and three Lords, it was manifestly perceived that they had an idea of three (for in another life there is given a communication of ideas), when yet it is expressly said in the Creed, that there are not three uncreate, nor three infinite, nor three eternal, nor three omnipotent, nor three Lords, but One, as is really the case ; thus they confessed, that with the mouth they indeed asserted God to be One, but still they thought, and some of them believed in three, whom they could in idea separate, but not join together ; the reason whereof is, because all arcana, even the deepest, are attended with some idea, for without an idea nothing can have place in the thoughts, or even be retained in the memory. Hence in another life it is manifest, as in open day, what kind of thought, and faith thence, every one has formed to himself concerning one God."—*A. C.* 2329.

almost all have an idea concerning the Lord as concerning another man, not only separate from the Divine, although they also *adjoin* the Divine to Him, but also separate from Jehovah, and what is more, separate also from the holy which proceeds from Him: they say indeed one God, but still they think three. and actually divide the Divine among three, for they distinguish into persons, and call each God, and attribute to each a distinct proprium ; hence it is said of Christians in the other life, that they worship three Gods, because they think three, howsoever they say one. But they who have been Gentiles, and converted to Christianity, in the other life adore the Lord alone ; and this by reason that they believed that it could not be otherwise than that the supreme God manifested himself on earth as a man, and that the supreme God is a divine man, and that if they had not such an idea of the supreme God, they could not have any idea, thus neither could they think about God, consequently they could not know him, and still less love him."—*A. C.* 5256.

Is there anything in this which savors of dementation? You may say, perhaps, that this character is to be predicated of his claim to a knowledge of the state of things in the other life. The doctrine, it may be said, may consist with a sound state of mind, but the disclosures bespeak hallucination. But we find the evidence of the truth of the disclosures in the character of the doctrines, which could never have been the product of a disordered intellect. It is the amazing intuition into the truths pertaining to the present life, so vastly transcending the reach of the highest unassisted genius, that assures us of his reliability in unfolding the truths that respect the life to come. They are all founded upon psychological laws of which we can judge from the testimony of consciousness. And as to the claim of converse with the spirits of the departed, it rests upon an asserted intromission into the world of their residence, which we understand as merely an opening of the spiritual senses, such as was accorded to the prophets and holy men of old, and which involves nothing incredible to one who admits the preternatural illapse that came upon their minds, and enabled them to look through the curtain of flesh made, for the time, transparent.

But on this point I do not, at present, propose to construct a plea. It is not so much Swedenborg himself, as it is the intrinsic truth of his teachings that stands before the bar of judgment. Upon this you are as competent to decide as upon the propoundings of any other system which appeals to Scripture and reason. If your verdict is adverse, it will be for reasons which stand definitely before your own mind, and which you will be able, with equal explicitness, to assign for the satisfaction, or, at least, the consideration, of others. Such reasons I have a great curiosity to see "set forth in order," especially by such an " excellent Theophilus," as I have always been happy to recognize in yourself.

Yours, &c.

THE END.